IMAGES
of America

WINSTON-SALEM

From the collection of
Frank B. Jones Jr.

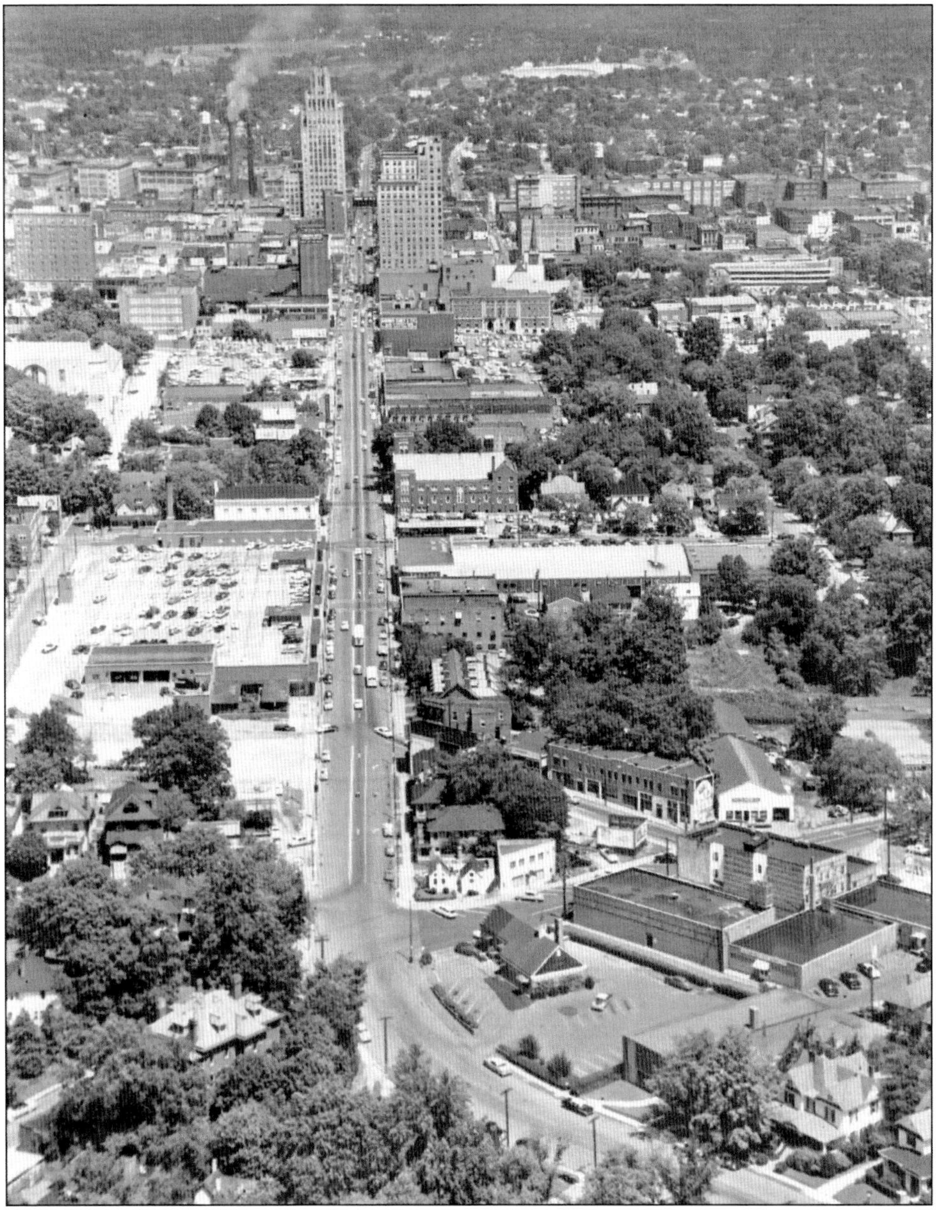

What a difference 50 years can make! In this 1957 birds'-eye view looking east on West Fourth Street, try to find the city's first drive-up bank, the retail store with rooftop parking, a hotel named for a Southern general, two churches nearly facing each other, a bank building originally designed as an auto garage, and a restaurant called the Toddle House. In 2006, some of these places are just a memory.

On the Cover: It's twilight in Winston-Salem, and the lights in the stores and on the street are coming on to help downtown shoppers and workers find their way to restaurants, shops, theaters, and homes. This 1940s view looking east on West Fourth Street shows the bustling downtown area, complete with Christmas decorations that foretell an even busier time to come for downtown merchants.

IMAGES
of America

WINSTON-SALEM

From the collection of Frank B. Jones Jr.

Molly Grogan Rawls

ARCADIA PUBLISHING

ISBN 978-0-7385-4324-6

Published by Arcadia Publishing
Charleston, South Carolina

Printed in the United States of America

Library of Congress Catalog Card Number: 2006926625

For all general information contact Arcadia Publishing at:
Telephone 843-853-2070
Fax 843-853-0044
E-mail sales@arcadiapublishing.com
For customer service and orders:
Toll-Free 1-888-313-2665

Visit us on the Internet at www.arcadiapublishing.com

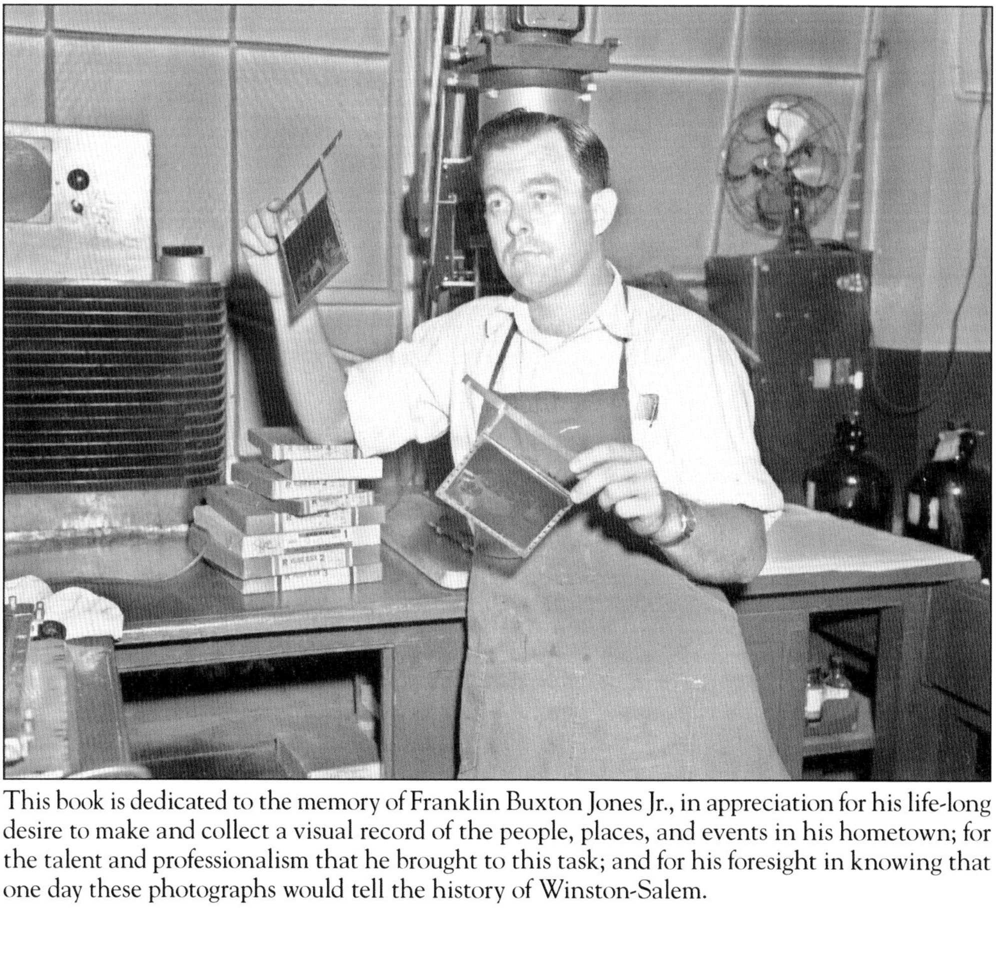

This book is dedicated to the memory of Franklin Buxton Jones Jr., in appreciation for his life-long desire to make and collect a visual record of the people, places, and events in his hometown; for the talent and professionalism that he brought to this task; and for his foresight in knowing that one day these photographs would tell the history of Winston-Salem.

CONTENTS

ACKNOWLEDGMENTS

The Frank B. Jones Jr. Photograph Collection was placed on permanent loan at the Forsyth County Public Library by the Wachovia Historical Society in 1983. The collection, mostly unidentified and uncataloged, arrived at the library in a variety of storage containers, from photographic paper boxes, to laundry carts, to shoe boxes.

In 1990, I was hired to bring order to the photograph collection and to make it usable. I have been fortunate to receive help from many individuals over the years who identified photographs and shared background information about the collection and Frank Jones. While I cannot name everyone individually, I would like to acknowledge those who have helped on an ongoing basis.

As I began to number and look through the 100-plus boxes of photographs, I recognized some individuals and places from my years of living and working in Winston-Salem. For the many remaining unidentified photographs, I turned to my father, Joseph C. Grogan Sr., a Winston-Salem native, and my mother, Angelia Mackie Grogan, a resident since 1938. Their willingness to help with early and ongoing identifications, with providing facts about the city, and with reading the book manuscript is invaluable.

Bob Whaling and Jane Pepper Masich are Winston-Salem natives who looked through stacks of unidentified photographs and noted people that they recognized or thought that someone else might know. They often went the extra mile and showed the photographs to the person in question, returning with identifications that greatly reduced the "unidentified" numbers.

Frank Jones's family and friends have always been willing to talk with me about Frank. I especially thank Tim Cahill, Roger Saunders, George Hege, Keith Hege, Homer Sutton, and Jane and Don Fuller. Their help is greatly appreciated.

This book could not have been written without the help and support from my husband, Jeffrey Rawls. Together we have researched locations for many of the photographs, sought historical background information, and investigated ways to provide better access to the photographs. For this book, he skillfully and patiently prepared the images for publication and photographed the "now" locations for the "Then and Now" chapter. Our sons, Curtis, Allen, and Kevin, have all helped with the collection over the years and have grown up hearing about Frank Jones and Winston-Salem history.

INTRODUCTION

When I was a little girl, I lived just outside of the Winston-Salem city limits. I rode the school bus to Old Town Elementary School, then to Northwest Junior High, then to North Forsyth High School. In the summers, I walked across the horse pasture (now Reynolda Manor Shopping Center) to swim at Crystal Lake, often staying all day. When I was older, my girlfriends and I would go downtown on Saturday. We might go to the Saturday Morning Kiddie Show at the Carolina Theatre, eat lunch at Morris Service, and shop at Thalhimers, Davis, or Mother and Daughter Store. In my early dating days, there were two choices of movie theaters, the Carolina or the Winston, both located downtown. After a movie, my date and I might go to one of the Staley's Restaurants for a snack. Or we might go bowling at Major League Lanes and have a pizza at the Triangle Drive-in Restaurant.

So where was Crystal Lake and what did it look like? Where was the Triangle Drive-in Restaurant and how did it get its name? Many places from our past only live in our memories or, if we're lucky, in photograph collections.

Winston-Salem is blessed with a rich social and industrial history that has been well documented with written and visual accounts. Historians recall how Forsyth County was formed in 1849 from Stokes County. The land for a new county seat, which included building lots for homes and businesses, was sold to the county by the Moravians, and the county seat was established at Winston, just north of Salem. Winston and Salem had existed independently, but gradually they began to share some municipal services. In May 1913, the towns joined officially to become Winston-Salem.

Even before the towns joined, Winston had established itself as a center of tobacco trade and manufacturing. Tobacco warehouses and factories dotted the town, and many businesses were born in support of the tobacco trade, such as boarding houses, cafés, stables, hardware stores, and banks. R. J. Reynolds Tobacco Company was founded in 1875, and its impact as an employer and a community supporter is still felt by the city today. Many other industries also had their start in Winston-Salem, such as Hanes Corporation, Piedmont Airlines, Wachovia Bank, and Krispy Kreme, to name some of those known nationally.

Frank B. Jones Jr. was born in 1914, just a year after the towns of Winston and Salem merged. He grew up in a family that had roots in Forsyth County, with Moravian ties that he continued to hold. Frank wanted to be a photographer and, even as a young boy, began to experiment with cameras and film, making photographs of family and places in town.

Frank realized his professional goal when he was hired as a staff photographer for the *Winston-Salem Journal* and *Twin City Sentinel* in 1937. For the next 38 years, he rose to the top of his profession, choosing to remain in Winston-Salem to live and work, surrounded by family and friends. During those years, Frank photographed people, events, and places mostly in Winston-Salem. He also traveled and photographed throughout North Carolina and overseas.

Many people recall seeing Frank at city events, always with at least one camera, taking photographs for the newspaper. Many people who were photographed by Frank have a "Frank

Jones story," usually involving their interaction during the photo shoot. Frank asked one woman whose photograph he was taking if she could "do something with her hair." The woman was taken aback for a few moments but answered honestly, "No, I can't." Years later, she recalled this conversation with a chuckle.

In addition to making photographs, Frank also collected photographs that had historical significance. His mission was to use these photographs to tell the history of Winston-Salem. Upon Frank's death in 1975, his photographs were willed to the Wachovia Historical Society. In 1983, the Wachovia Historical Society placed Frank's photograph collection on permanent loan at the Forsyth County Public Library. The historic images in this book were taken from the Frank B. Jones Jr. Photograph Collection.

The images chosen for this book show Winston-Salem from the late 1930s to the early 1970s, arranged by decade. Most of the photographs were used in the newspaper to accompany news or feature articles, showing people and events during the day-to-day happenings of a city. The last chapter of the book, "Then and Now," compares historical views of the downtown area with photographs taken in 2006.

So where were Crystal Lake, Staley's Restaurant, and the Triangle Drive-in Restaurant, and what did they look like? They're in the book; start reading!

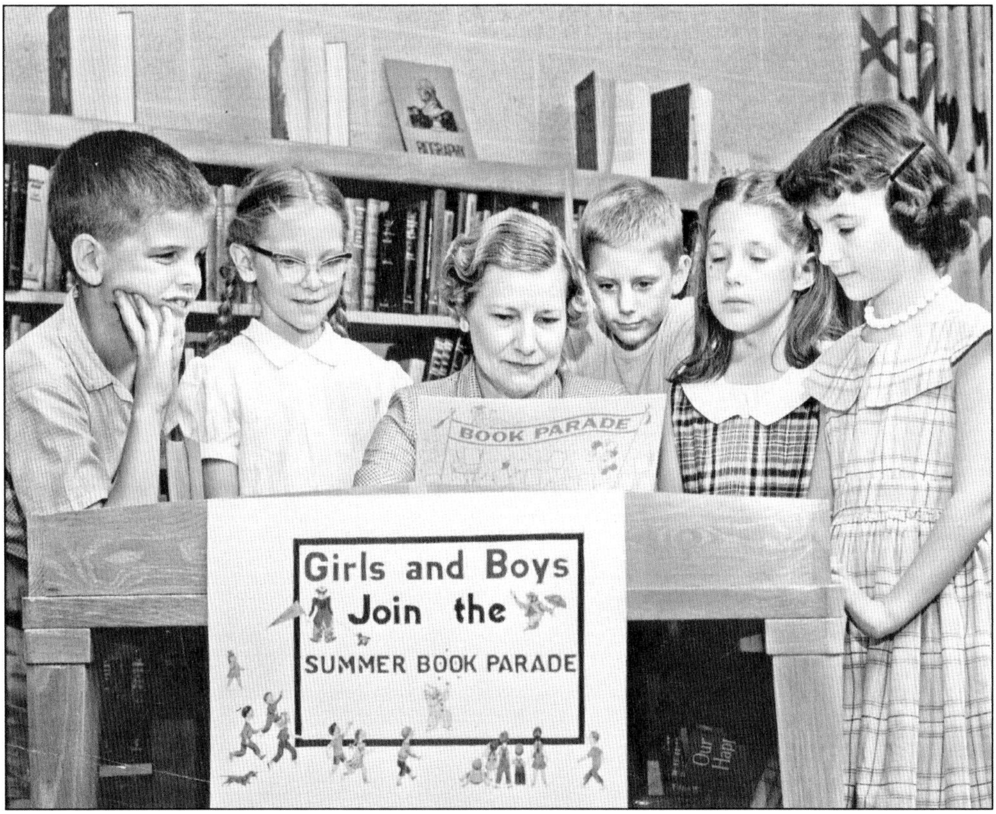

Children crowd around Miss Katherine Reid as she explains the summer reading program at the Forsyth County Public Library. Miss Reid was the children's librarian at the downtown library for many years, retiring in 1967. Summer reading programs bring children and parents to the library, and each year, the librarians find creative ways to introduce the younger set to the joy of reading and lifetime learning.

One

Frank B. Jones Jr.

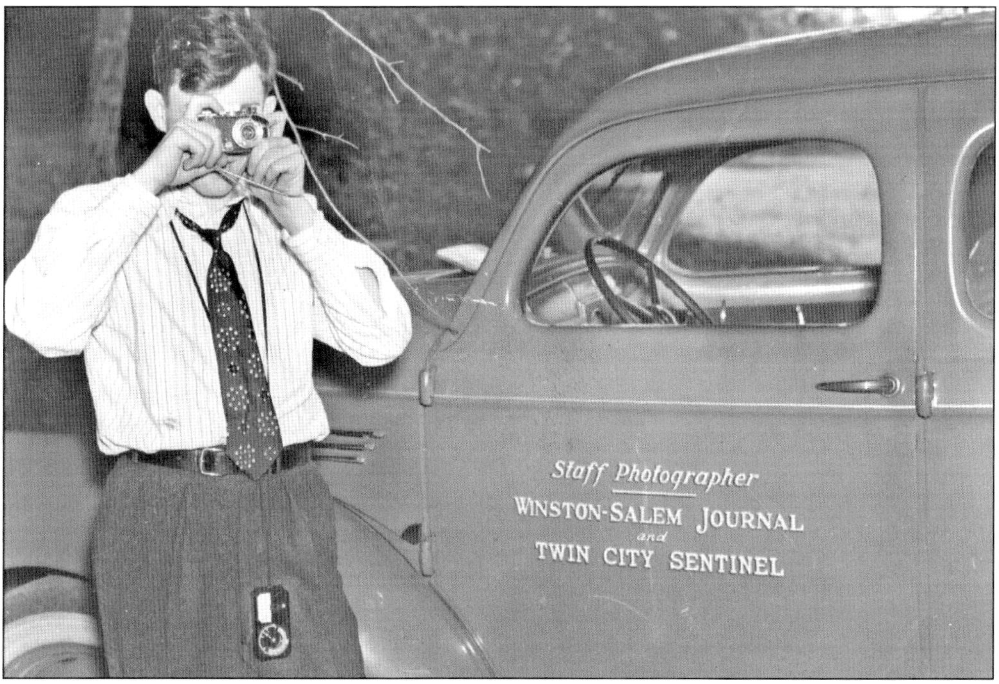

Some people claim that Frank Jones was born with a camera in his hands. Even before he joined the staff of the *Winston-Salem Journal* in 1937, he made photographs of his family and friends and places in Winston-Salem. As staff photographer for the newspaper, he was a familiar sight at every sort of event imaginable. Frank is shown here in 1938, with his first staff car, a blue Willys.

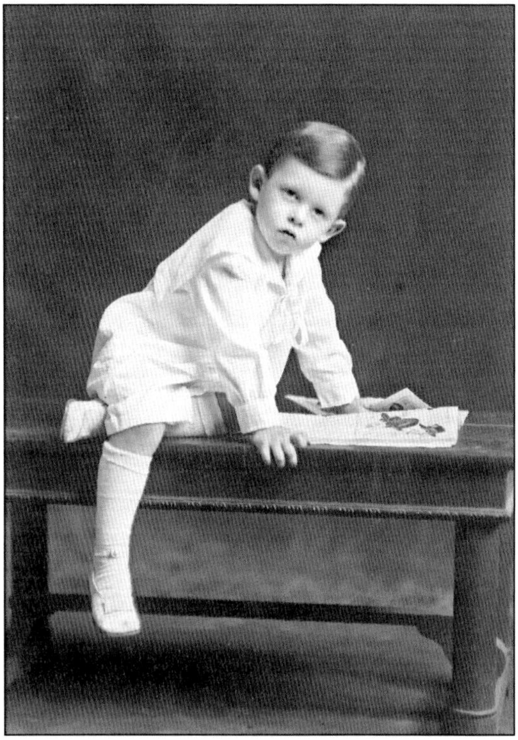

Franklin Buxton Jones Jr. was born March 26, 1914, in Winston-Salem, the only child of Franklin Buxton Jones Sr. and Carrie Keith Jones. He was born at the home of his grandparents, Wiley F. and Isabelle Transou Keith, on Brookstown Avenue. Frank's father was born in Oxford, North Carolina, and he married Carrie, a Winston-Salem native, in 1910. Frank's father worked for several years as a salesman for C. D. Kenny Company, a wholesale tea and coffee business.

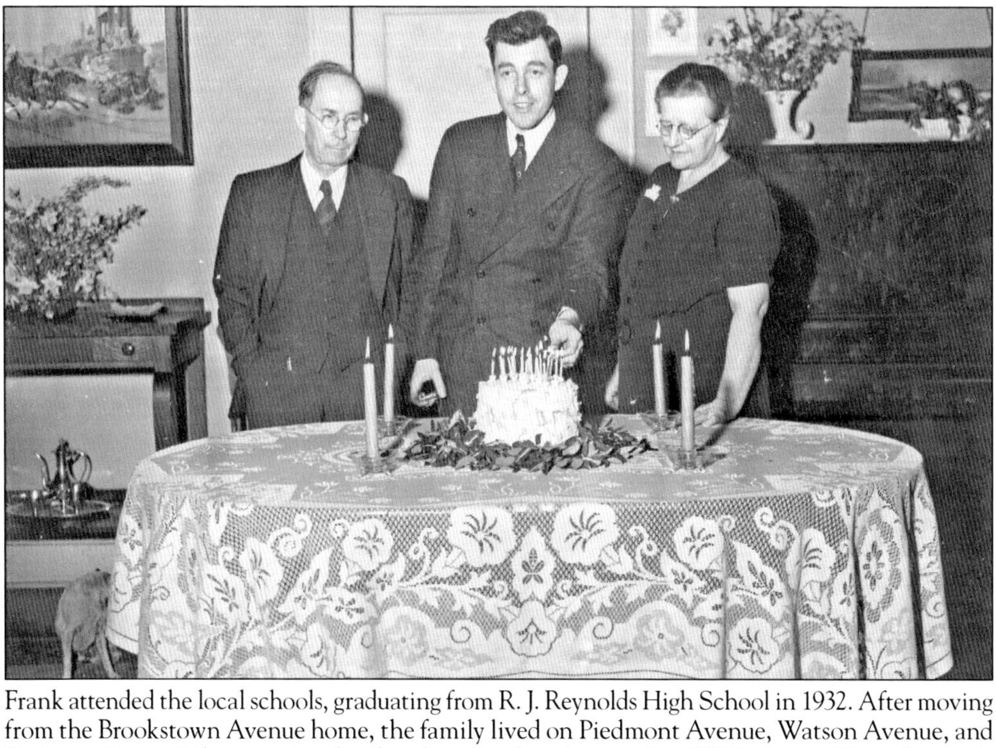

Frank attended the local schools, graduating from R. J. Reynolds High School in 1932. After moving from the Brookstown Avenue home, the family lived on Piedmont Avenue, Watson Avenue, and Fenimore Street. The occasion for the photograph, taken in the 600 Fenimore Street home, is Frank's 24th birthday in 1938, as Frank poses with his parents, Frank Sr. and Carrie.

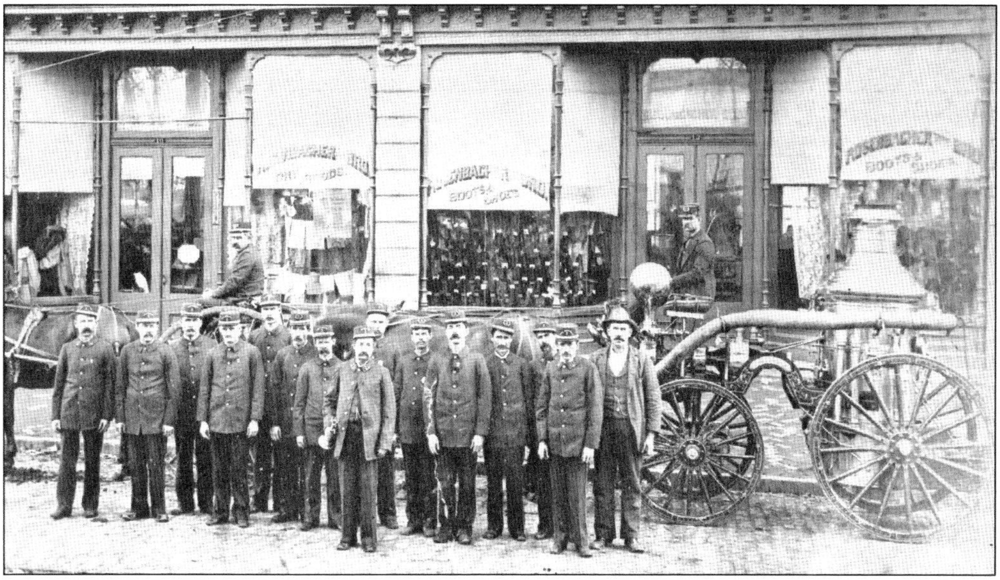

Standing in front of Winston Fire Department Number 1 is Wiley F. Keith, Frank's grandfather and organizer in 1882 of Winston's first fire department. Keith persuaded the aldermen to purchase a fire engine, then organized a volunteer company of 40 men. Captain Pace was in charge of the company, and Keith operated the engine and installed the fire alarm system. Keith lost an arm in 1897 when the cannon he was loading misfired.

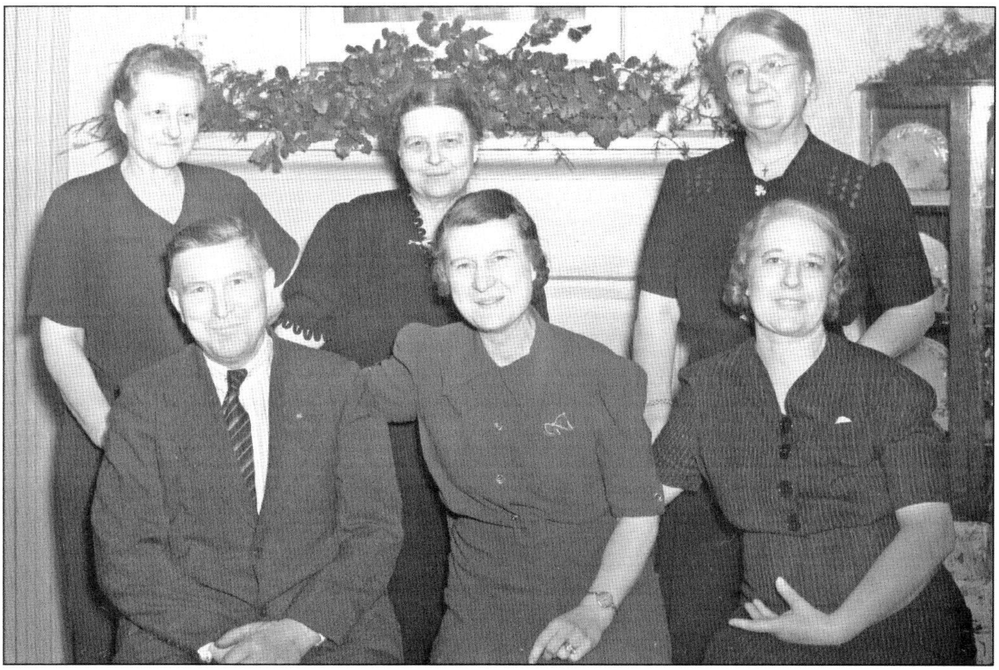

Wiley F. and Isabelle Transou Keith had six children, five daughters and one son, pictured here in 1940. The children from left to right are (first row) Thomas Keith, Virginia Keith Montgomery, and Helen Keith Cahill; (second row) Carrie Keith Jones, Margaret Keith Mickey, and Kate Keith Hege. The sisters and their brother, along with their spouses, lived in Winston-Salem for most of their lives and were loving aunts and uncles to Frank and his cousins.

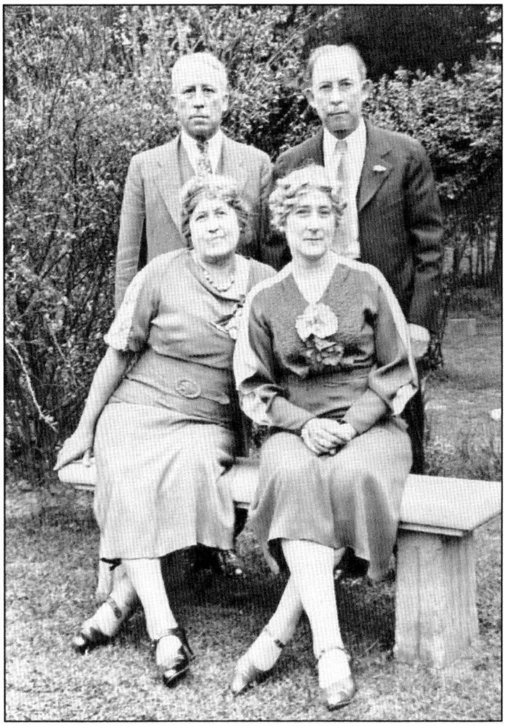

Franklin Buxton Jones Sr. was the son of Manly Basil and Mary Jane Minor Jones. Four of their seven children are shown from left to right in this photograph: (first row) Elizabeth Jones Cox and Mamie Jones Tomlinson; (second row) Fred Jones and Frank Jones Sr. Elizabeth and Mamie lived in Thomasville with their families. Fred and another brother, Charles, lived in Maysville, Kentucky. Family photographs record that the families visited often, sometimes with the Keith relatives.

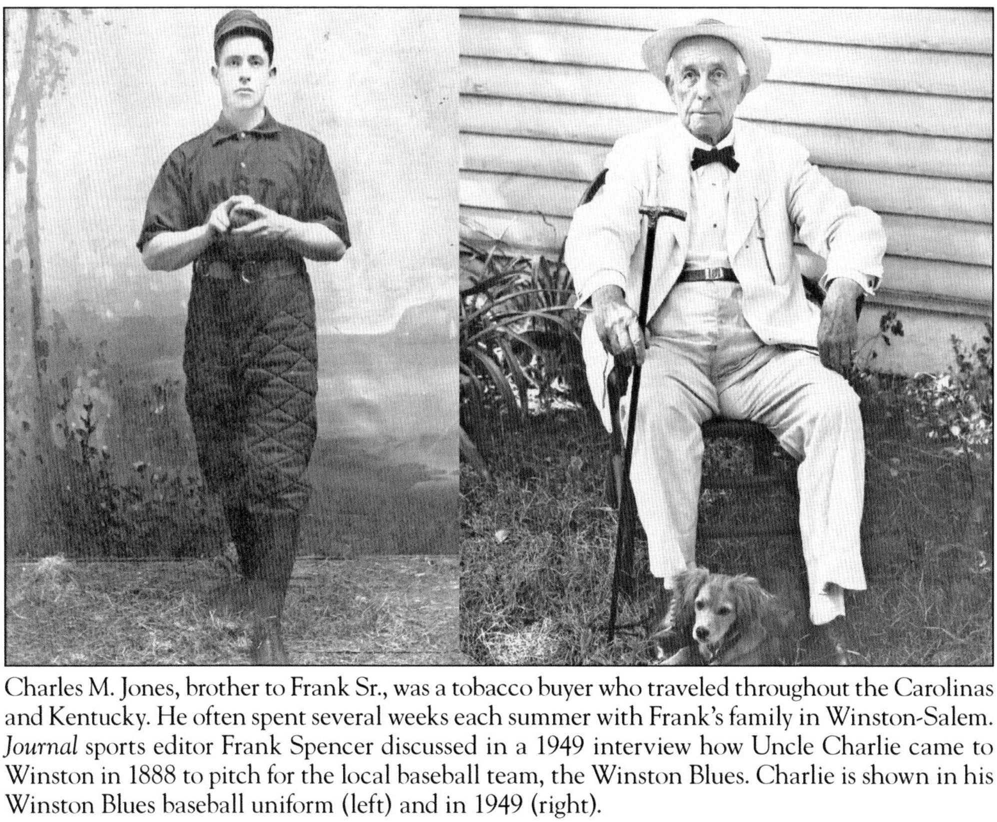

Charles M. Jones, brother to Frank Sr., was a tobacco buyer who traveled throughout the Carolinas and Kentucky. He often spent several weeks each summer with Frank's family in Winston-Salem. *Journal* sports editor Frank Spencer discussed in a 1949 interview how Uncle Charlie came to Winston in 1888 to pitch for the local baseball team, the Winston Blues. Charlie is shown in his Winston Blues baseball uniform (left) and in 1949 (right).

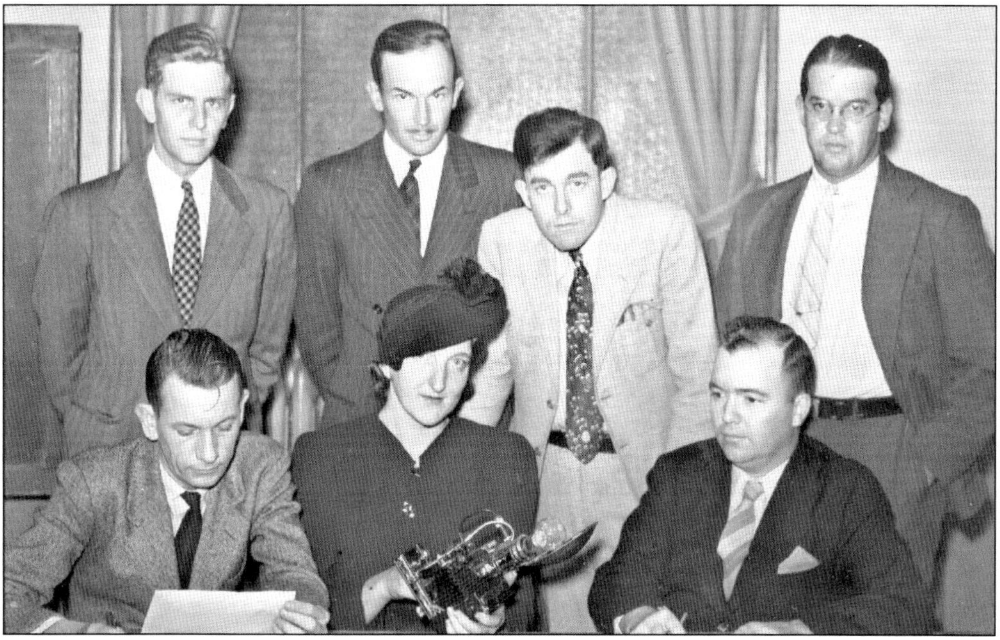

Winston-Salem's first camera society was formed in 1938 to promote better picture-making and to sponsor local exhibits of prints made by club members. The initial society meeting at the YMCA attracted 30 camera fans. One plan for the club was to outfit a darkroom for use of all members. The officers pictured from left to right are (first row) Ben Shepherd, Nona Hanes, and Sam Vance; (second row) Connley Guerrant, Galloway Reynolds, Frank Jones, and Fred O'Brien.

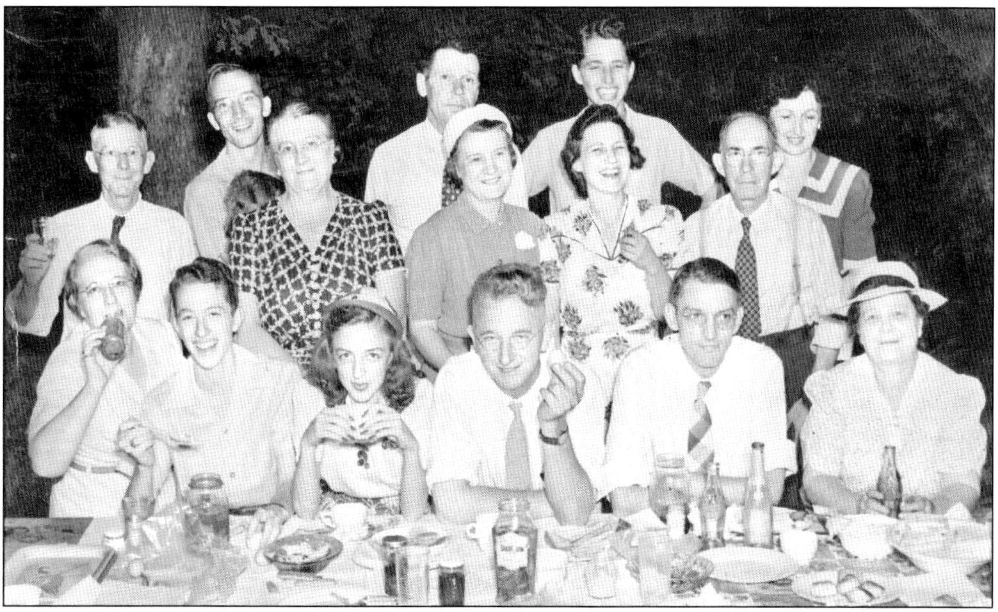

It was a family gathering at Washington Park in September 1942 that prompted this photograph, one of the last taken of the group before Frank joined the navy the next month. The family often celebrated special occasions together. The younger folks in this photograph are Frank's cousins Tim Cahill and Jane Church (first row, second and third from left), Helen Spencer (second row, second from right), and Oscar Hege and Ben Cahill (third row, second and fourth from left).

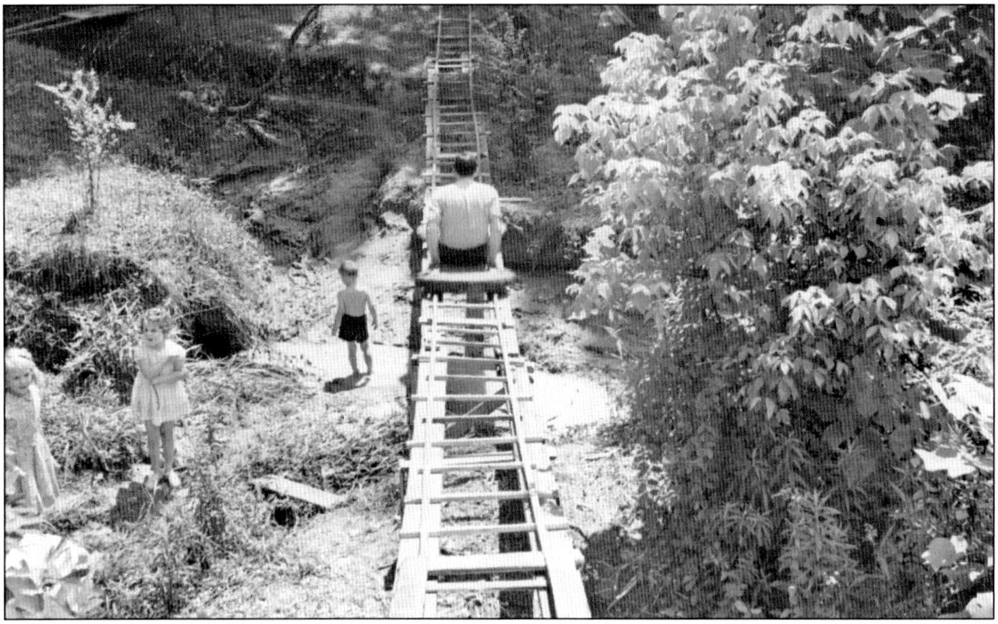

John W. Clay, friend of Frank Jones, built the "Sunnyside Avenue Express" in his 1805 Sunnyside Avenue backyard in June 1942, for children of all ages. The 150-foot railroad line had rails and cross ties, joined by strips of scrap metal, and cost just $3 to build. A railroad car fit on the rails, taking the rider down a slope, across a creek, and back up a bank, finally resting at the bottom of the dip.

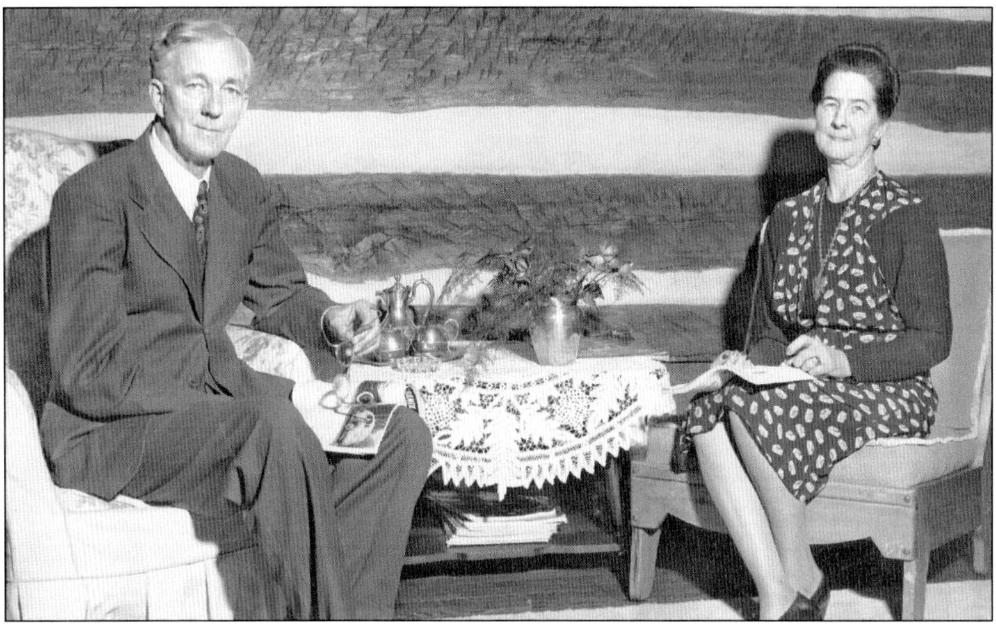

John Wesley Clay and his wife, Myrtle Brown Hendley Clay, did not confine their activities solely to entertaining neighborhood children. The couple served as missionaries in Brazil and established Clay Printing Company in Hickory and Winston-Salem. They were also the parents of 6 children and had 13 grandchildren. Clay was probably best known as teacher of a 300-member Bible class at Centenary Methodist Church and the writer of a newspaper column called "My Notions."

The November 15, 1942, issue of the *Winston-Salem Journal and Sentinel* newspaper paid tribute to the 55 former employees who left to serve their country. Names, photographs, and ranks filled the page and noted that 23 were in the air corps, 22 in other branches of the army, 8 in the navy, and 2 in the Marines. Frank Jones was listed as Specialist Photographer, Second Class, Naval Air Station, Anacostia, D.C.

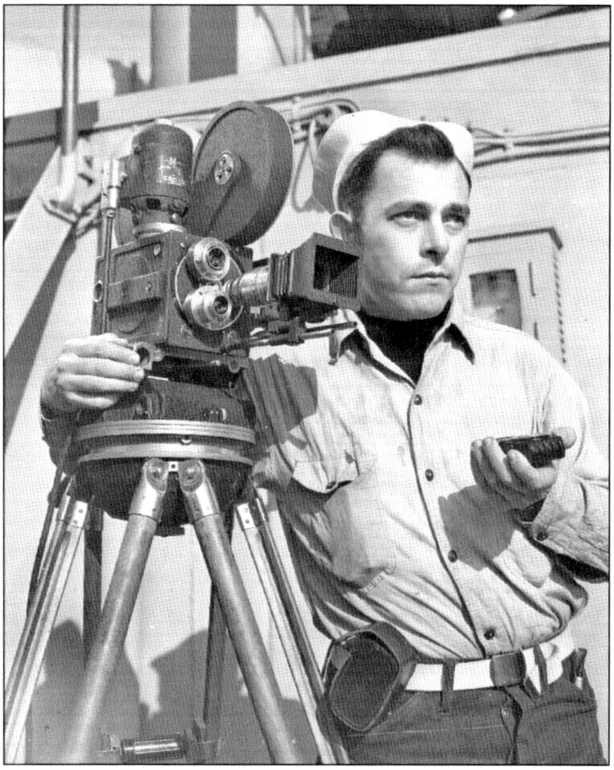

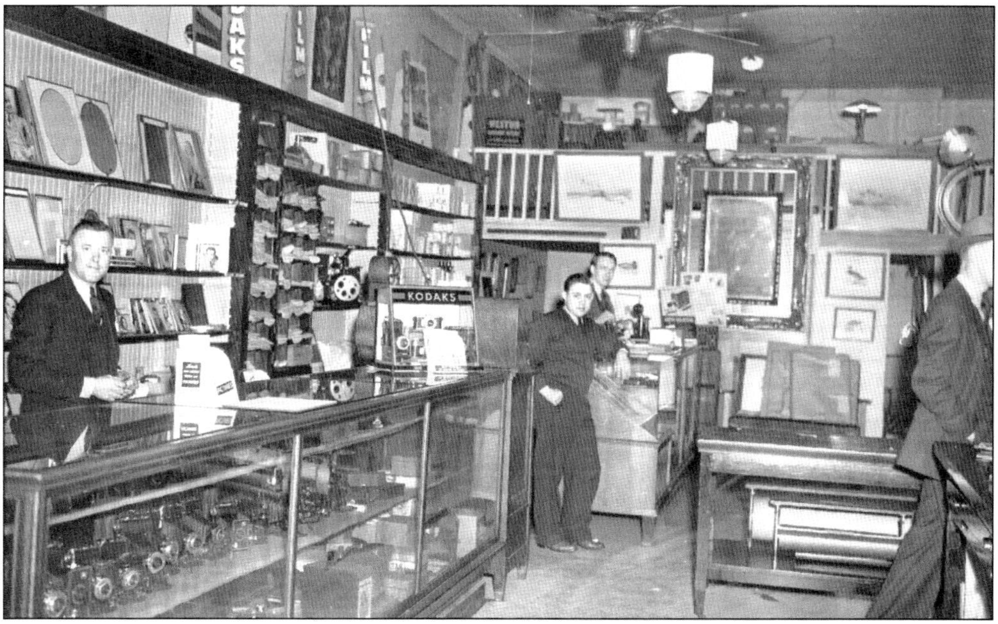

Barber Photo Supply, later owned by Henry Lindley and called Lindley Photo, was located on West Fifth Street, across from the post office. The store carried cameras, film, picture frames, and all types of equipment necessary for the amateur and professional photographer to take photographs and movies. They also processed film and mounted prints. Frank Jones worked at Barber Photo Supply before he began his career with the newspaper.

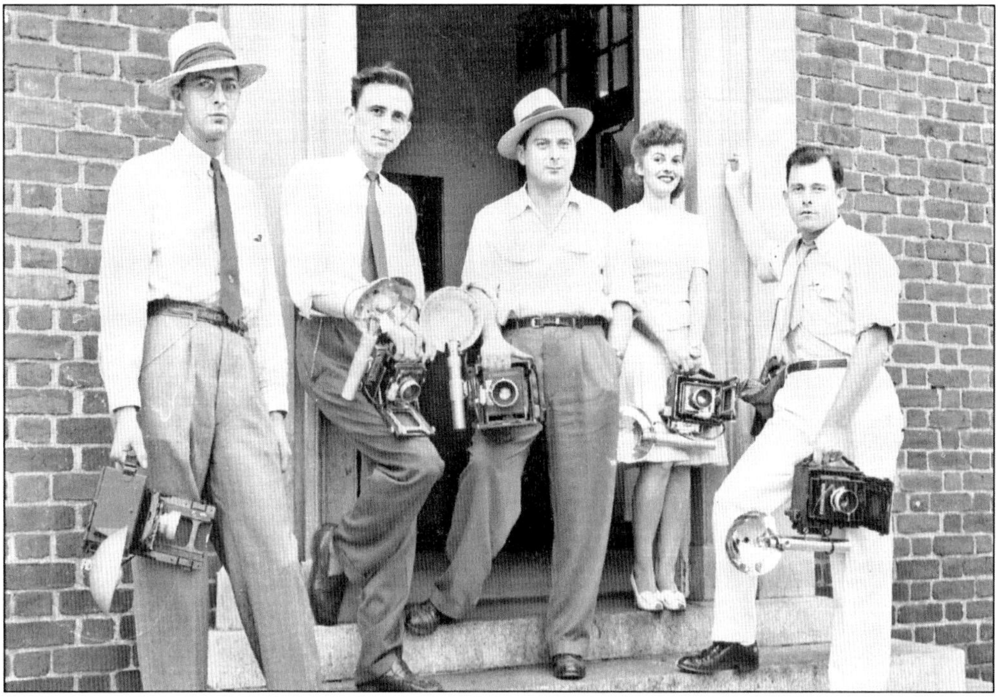

Winston-Salem Journal and Sentinel photographers paused from their busy assignment schedules about 1946 to pose with their camera equipment outside of the *Journal* building on Marshall Street. The photographers from left to right are Tom Pitts, Bill Ray, Jim Wommack, Jean Cunningham, and Frank Jones. Bill Ray took Frank's place at the newspaper when Frank went into the navy. Bill also had a tour of duty and returned to the newspaper, retiring in 1984.

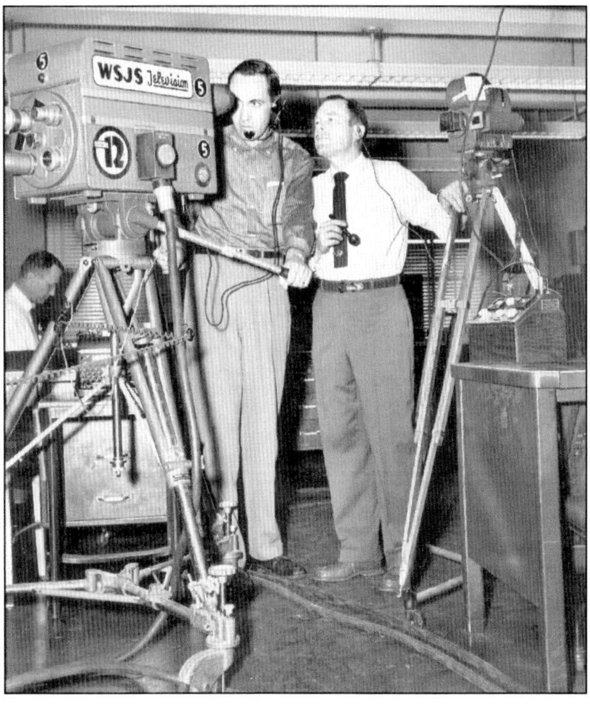

Washington, D.C., came to the *Winston-Salem Journal* newsroom in April 1958 in the form of Dave Garroway and Wide Wide World Sunday. After four-and-a-half days of equipment installation and office preparation, the four-and-a-half-minute segment showed how news stories were handled locally. Robert Van Horn (left), known to television viewers as Bob Gordon, manned the camera for WSJS television. Frank Jones (right) photographed the day's events.

Margaret Keith Mickey, Frank's aunt, came to live with the Jones family when Frank's mother, Carrie, was ill. When Carrie died in 1941, Aunt Margaret kept house for Frank and his father. A Dr. Pepper Company contest in 1955 guaranteed payment of $10 if a carton of the soft drink was found in the refrigerator. Margaret showed her carton and received her cash reward, in silver dollars.

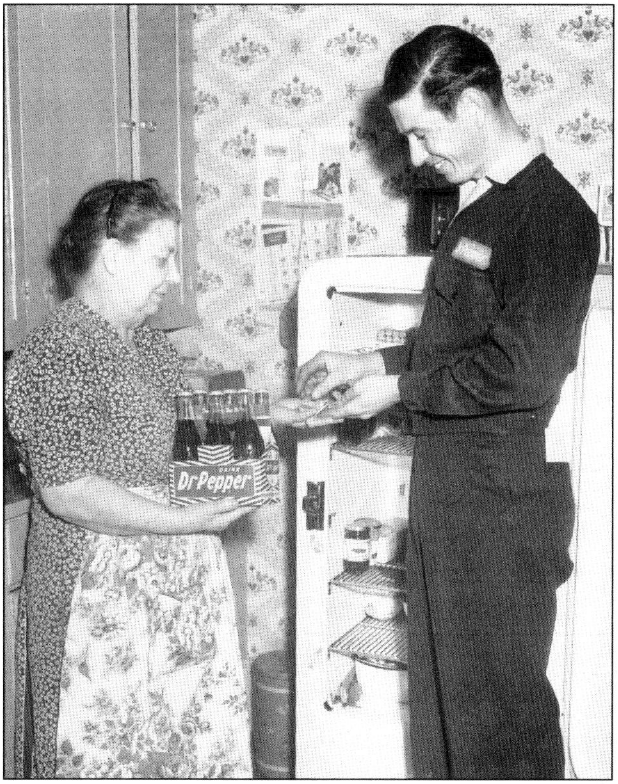

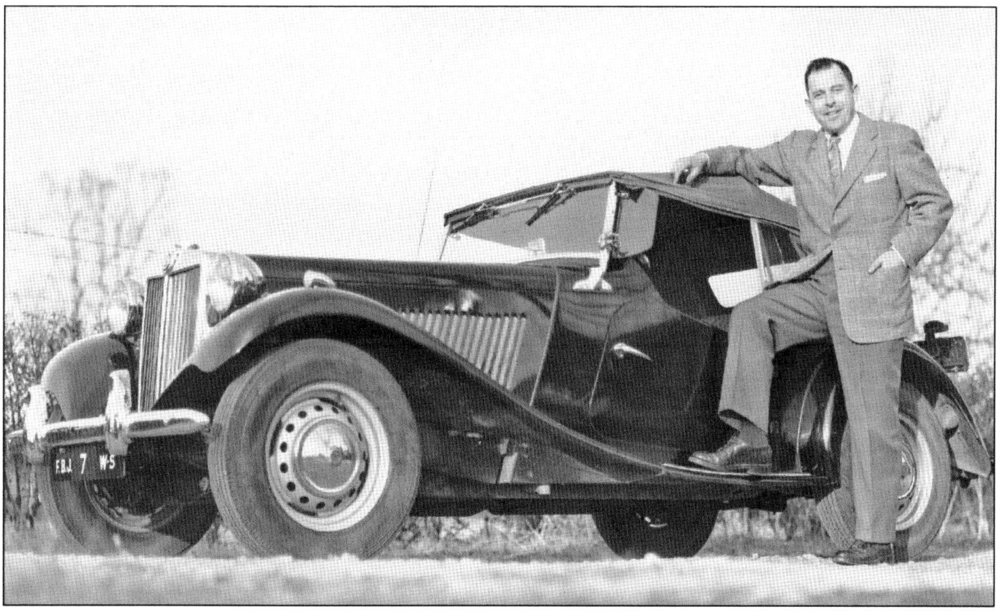

Frank owned several cars during his lifetime, all of which were unusual for the time. He reportedly owned the first MG in Winston-Salem and is shown with a 1952 model, the first type that was imported to the United States. Keith Hege, a younger cousin, said that Frank would give Keith and his brothers a ride home from Calvary Moravian Church on Sundays if they behaved in church.

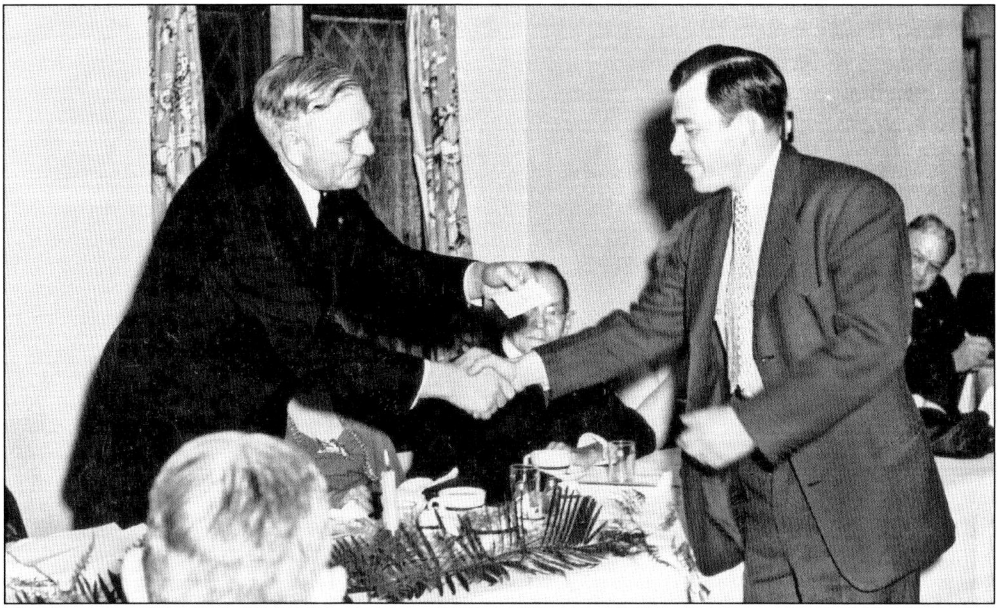

Frank was often called upon to write and speak about his profession and to share advice and techniques with amateur and professional photographers. In 1939, he wrote a column in the newspaper called "Through the Lens," in which he passed along news concerning film, cameras, and picture taking. He also received many awards for his photographs over the years, such as the one being given by Gov. Gregg Cherry about 1951.

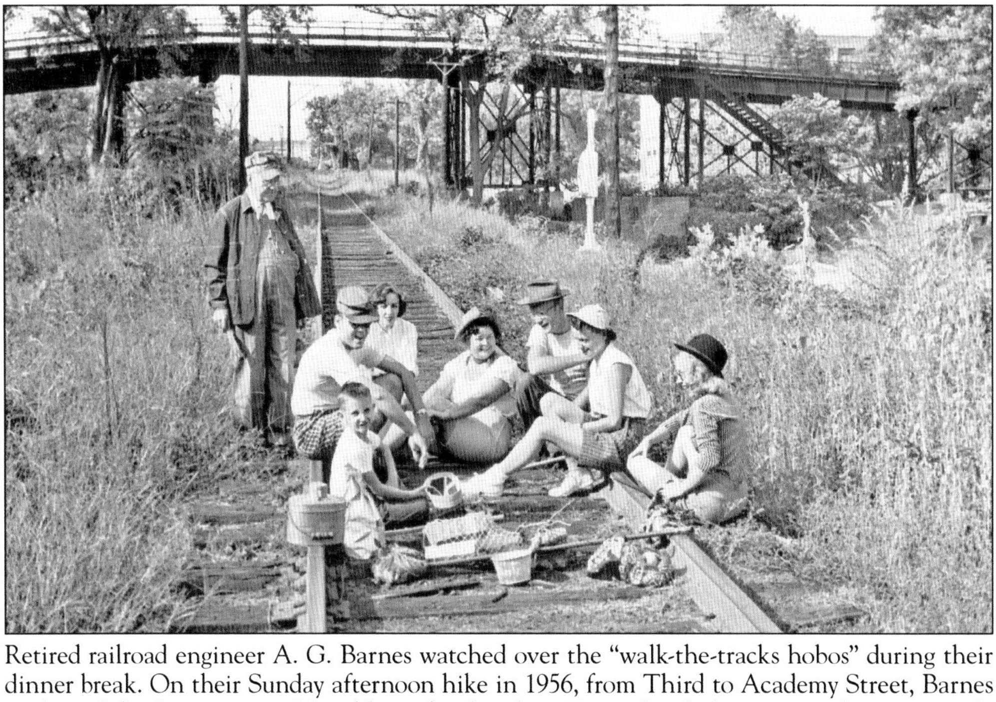

Retired railroad engineer A. G. Barnes watched over the "walk-the-tracks hobos" during their dinner break. On their Sunday afternoon hike in 1956, from Third to Academy Street, Barnes explained the finer points of Southbound railroading. Dressed in hobo attire and carrying only their dinners were Frank's good friends Scooter and Homer Sutton, Jane Fuller, Mildred Floyd, Roger Saunders, Katy Sutton, and Dorris Highsmith.

Frank Jones loved to travel and had several opportunities to do so, both in the United States and abroad. Sometimes he traveled as part of an official delegation and sometimes just as a tourist. *Journal* photographer Jim Keith snapped Frank in his Russian Cossack outfit as he tells fellow journalists about his trip to Russia in 1960. Frank mentioned that Russians loved American postcards, and he left Winston-Salem postcards everywhere he went.

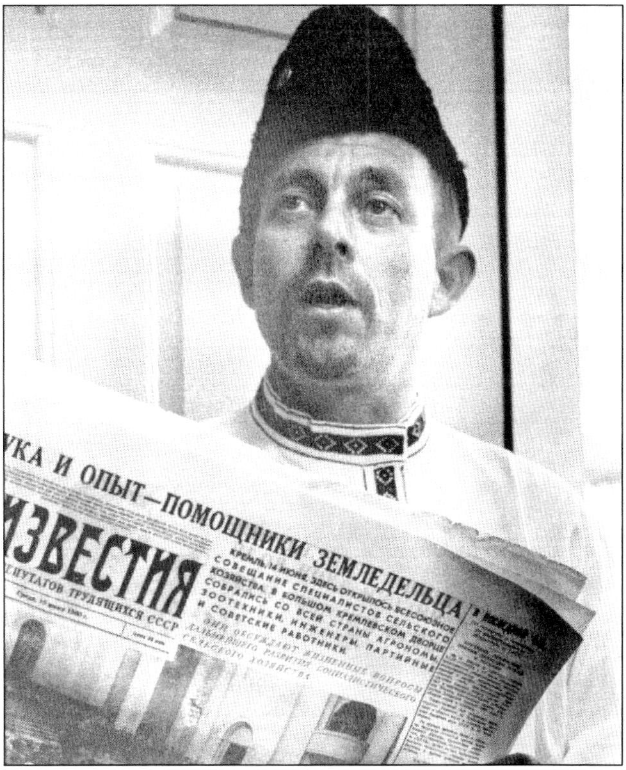

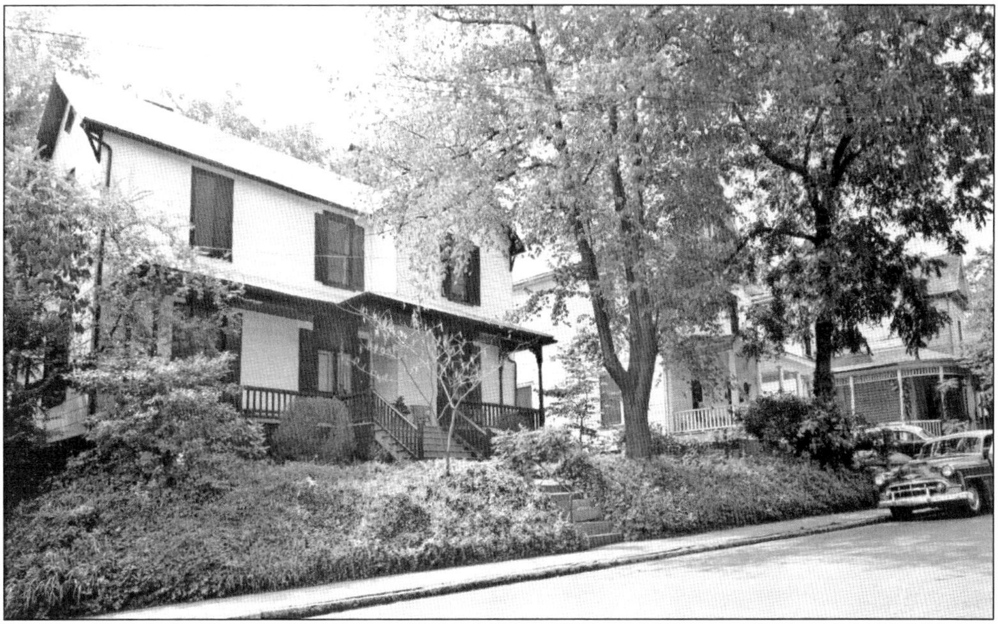

Wiley Keith came to Winston in 1875 and worked as a plasterer. He roomed with a Lee Keith (kinship unknown) on West Fifth Street. Wiley and Lee married Transou sisters, Isabelle and Jane, and the families lived side-by-side on Brookstown Avenue. Wiley Keith died in 1931, and Frank's family moved to the Keith homeplace (left) about 1940. Frank bought the house about 1945 and lived there until he died in 1975.

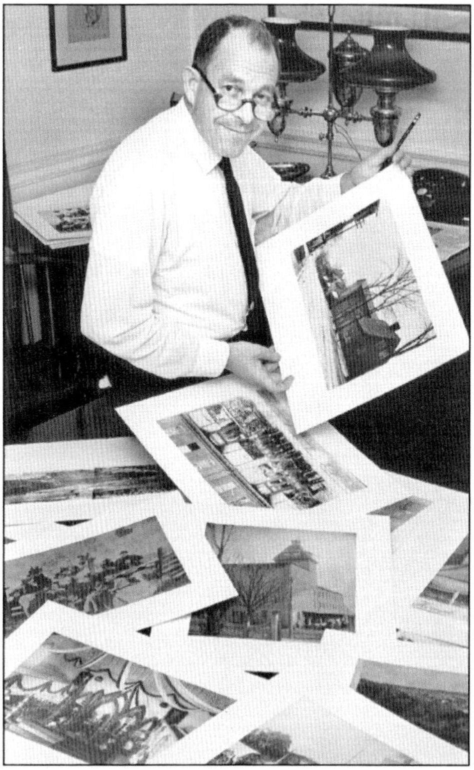

"Unless someone collects these old photographs, there'll be no visual record of what went on in the past." These were Frank Jones's words as he described an exhibit he prepared in celebration of Salem's 200th anniversary in 1966. His preparation included hunting down, copying, enlarging, and mounting over 200 photographs, a project that took 18 months to complete. The images were displayed for a month at the Salem Fine Arts Center.

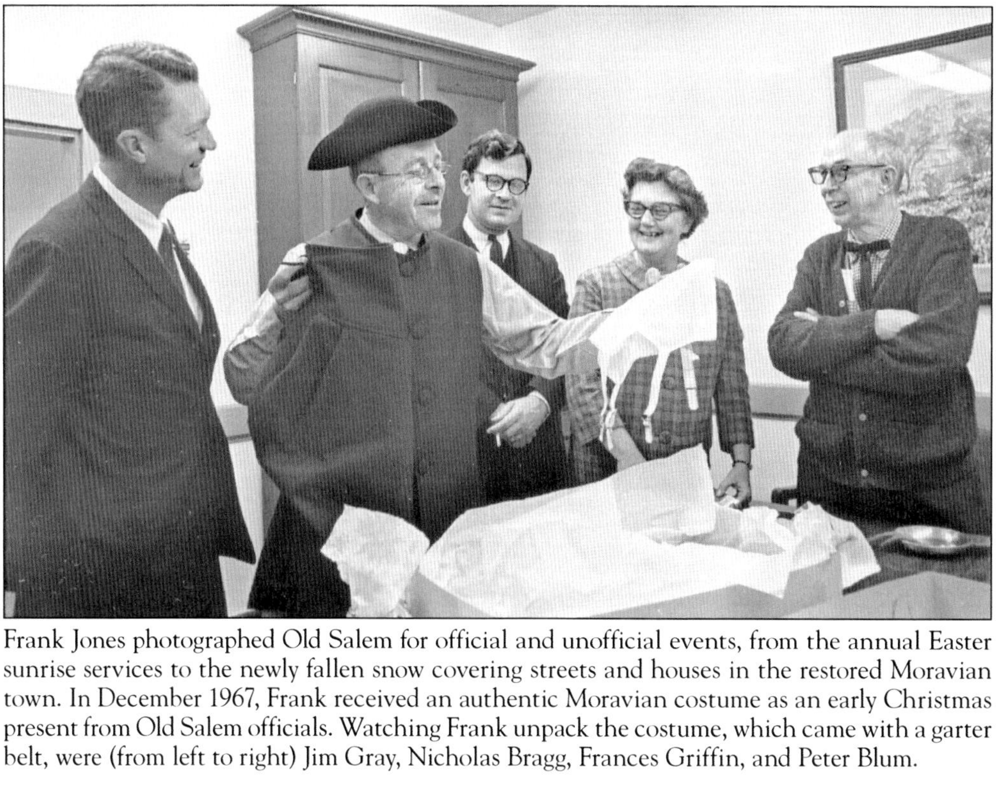

Frank Jones photographed Old Salem for official and unofficial events, from the annual Easter sunrise services to the newly fallen snow covering streets and houses in the restored Moravian town. In December 1967, Frank received an authentic Moravian costume as an early Christmas present from Old Salem officials. Watching Frank unpack the costume, which came with a garter belt, were (from left to right) Jim Gray, Nicholas Bragg, Frances Griffin, and Peter Blum.

Two

The 1930s

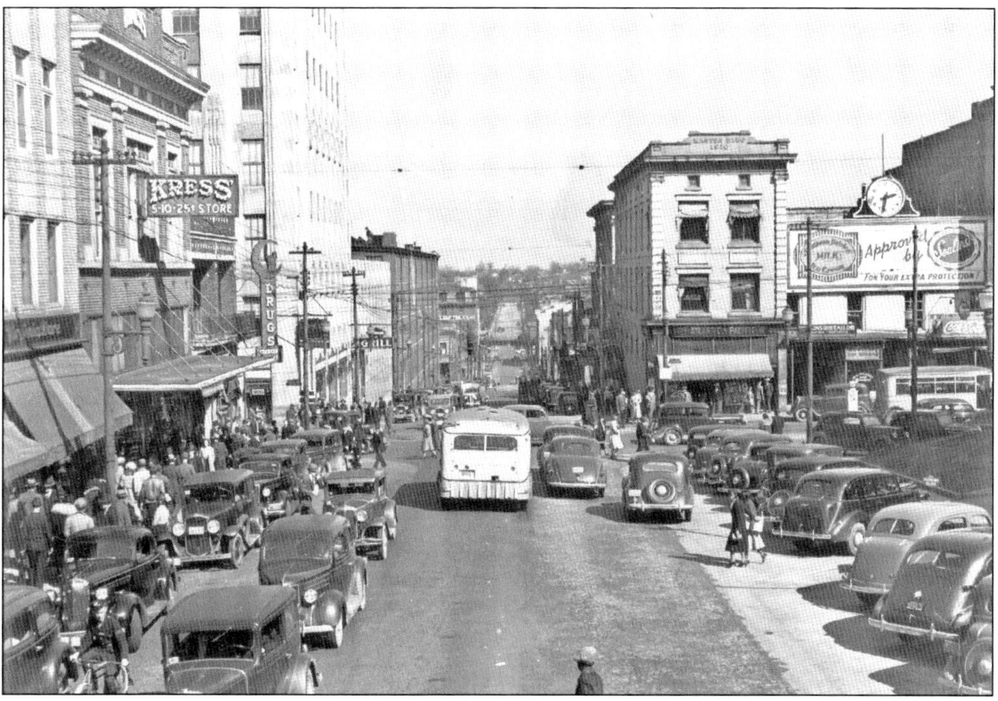

The streets surrounding the courthouse were filled with cars, buses, and people in April 1938 when this photograph was taken. On Fourth Street, looking toward Main, the Reynolds Building is on the northeast corner with the Masten Building on the southeast corner. The courthouse is out of sight on the right, and across the street are Crescent Drug Company, Family Shoe Store, S&H Kress, and Raylass Department Store.

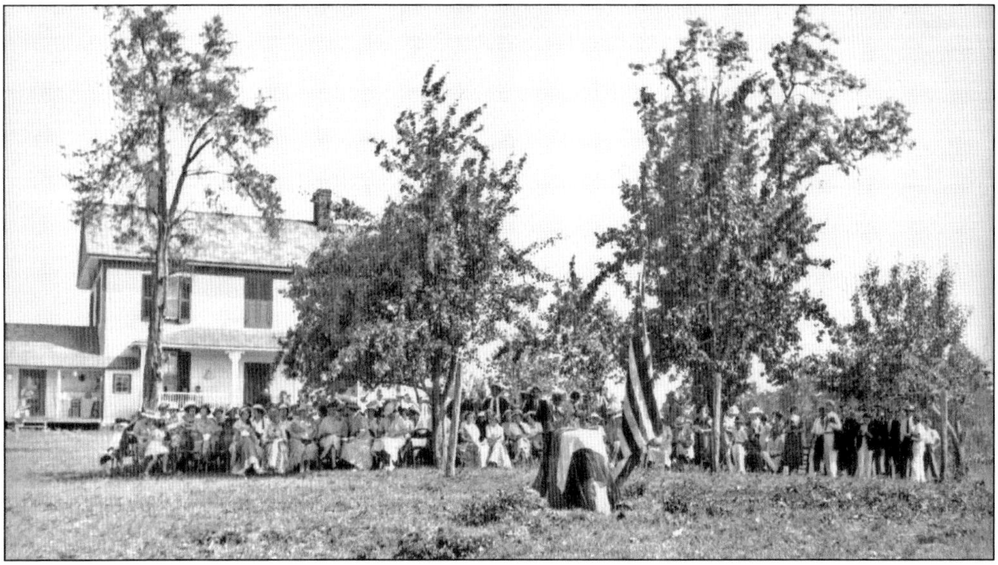

On a warm June day in 1936, 200 citizens gathered in Germanton to commemorate the home site of Col. Joseph Winston, for whom the town of Winston was named. A large boulder was placed on the home site, with a bronze marker attached to the boulder. The marker was provided by the General Joseph Winston Chapter of the Daughters of the American Revolution, the group that organized the ceremonies. Mayor W. T. Wilson delivered the principal address, and Rev. Douglas Rights offered the invocation. Mayor Wilson talked about Colonel Winston, his heroic record in the American Revolution, and his service as a state senator from Stokes County. A quartet provided musical entertainment, and a young girl gave a patriotic reading of "Why I Love the Flag." Other participants included a National Guard bugler, Boy Scouts in uniform, and girls wearing Colonial costumes.

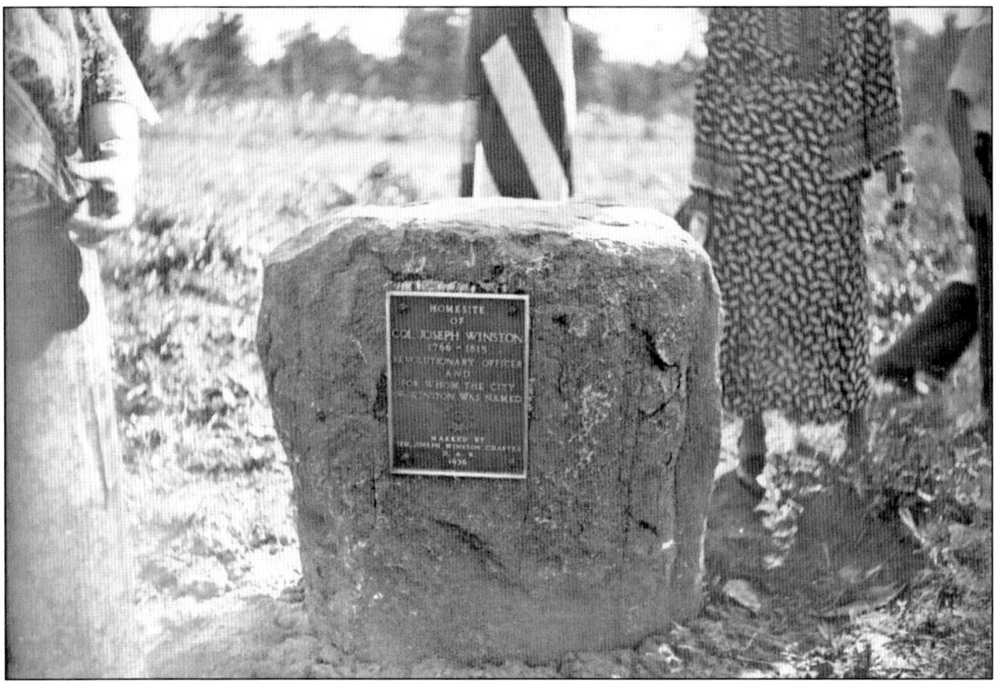

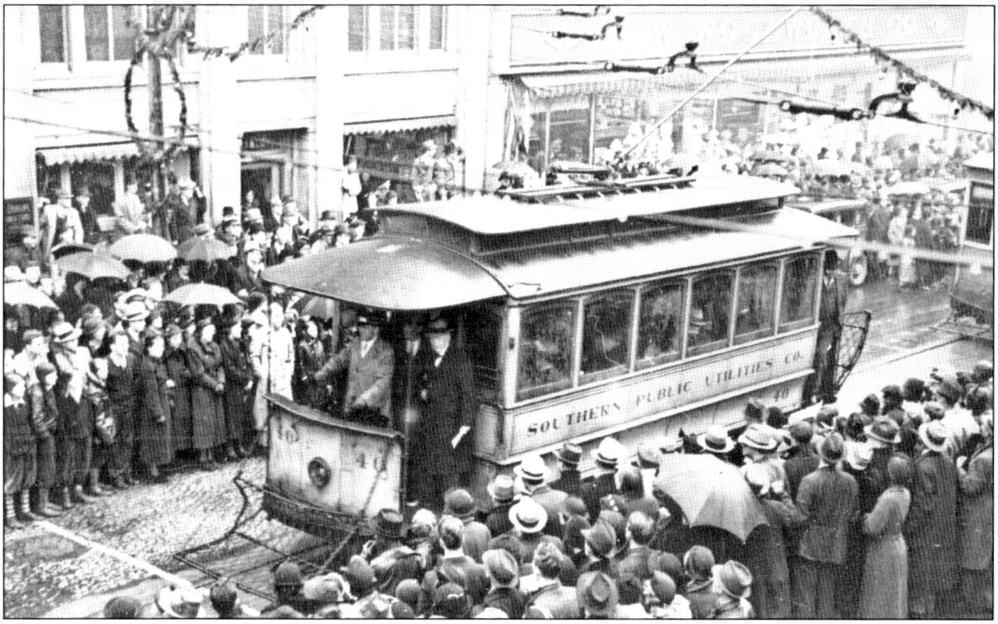

Charles K. Norfleet was general chairman of the "Romance of Transportation" parade, held December 30, 1936, which marked the end of the city's 46-year-old streetcar system. Wearing raincoats and holding umbrellas, spectators lined Liberty Street to see every type of vehicle imaginable roll past. Standing at the front of the streetcar was Henry E. Fries, who was instrumental in bringing the streetcar system to Winston-Salem. Riding with him in the car were motormen with 30 or more years of service. In addition to the streetcars, other vehicles in the parade included an ox cart, several generations of fire trucks, the Salem stage coach carrying women dressed in antebellum attire, bicycles, Model Ts, and a hearse. Immediately following the streetcar were the new buses, one of which carried the Exchange Club band, playing music as the city bade the streetcar farewell.

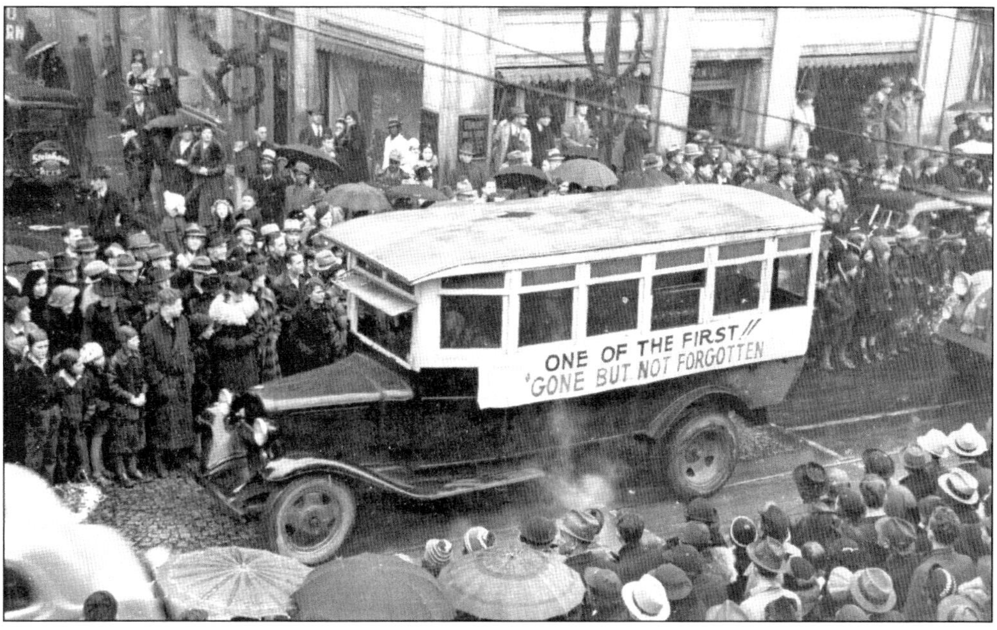

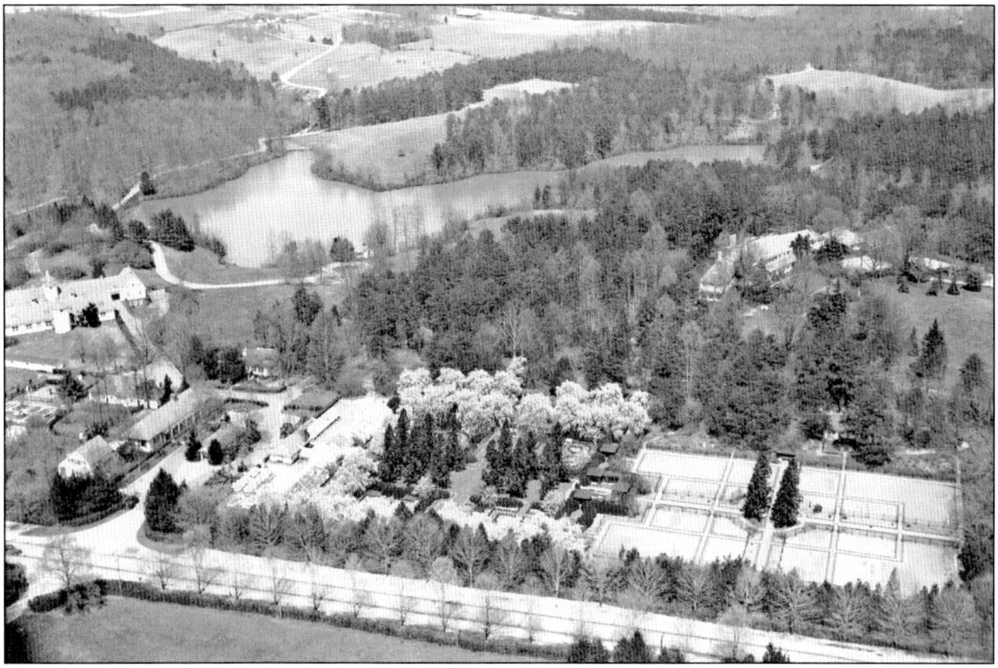

Reynolda House, gardens, barns, and other village buildings are clearly seen in this 1938 aerial, with Reynolda Road at the bottom of the photograph. Noticeable are the young trees lining Reynolda Road and the expansive Lake Katherine, named for Katherine Smith Reynolds, wife of Richard J. Reynolds. Reynolda House underwent an expansion and restoration, reopening in April 2005. The addition included a museum shop, library, auditorium, classrooms, and gallery space.

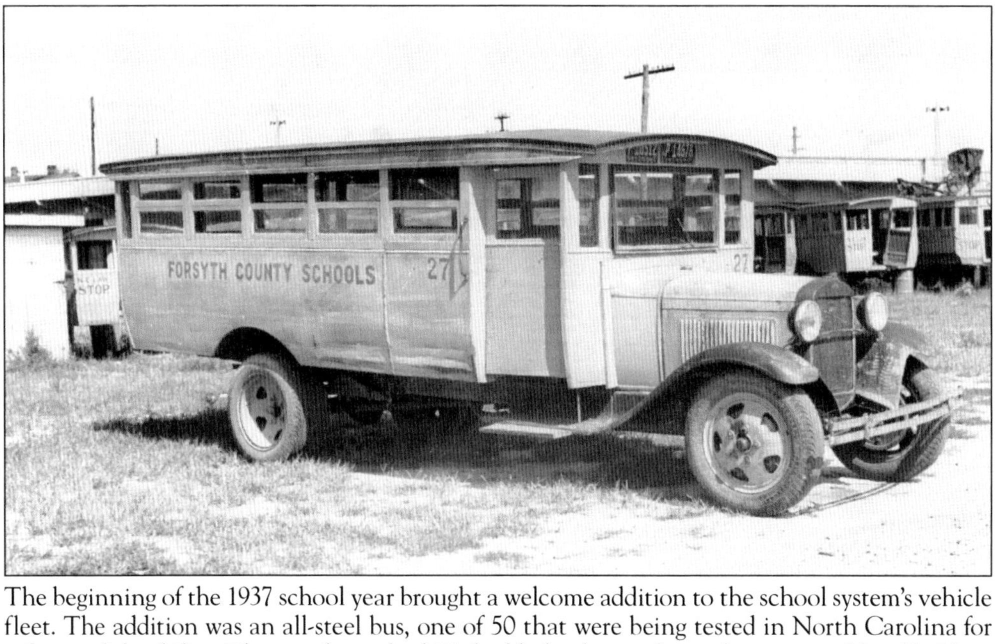

The beginning of the 1937 school year brought a welcome addition to the school system's vehicle fleet. The addition was an all-steel bus, one of 50 that were being tested in North Carolina for safety and durability. The new buses had 18 double leather-cushioned seats, capable of holding 36 children in comfort, and more reliable brakes. The other vehicles being used at this time were wooden buses, shown above.

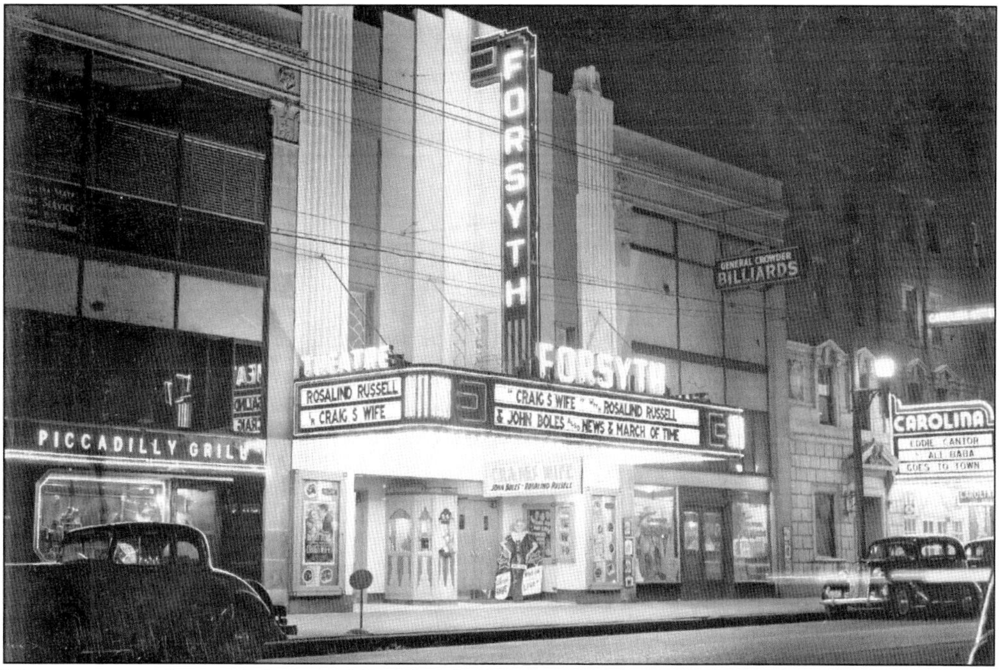

Movie-goers welcomed the new Forsyth Theatre to the city on January 13, 1937. Located on West Fourth Street, near the already-popular Carolina Theatre, the Forsyth Theatre featured air conditioning and the new Western Electric Mirrophonic Sound System. *Palm Springs* was the opening movie attraction, starring Sir Guy Standing, Frances Langford, Ernest Cossart, and David Niven. Also featured were a Laurel and Hardy comedy and a color cartoon titled "Neighbors."

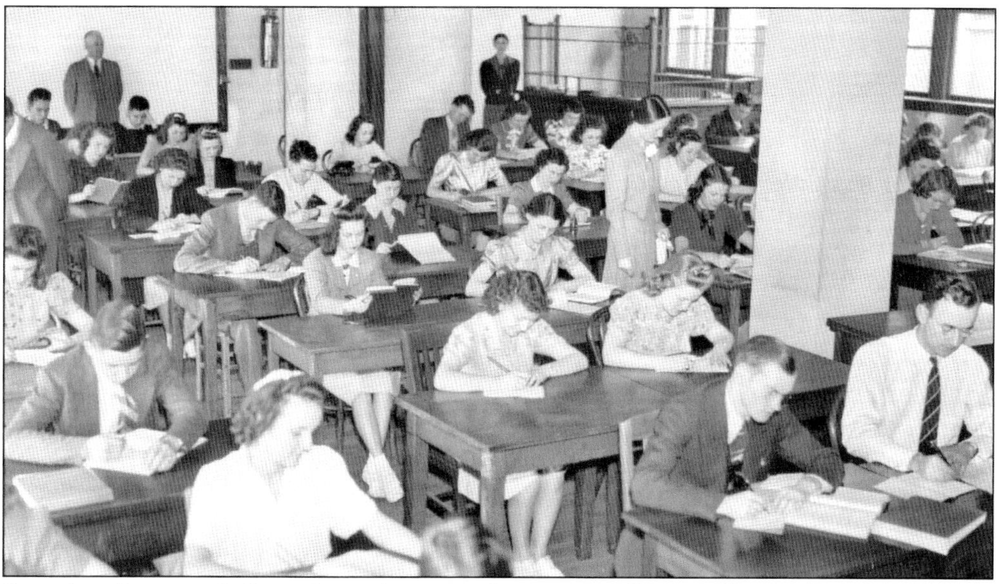

Draughon Business College, shown here in 1939, was initially started in Nashville, Tennessee, by John F. Draughon in 1890. He established branches in other cities and allowed managers to become owners of the schools. W. R. Middleton opened the school in 1924 in Winston-Salem, which was located after 1927 at 632 West Fourth Street. Carolyn Westmoreland, who later bought the school, had been a Draughon student and teacher.

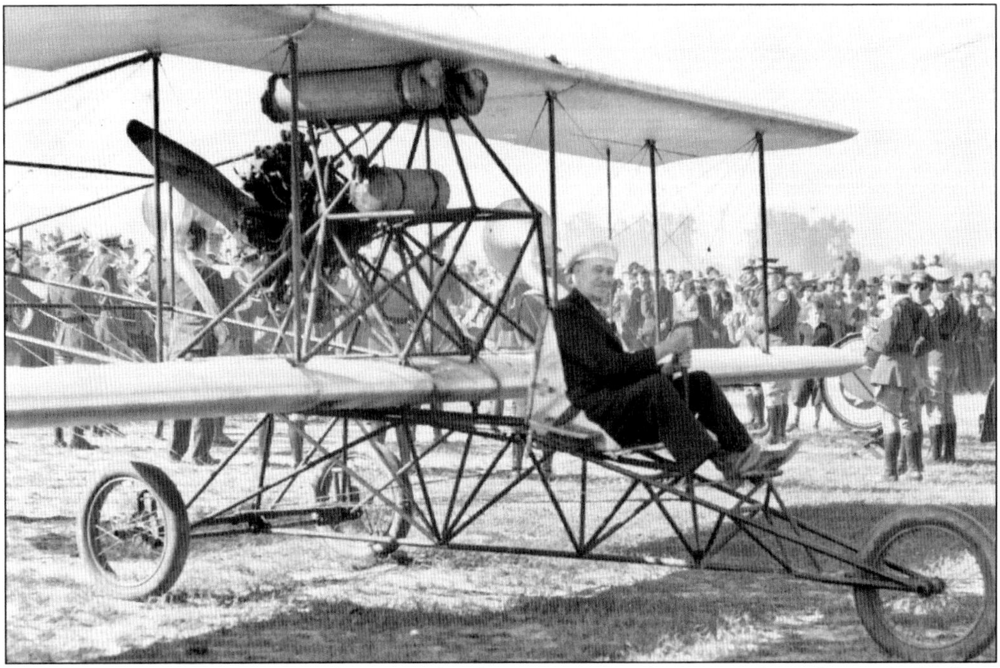

J. G. Stratton, shown above at the controls of a 1910 Curtis plane, was the only "Early Bird" in North Carolina at the time of the October 1939 air show. An Early Bird did active flying before 1916. Winston-Salem resident Stratton did exhibition flying with the Wright brothers in 1911. The air show was sponsored by the Exchange Club and drew a crowd of about 65,000 at Miller Field (below). There were 11 features in the show, complete with individual stunts, flying in formation, barrel rolls, power dives, loops, and flying upside down. For the finale, one daredevil rolled out of his plane from a mile up, and plummeted 4,500 feet before opening his parachute. While falling, he ripped a hole in a 50-pound bag of flour and left a flour-trail for about a mile as he descended.

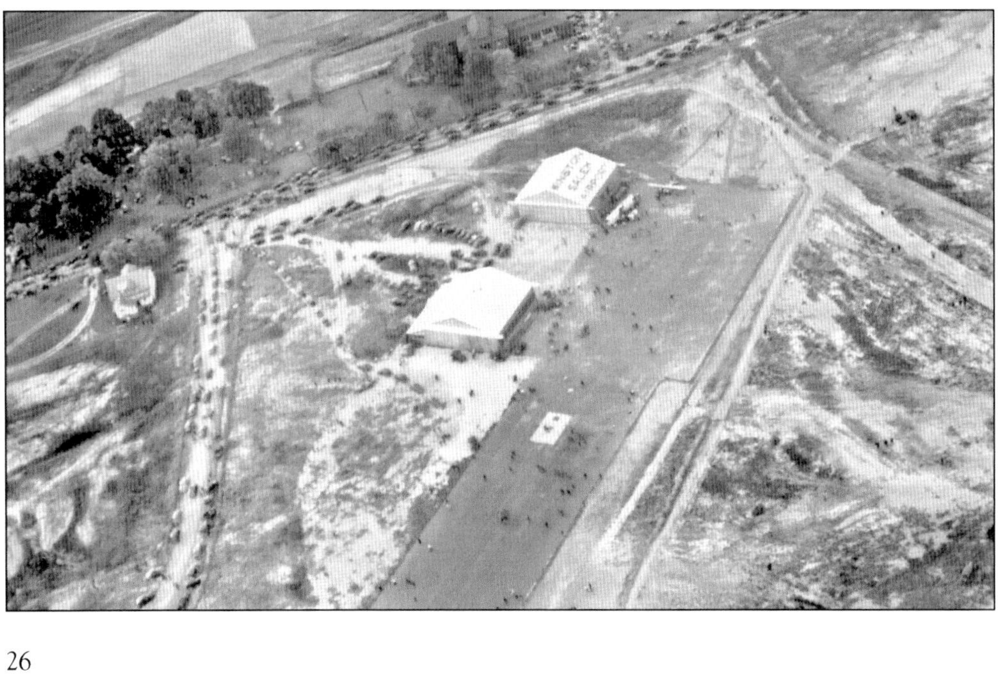

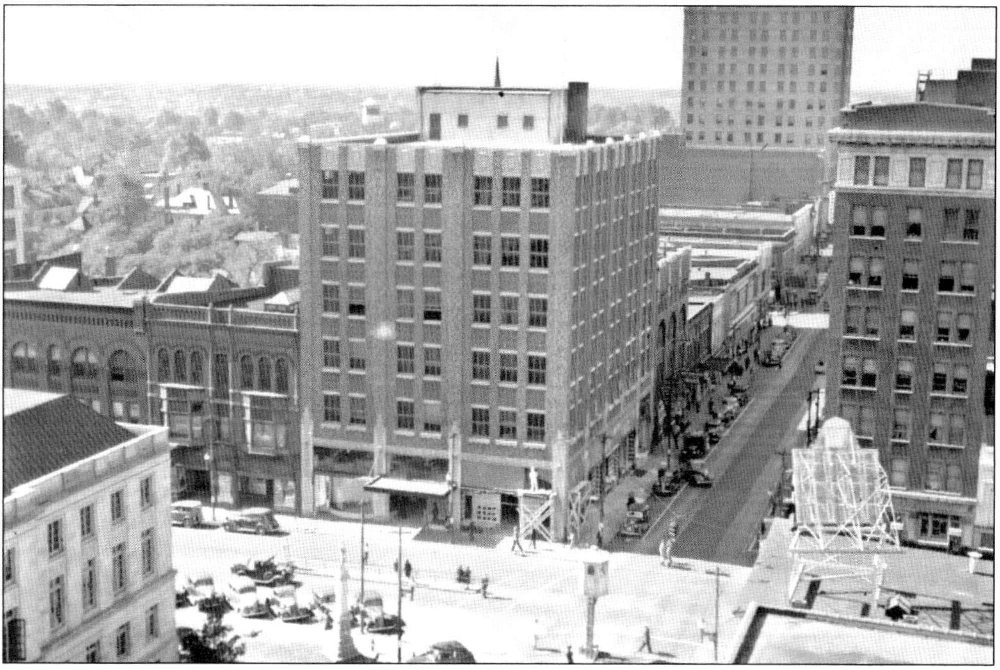

Huntley-Hill-Stockton Furniture Company opened in the Van Dyke Building (center) at Fourth and Liberty Streets on November 2, 1939. The company, formed in 1900, was previously located on North Trade Street. The founders of the company were B. F. Huntley, W. P. Hill, and M. D. Stockton. Twenty-six employees, plus the store manager, were available to assist customers in the new departments, and two elevators were installed to carry them between floors. Radios, lamps, rugs of all sizes, a Victorian furniture department (shown below), modern heating and ventilating systems, and elaborate overhead lighting were all new features for the store. An unusual innovation of the store was the revolving show window on the Liberty Street side, divided into sections and outfitted to resemble actual rooms. To celebrate the opening, everyone who attended received a genuine rabbit's-foot key ring.

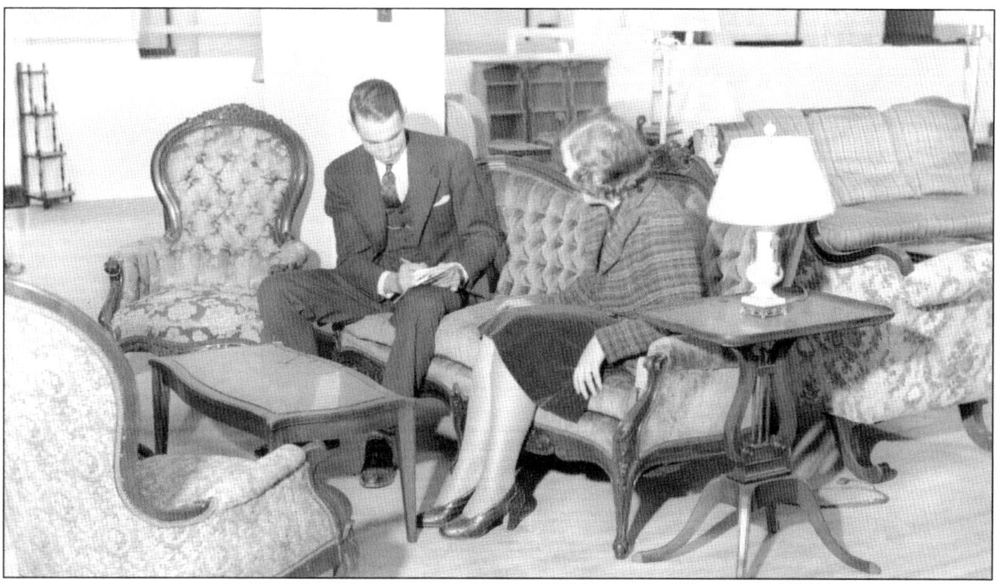

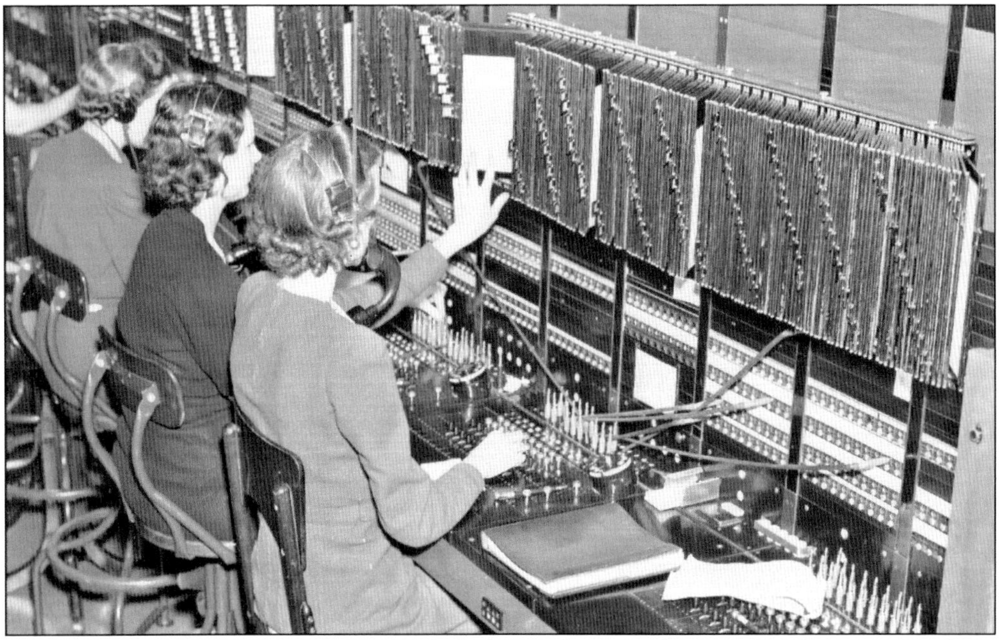

Some of the busiest people in town, particularly during the 1939 Christmas holidays, were Southern Bell Telephone and Telegraph switchboard operators. Working from their West Fifth Street office, the 47 operators underwent extensive training and practice to prepare them for the variety of calls received daily. The dial system for local calls was just beginning, so most operators handled only long-distance and information calls.

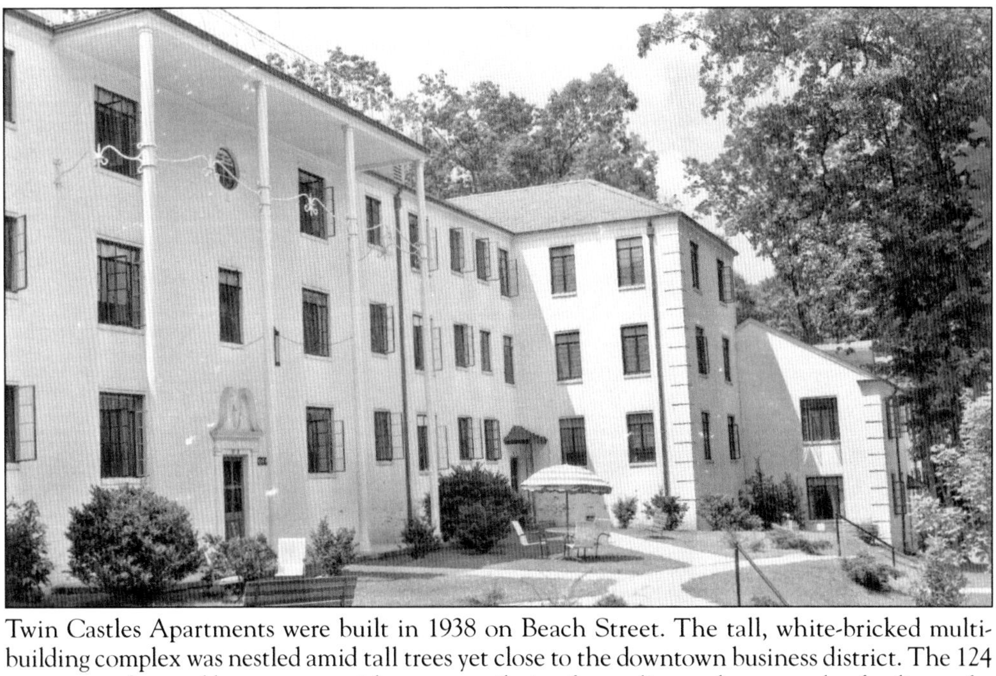

Twin Castles Apartments were built in 1938 on Beach Street. The tall, white-bricked multi-building complex was nestled amid tall trees yet close to the downtown business district. The 124 apartments featured large rooms, with cross ventilation for cooling and a new style of radiators for heating. Tiled bathrooms, large closets in the bedrooms, and compact but well-equipped kitchens offered all the amenities to prospective renters, including outdoor sandboxes for children.

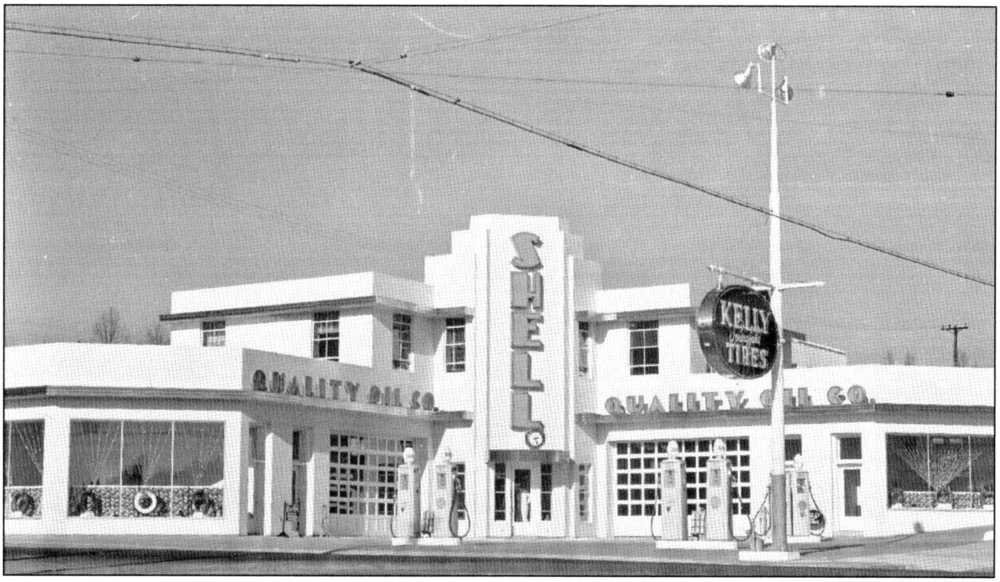

The new T-shaped brick-and-terra-cotta-tile building that opened on the corner of Reynolda Road and Northwest Boulevard was built to house Quality Oil Company. The opening took place on December 10, 1938, and was "dedicated to the satisfaction of the motoring public." The business started in 1930, and the five partners in 1938 were Bert and Paul Bennett and Joe, Archer, and James Glenn.

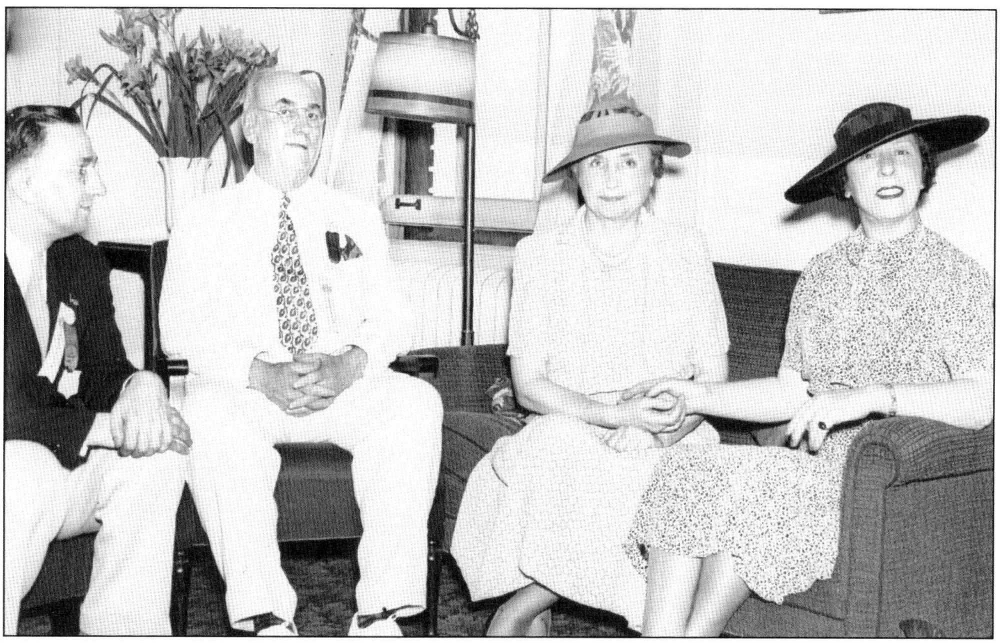

Helen Keller (second from right) and her companion, Polly Thompson (right), took the stage at the Carolina Theatre in June 1939 to speak at the State Lions Convention. Representing the American Foundation for the Blind, Miss Keller spoke on behalf of blind people. Miss Thompson interpreted the audience's questions with fingers in hand motions for Miss Keller, who was blind and deaf. Miss Thompson replaced Miss Keller's longtime companion, Anne Sullivan Macy, who died in 1936.

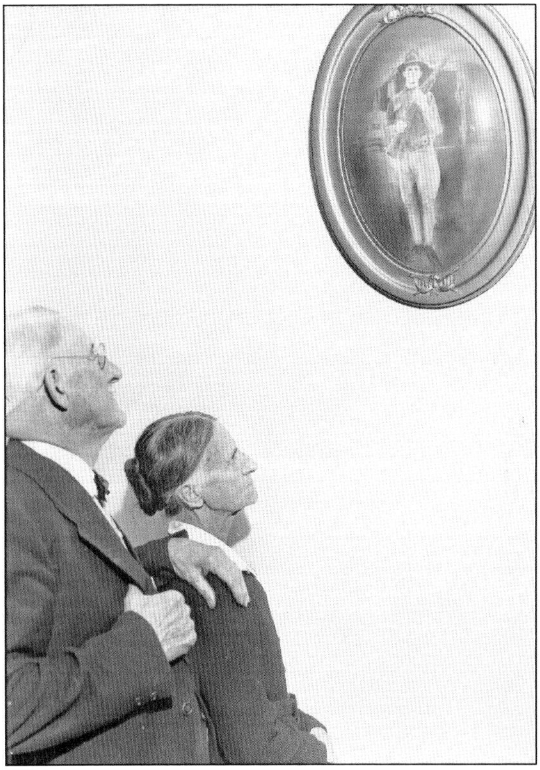

Mr. and Mrs. Charles W. Bolling reminisce about their son, Clyde (shown in the wall portrait), who was the first man from Winston-Salem to be killed in World War I. The occasion was Armistice Day in 1938, and they recalled that their son died in France on May 11, 1918, as a soldier in the 18th Infantry. In 1920, the Forsyth County American Legion named their post in honor of Clyde W. Bolling.

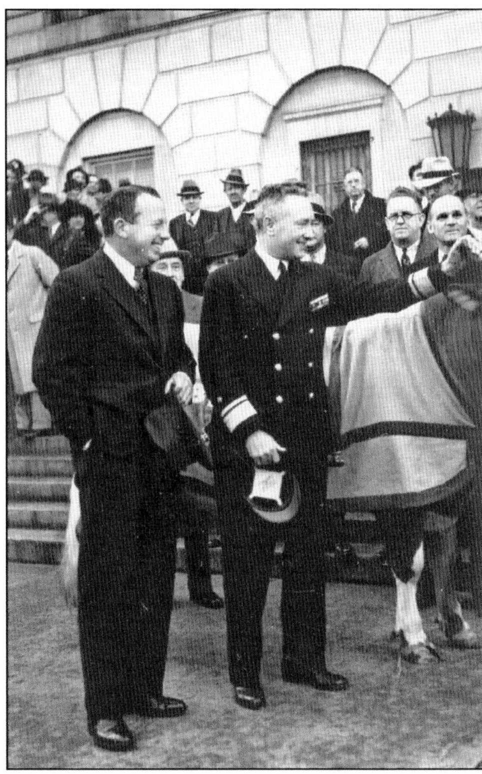

Adm. Richard E. Byrd (in uniform), the famous Antarctic explorer, visited Winston-Salem in March 1936 and posed for pictures with Klondike Iceberg, owned by Thurmond Chatham (left). Klondike Iceberg was the famous bull born to Klondike Nira in the Antarctic. Admiral Byrd made his third trip to Winston-Salem to discuss his experiences and to show his moving pictures at Reynolds Auditorium. Thurmond Chatham furnished a cow and blankets for Byrd's polar expedition.

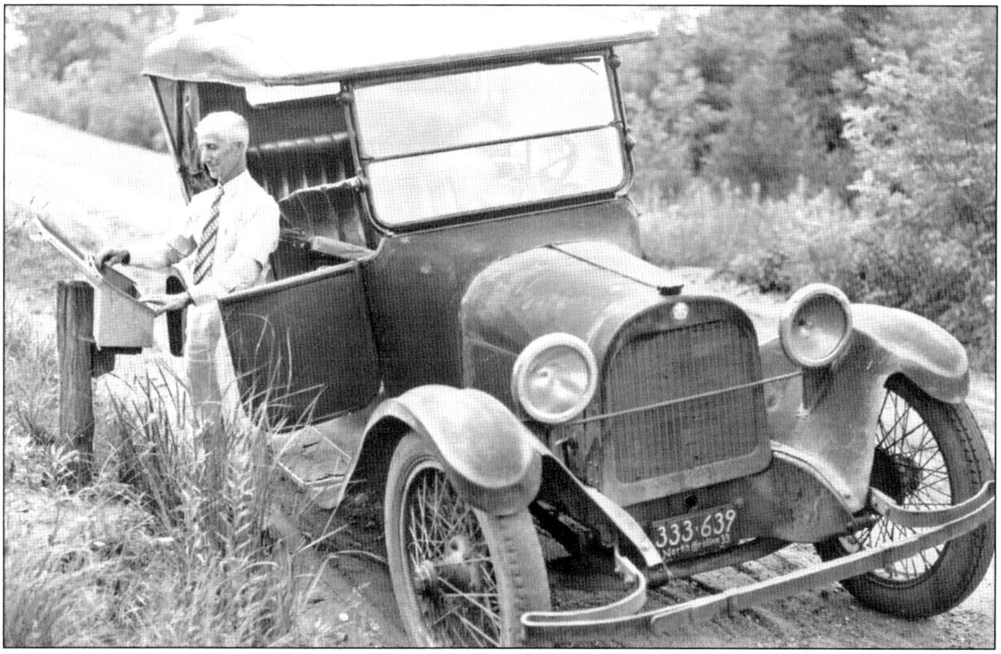

T. E. Woosley, a rural mail carrier, used the same car on his six-day route for 20 years. The deluxe model touring car cost $1,145 in 1919, and in 1939, it was traveling 53.9 miles a day, getting 22 miles to a gallon of gas. Mr. Woosley delivered mail to 1,500 to 2,000 people each day in Forsyth County and pointed out that it never had a dented or replaced fender.

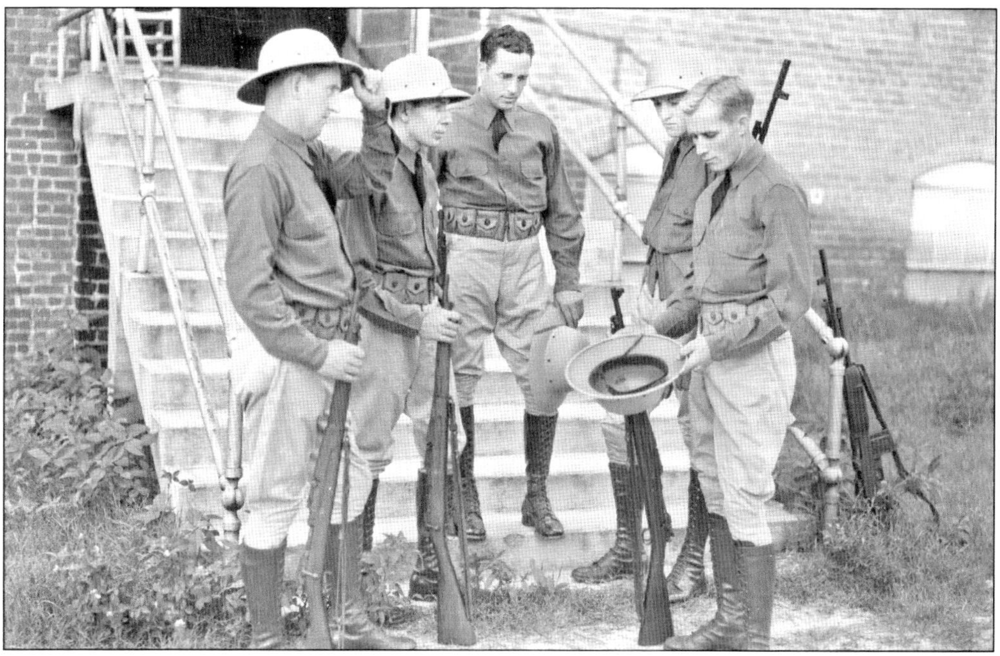

Soldiers in Winston-Salem's National Guard Company A of the 105 Quartermaster's Regiment left for their two-week summer camp in July 1939. The men sported new tropical helmets to help relieve the heat they would encounter at Fort McClelland, Alabama. At that time, Company A was the only motorized company in the state, with seven recently purchased trucks.

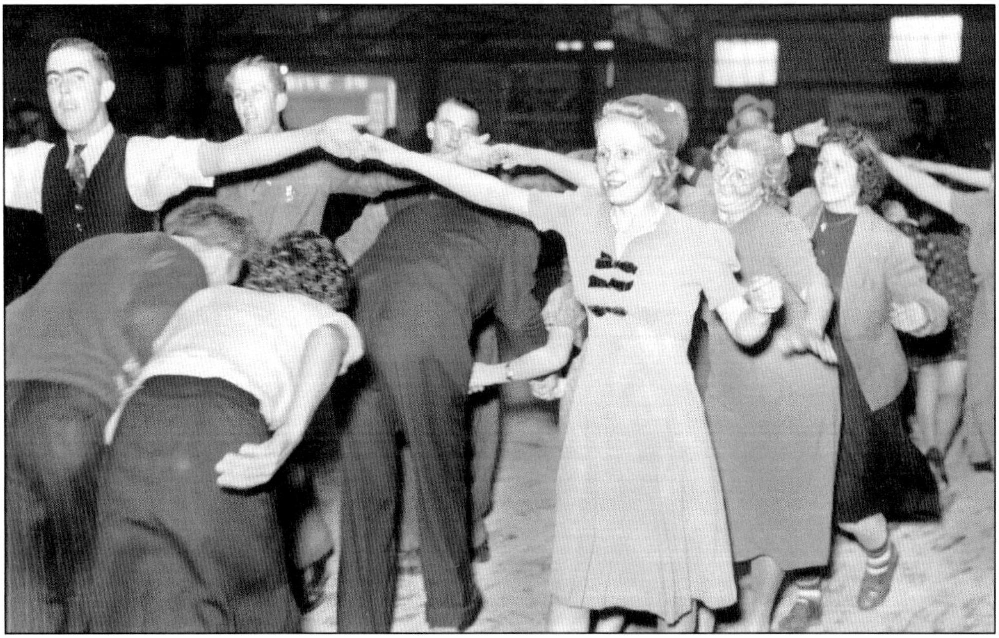

The City of Winston-Salem threw a Christmas party for a group of 30,000 people, tobacco growers and their families, in December 1939. The party was a "thank you" for the patronage of the tobacco growers, who together marketed over 54 million pounds of tobacco during 1939. The festivities of the day included fireworks, square dancing, prize drawings, and bagged treats of fruits and toys distributed to 9,000 children.

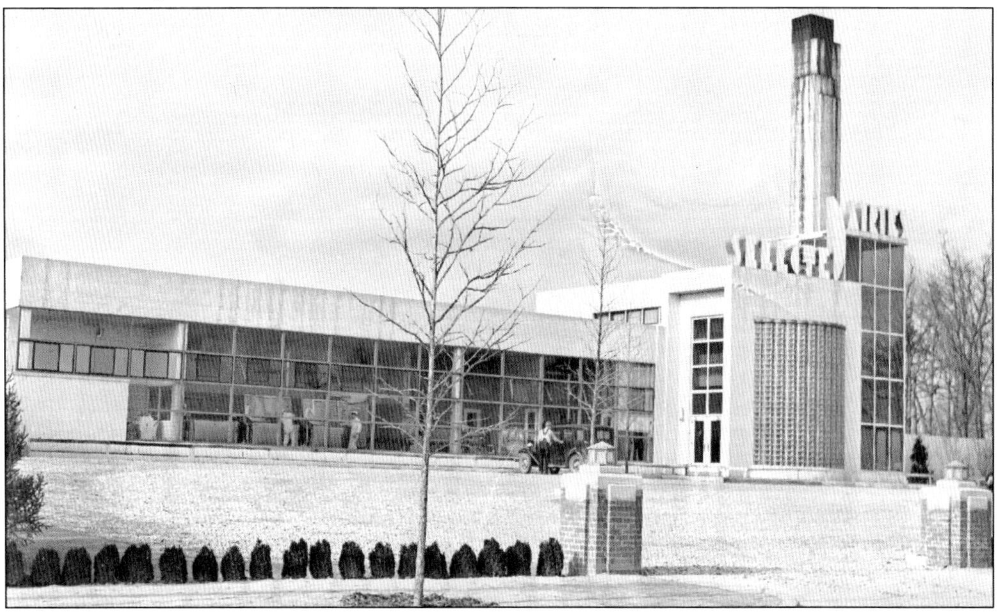

Selected Dairies was incorporated by T. Holt Haywood, owner of Arden Farms; Thurmond Chatham, owner of Klondike Farm; and John C. Whitaker, owner of Whit-Acres Farm. The business was established to handle dairy products from these farms and at least three others. Selected Dairies opened in March 1938 on South Stratford Road in a building designed by a national dairy architect in the most modern style.

Three

THE 1940S

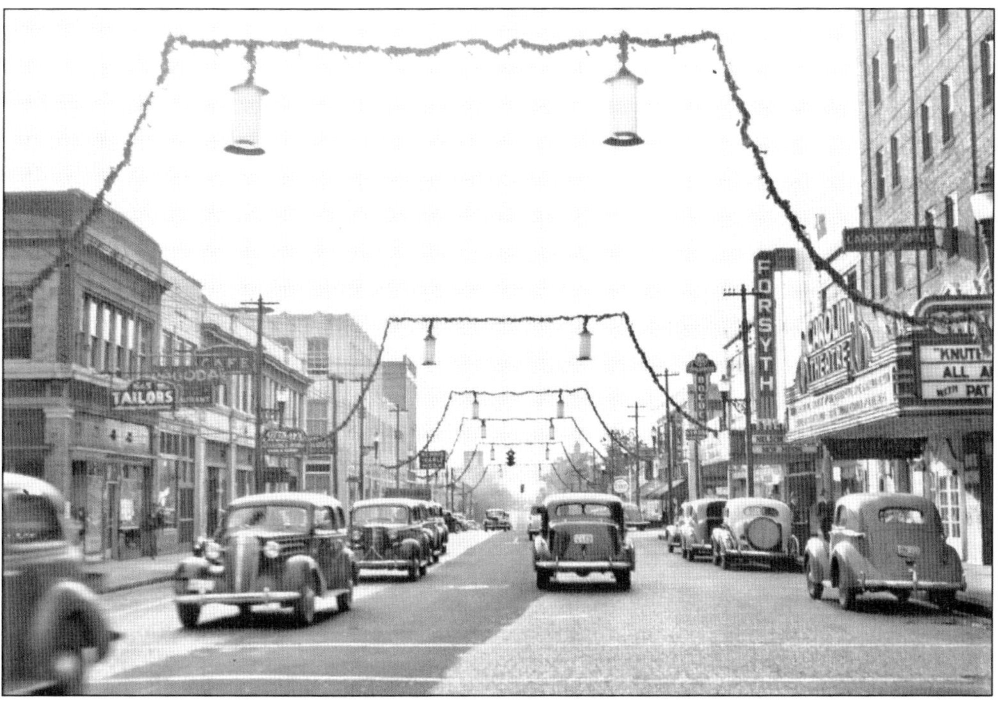

More spectators than usual came to town in November 1940 to see the new Christmas decorations. Despite unseasonably warm weather, the new garlands and red lanterns attracted shoppers to the downtown stores for the opening of the yuletide season. This view looking west on Fourth Street, at the Marshall Street intersection, shows two-way traffic and the paved center street section previously consumed by streetcar tracks.

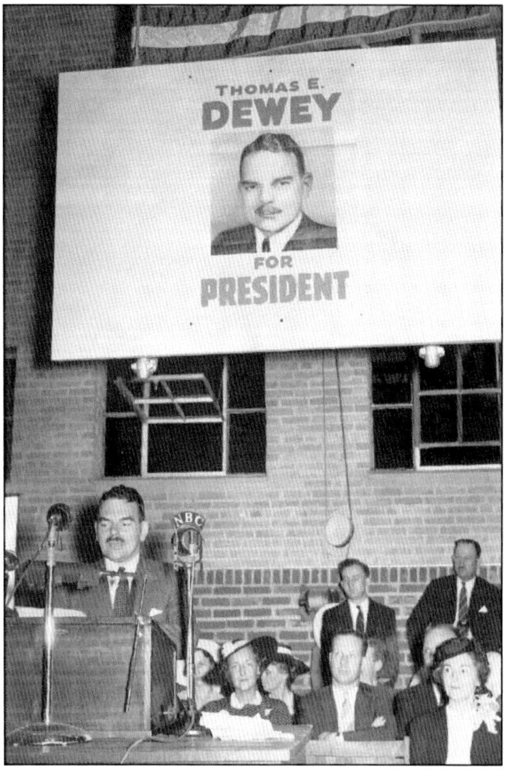

Thomas E. Dewey, candidate for the Republican presidential nomination, spoke to a capacity crowd at Reynolds Park gymnasium on June 8, 1940, on the topic "What America Faces." Dewey, a New York district attorney, visited Winston-Salem as part of a Western North Carolina counties tour, accompanied by his wife. Dewey's speech touched on many points related to his campaign, including those that criticized President Roosevelt's "New Deal."

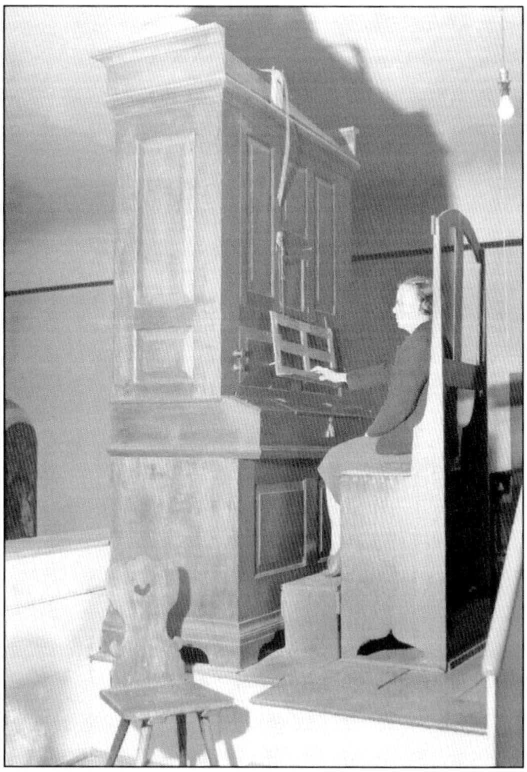

Miss Pearl Strupe sat at the organ console in Bethania Moravian Church in November 1941. Built in 1773 by Joseph Bullitschek, the organ featured reverse coloring of the keys; the keys normally colored white are black and vice versa. The organ, used regularly for Sunday worship, was destroyed along with other interior furnishings in a November 1942 fire. A new pipe organ was dedicated in the restored church in 1946.

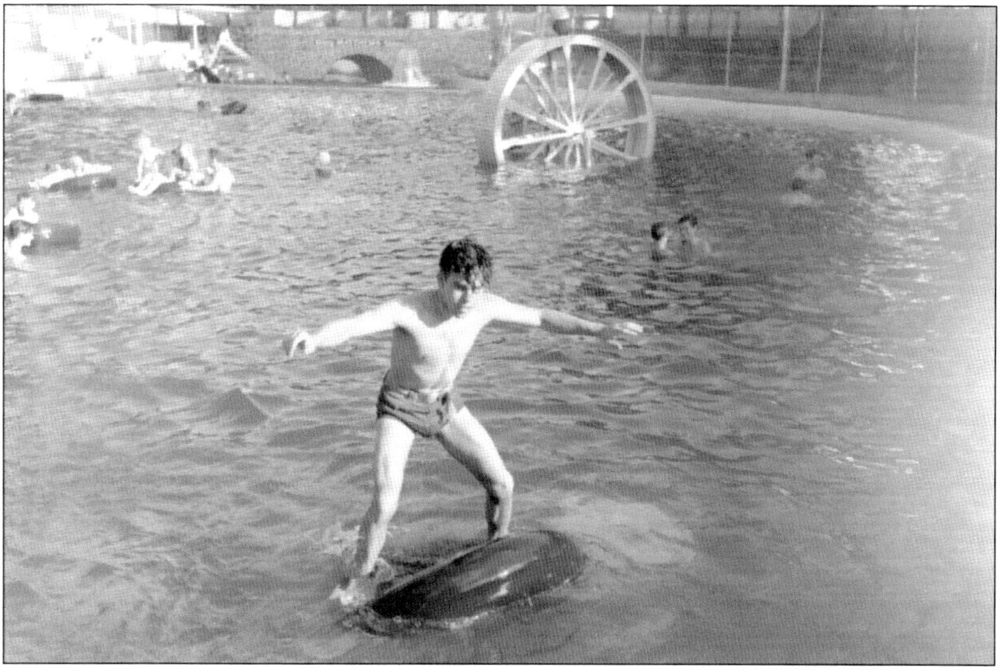

At Crystal Lake, off Reynolda Road, many children and adults spent their summers swimming in the large pool, with divided sections for different water levels. In this 1940 photograph, a waterwheel is shown in the center of the pool. The children's area featured a slide and waterfall. Owned by the Davis family, Crystal Lake also offered multi-level diving boards, boating and fishing lakes, a pavilion for dancing or socializing, and picnic shelters.

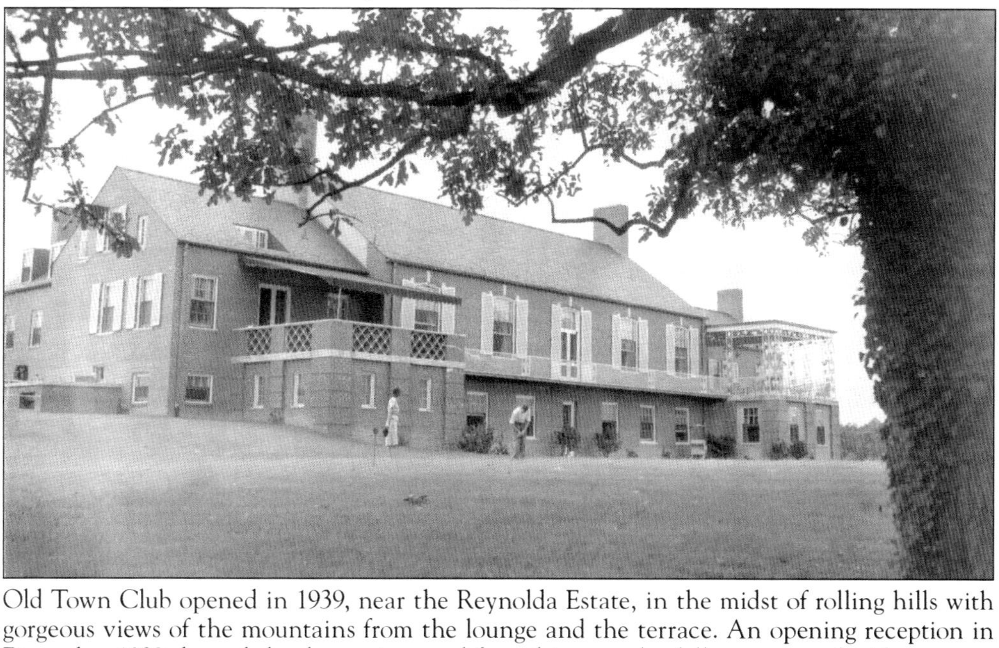

Old Town Club opened in 1939, near the Reynolda Estate, in the midst of rolling hills with gorgeous views of the mountains from the lounge and the terrace. An opening reception in December 1939 showed the decorations and furnishings to the fullest, accented with greenery for the Christmas season. The terrace, shown at the right in this 1940 photograph, featured an iron rail with scrollwork of grapes.

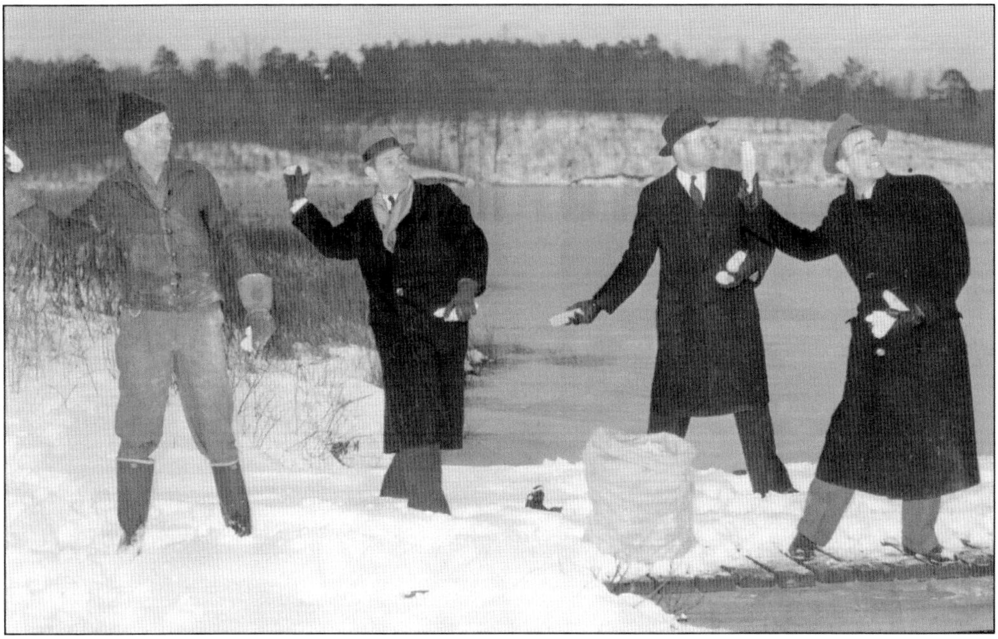

Izaak Walton was an English author who wrote a book on fishing in 1653 titled *The Compleat Angler.* The book contained practical information on fishing, along with songs, poems, and descriptions about the English countryside. The Izaak Walton League of America was founded in 1922 as a conservation organization. On a cold January night in 1940, local members of the organization fed corn to destitute ducks on the city pond.

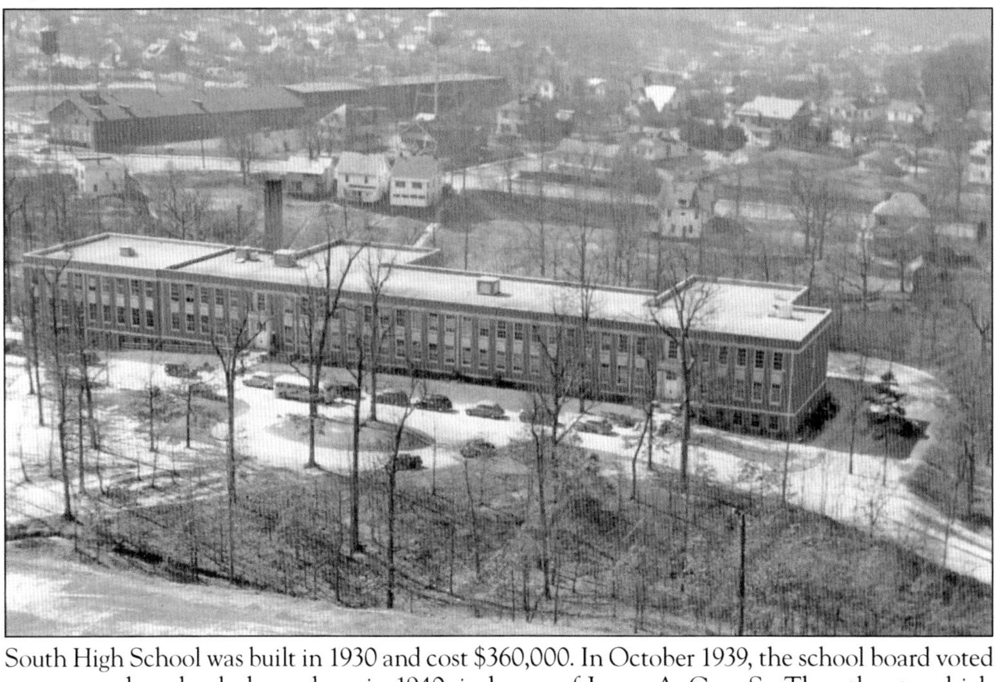

South High School was built in 1930 and cost $360,000. In October 1939, the school board voted to rename the school, shown here in 1940, in honor of James A. Gray Sr. The other two high schools, Richard J. Reynolds and John W. Hanes, were also named for city leaders. Mr. Gray took an active part in establishing the local public school system, which was approved in 1883.

It took a lot of imagination to see that new items, such as shoe heels and brush handles, could be made from old tires. These 543 old automobile tires were on their way to Charlotte in 1942 for shipping to factories that would reclaim the rubber for new uses. The reclamation was a defense project, with tires and tubes collected by the local Goodrich-Silvertown Station, in exchange for defense stamps.

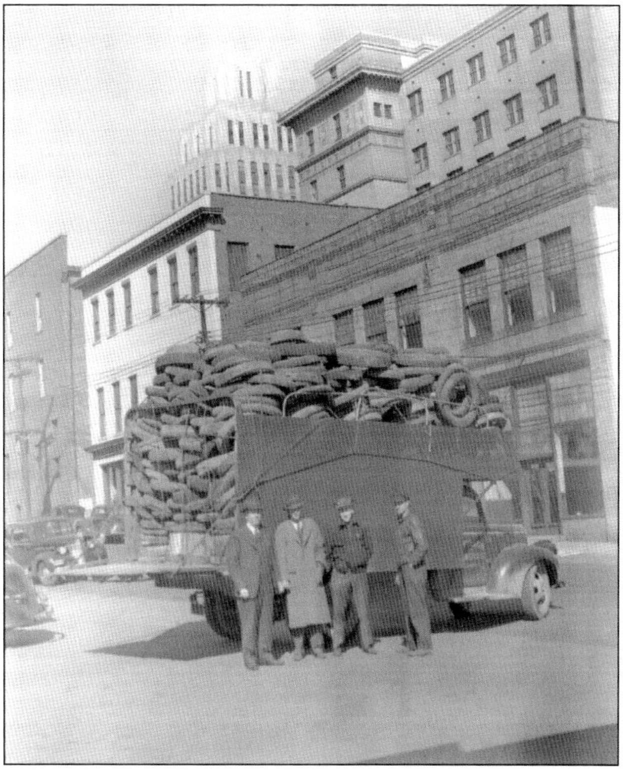

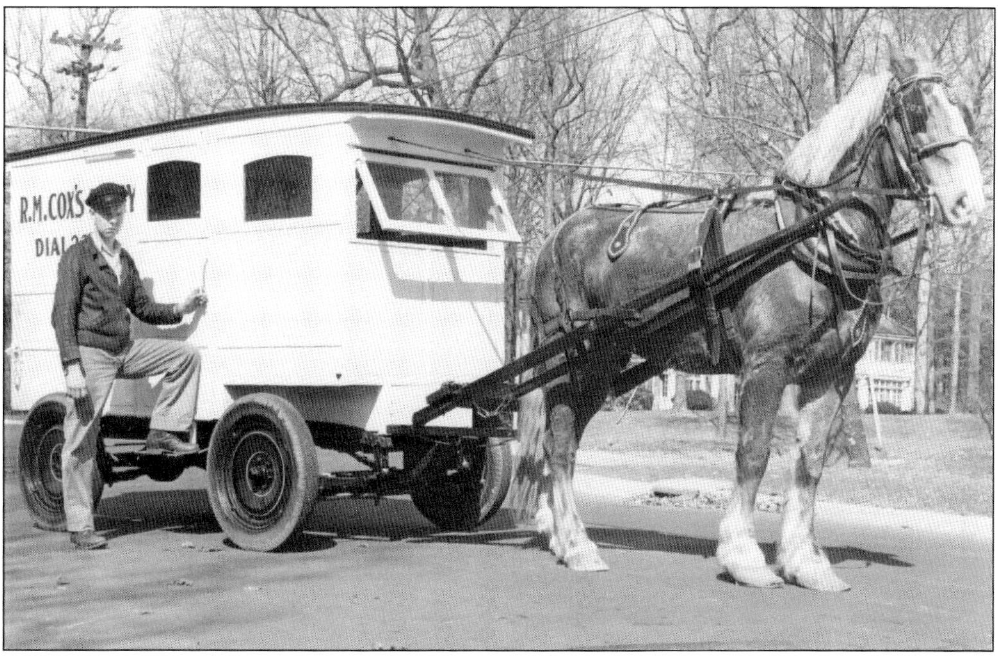

While old tires were being recycled in 1942, new tires were difficult to acquire. New truck tires were banned for certain uses, including house-to-house milk delivery. Home delivery companies had to be creative, so R. M. Cox's Dairy combined a horse with a wagon that used obsolete tires that were not rationed. Cox made a test run on the route, which covered 8 to 10 miles in six hours.

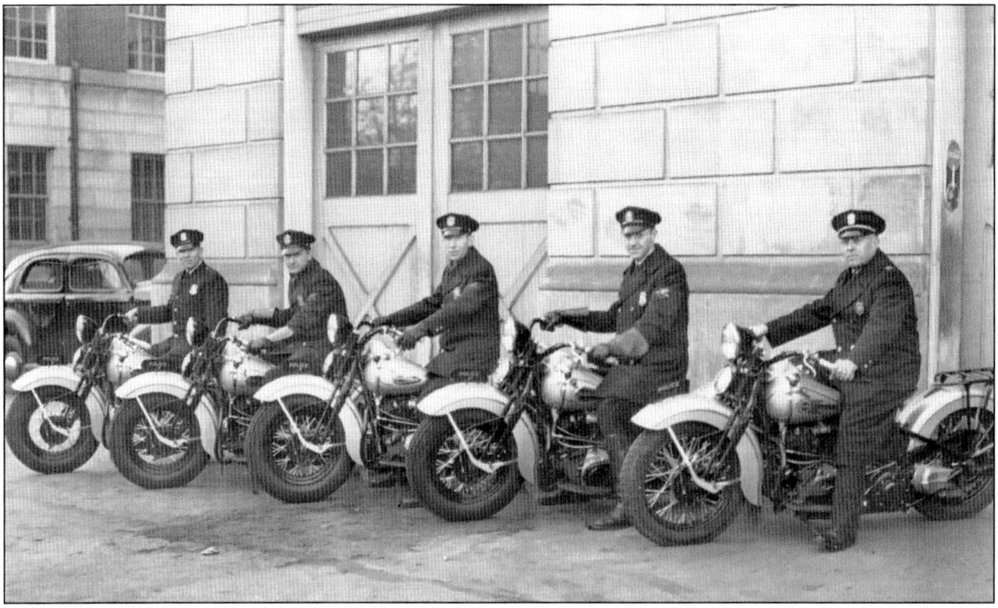

Five new motorcycles were added to the rolling stock for the Winston-Salem Police Department in January 1940. The new motorcycles were two-cylinder Harley Davidson models, replacing the four-cylinder Indians that the department previously owned. One month later, during Boy Scout Anniversary Week, two scouts struck a policeman's pose on the new motorcycles. This was the day that youth, represented by 60 Scouts, ruled city government by taking the places of officials for an hour. Some officials replaced were the mayor, aldermen, commissioners of various departments, and personnel in the police and fire departments. Scouts looked forward to special events each day, including a banquet, a movie at State Theatre, a rally at the armory, and church services on Sunday. The Scouts issued a proclamation of appreciation to the city for the hands-on civics lesson.

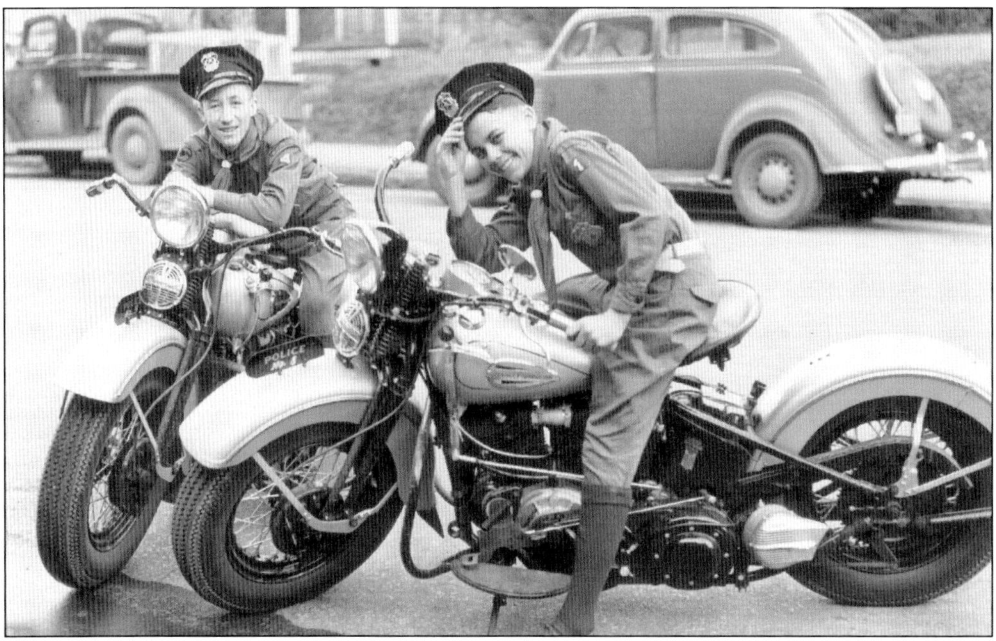

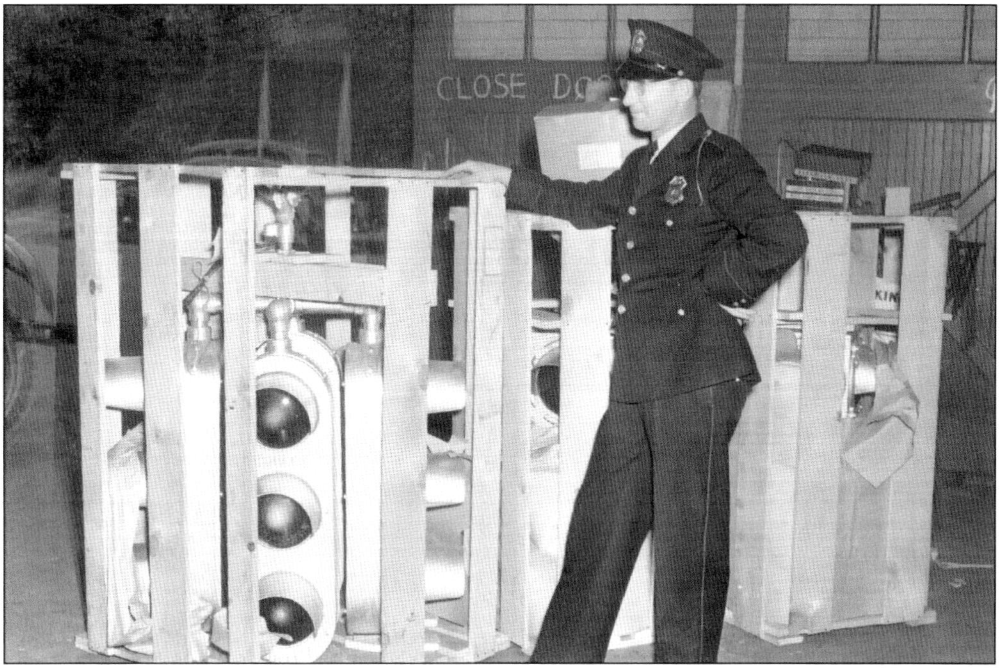

A new and heavier type of electric stoplight began to appear in Winston-Salem in 1939, replacing traffic policemen and some of the lighter signals installed earlier. Before the electric signal lights, policemen would hand-direct vehicles from a booth above the traffic at the intersection of Fourth and Liberty Streets. Three of the heavier lights installed in 1940 are shown above with a patrolman from the police department. One signal was adjustable for the three-point intersection of Eighth, Liberty, and Main Streets, with arms that moved to face different angles. In August 1941, the concrete safety islands (below) around the courthouse square were removed. The safety islands gave streetcar and bus passengers a place to load and unload safely in the middle of the street. When the buses began to stop at the curbs, the safety islands were no longer needed.

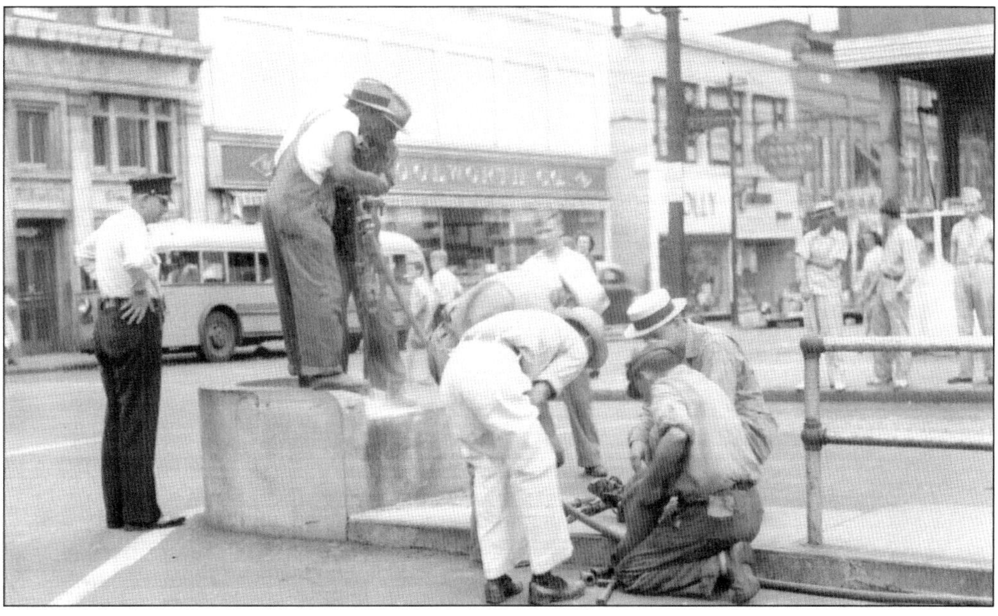

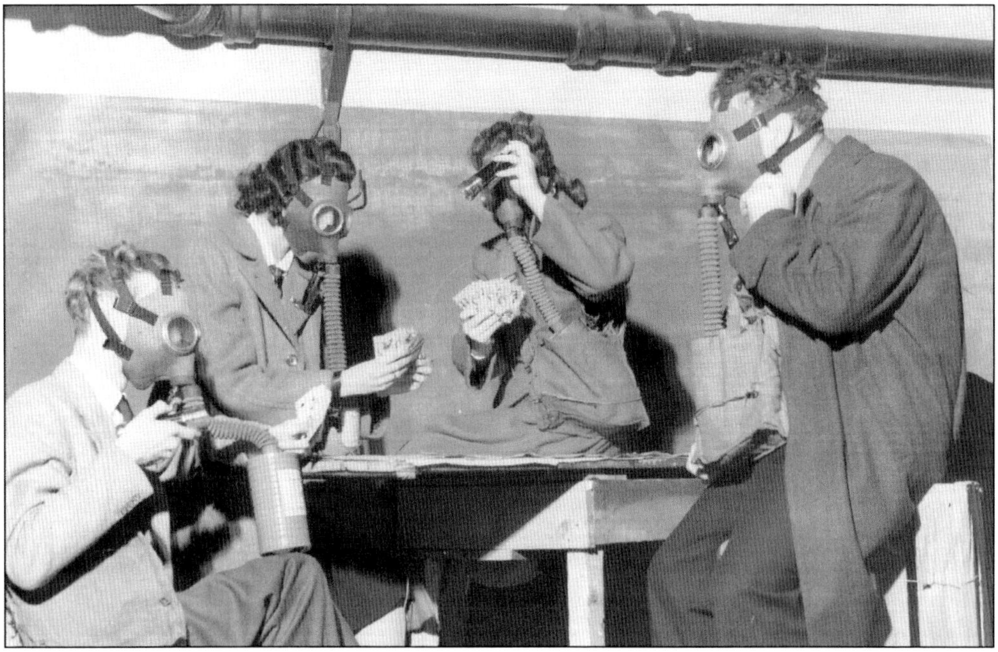

While newspapers of 1942 were filled with war news, local citizens were preparing themselves for what might be coming. Civilian defense workers were being trained as auxiliary firemen and policemen, air raid wardens, fire watchers, emergency medical personnel, and public works and utilities repair squads. Little Theatre members demonstrate how to don gas masks and wait out the air and gas raids while playing bridge.

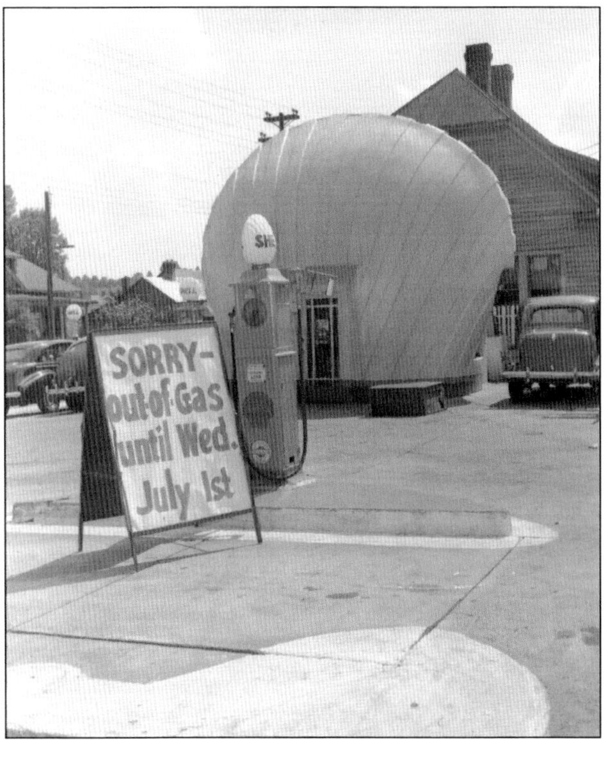

The Shell gasoline station at the corner of Main Street and Park Avenue sported a familiar sign in late June 1942. Many stations in town faced the same problem as residents drained local gas resources in anticipation of a gas price increase. The next month's gas allotment would be available July 1. But after July 22, the allotment system would be abolished and replaced by coupon gas rationing.

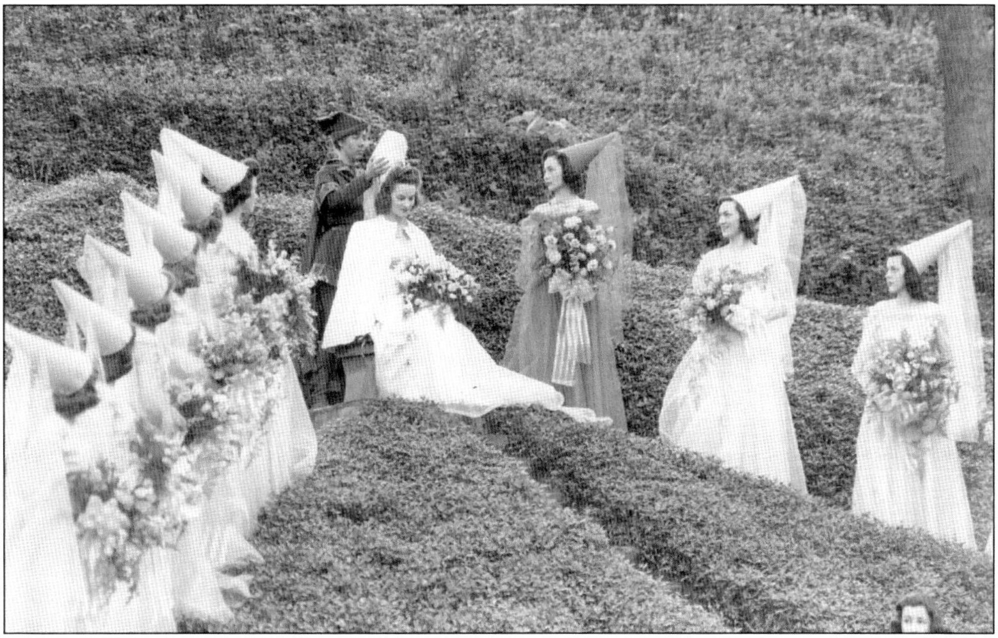

For many years, Salem College celebrated May Day with activities that often began early in the school year. The highlight of May Day was crowning the May Queen and watching the pageant that culminated in the dance around the colorful maypole. In 1941, Katherine King was crowned Queen of the May before 4,000 spectators in Salem College's May Dell, surrounded by her lovely attendants.

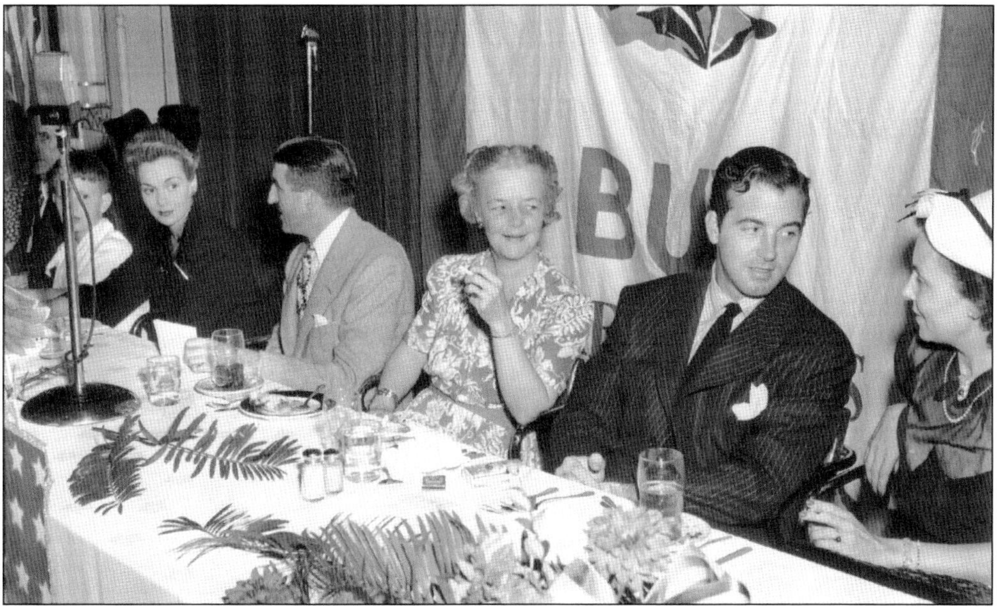

Movie stars Jane Wyman (left) and John Payne (second from right) were guests at the Victory Bond Drive dinner at the Hotel Robert E. Lee in September 1942. Sitting at the head table with the guests of honor were Mr. and Mrs. Robert Hanes (second and third from left). Miss Wyman and Mr. Payne entertained the group with songs and then autographed bonds that were purchased by the dinner attendees to raise money for the bond effort.

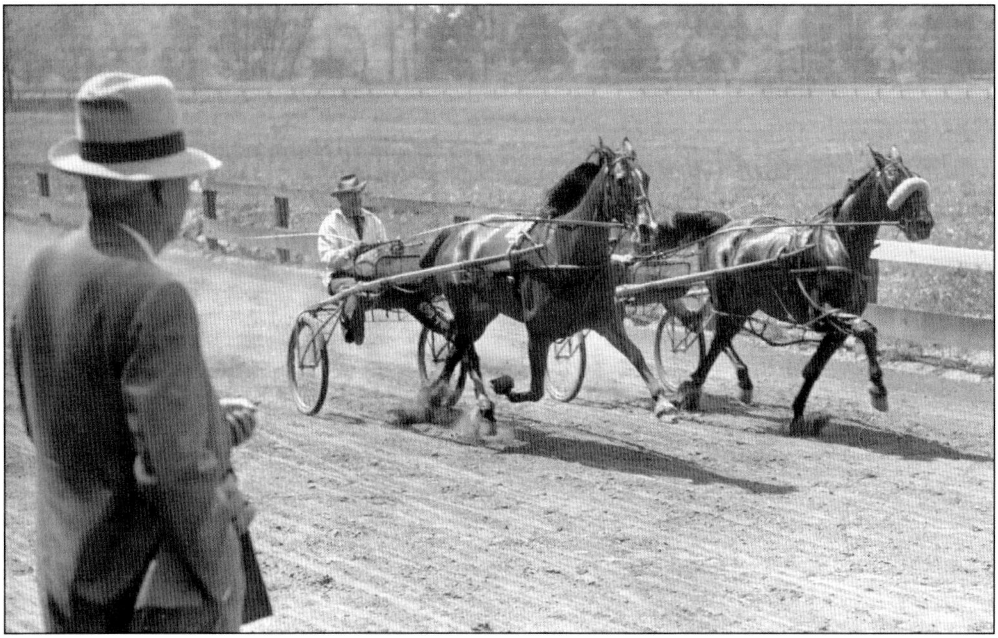

For racehorse owners, spring brings thoughts of the upcoming racing season. William Neal Reynolds is shown clocking two of his trotters at his Tanglewood Farm. He was preparing to ship 10 horses to Westbury, New York, for the opening of the summer season on May 24, 1946. Mr. Reynolds had recently returned from Florida, where his Grand Circuit horses trained during the winter.

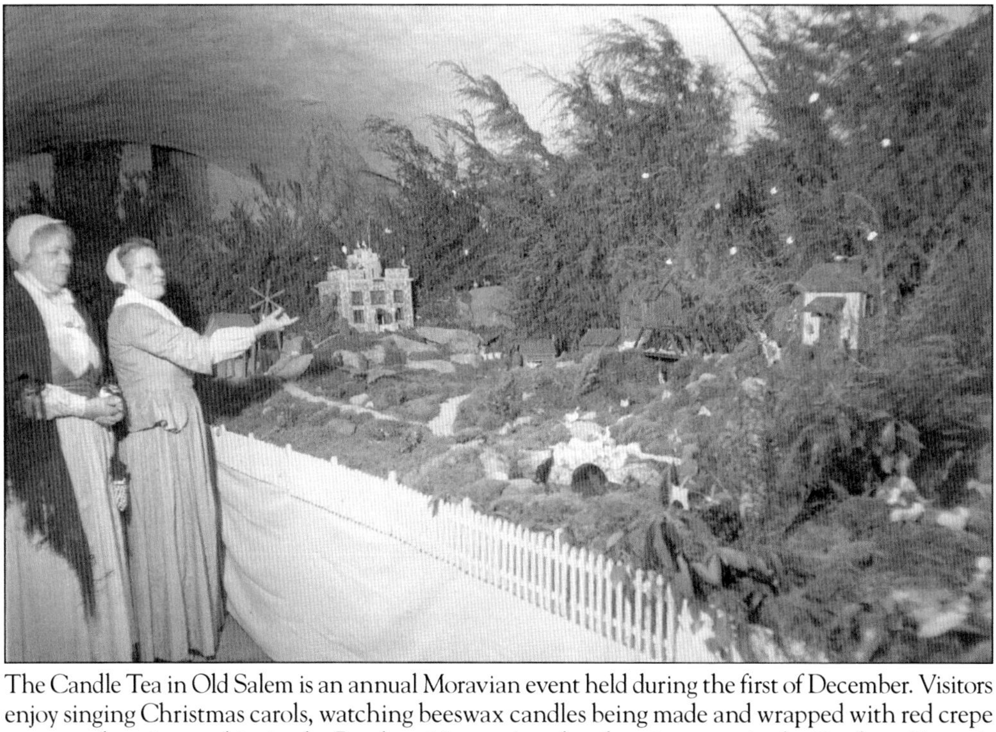

The Candle Tea in Old Salem is an annual Moravian event held during the first of December. Visitors enjoy singing Christmas carols, watching beeswax candles being made and wrapped with red crepe paper, and tasting cookies in the Brothers House. Another favorite scene in the Brothers House is the Christmas putz, being admired in 1946 by Miss Ellen Ebert (left) and Miss Ann Dills.

Mary Davis (Mrs. F. Murray Davidson) is the lovely lady posing for the photographer at her dressing table. The photograph was taken about 1946. Mrs. Davidson remembered the photograph when she was contacted several years ago, and when asked the occasion for the photo shoot assignment, Mrs. Davidson answered that Frank was "just practicing."

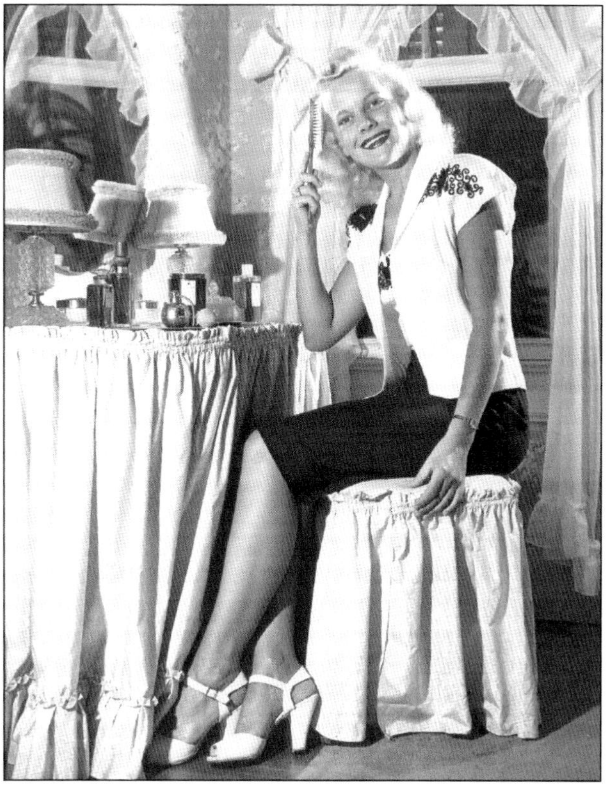

Joe Dudley was concentrating on sinking his putt when a helicopter interrupted his golf game at Old Town Club in the late 1940s. The company that owned the helicopter had a deal for Joe. They wanted to carry him from shot to shot during his game, to prove the adaptability of the helicopter. Joe consented to the arrangement and afterward received a helicopter ride around town for being a good sport.

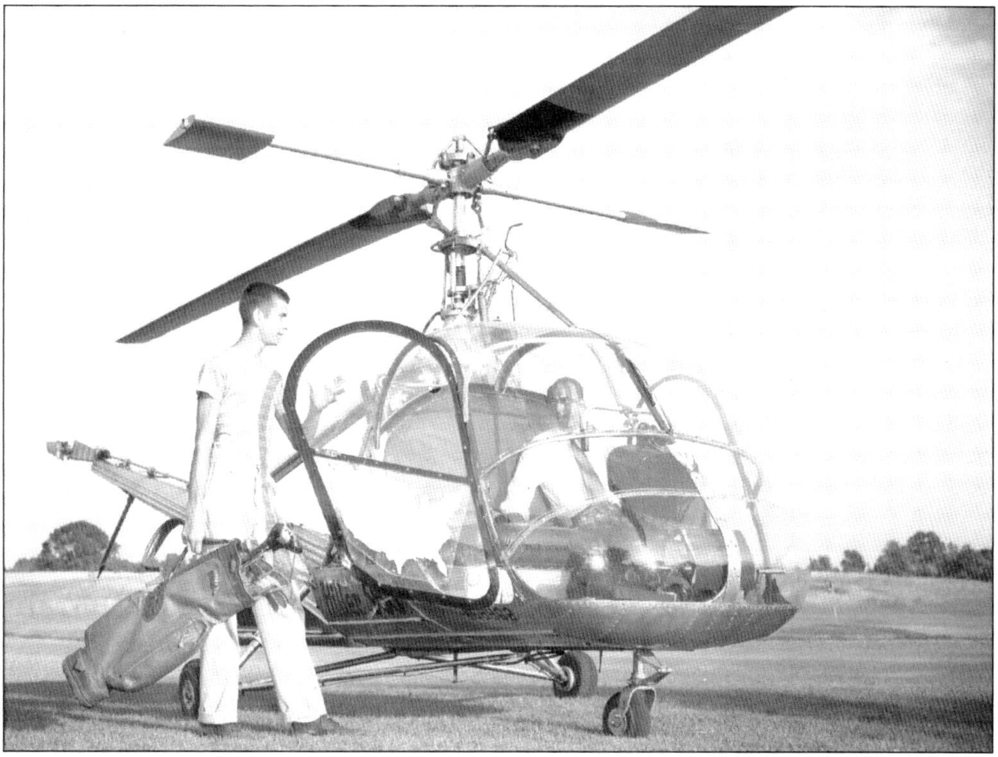

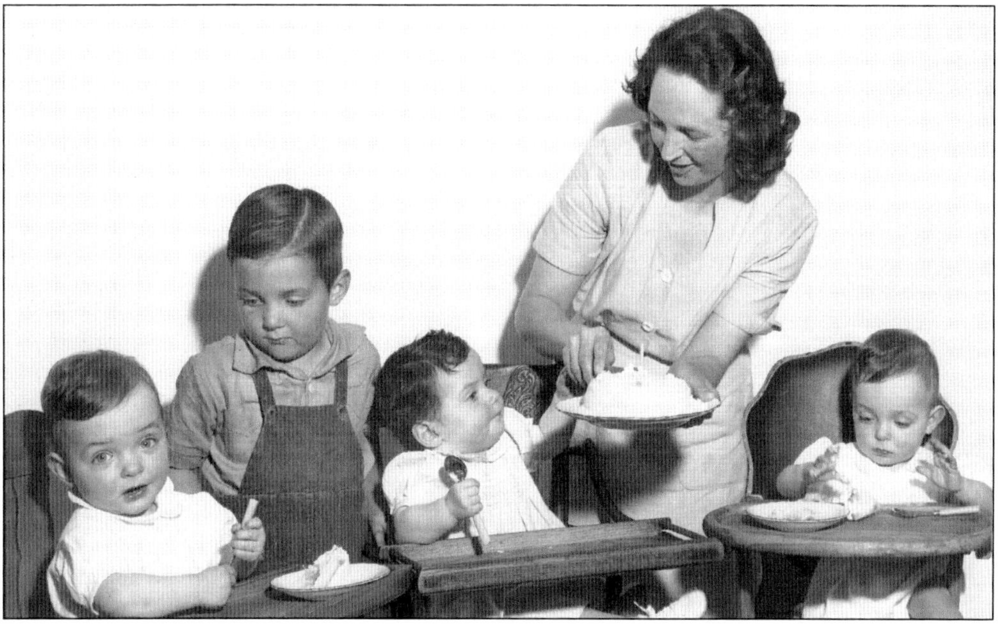

Rural Hall marked a special event in April 1946 when the population increased by three in a very short time. Proving that good things often come in threes, triplets Michael (left), Mary Anne (middle), and Marcus Tuttle celebrated their first birthday with a party. Their big brother, Leslie Gray, and mother, Mrs. D. L. Tuttle, watched as each child skipped the spoons and experienced their cake firsthand.

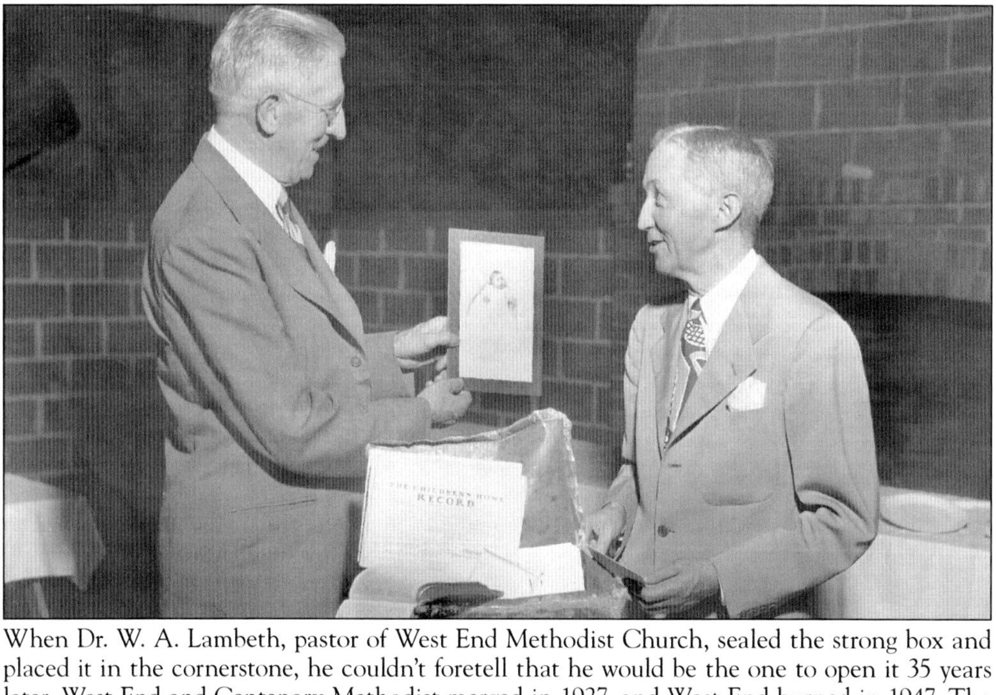

When Dr. W. A. Lambeth, pastor of West End Methodist Church, sealed the strong box and placed it in the cornerstone, he couldn't foretell that he would be the one to open it 35 years later. West End and Centenary Methodist merged in 1927, and West End burned in 1947. The fire occasioned the box opening, with Centenary members B. S. Womble (left) and Norman Stockton examining the contents.

The newspapers in the 1940s often featured fashion layouts showing clothing styles for the coming season. In January 1947, the Sunday newspaper had a full-page article about what the well-dressed Winston-Salem men, women, and children would be wearing for spring. Louise Casperian posed for this fashion photograph, wearing a rich wool ensemble highlighted with silk scarves. Miss Casperian was a local model who later became Mrs. Henry S. Mingus.

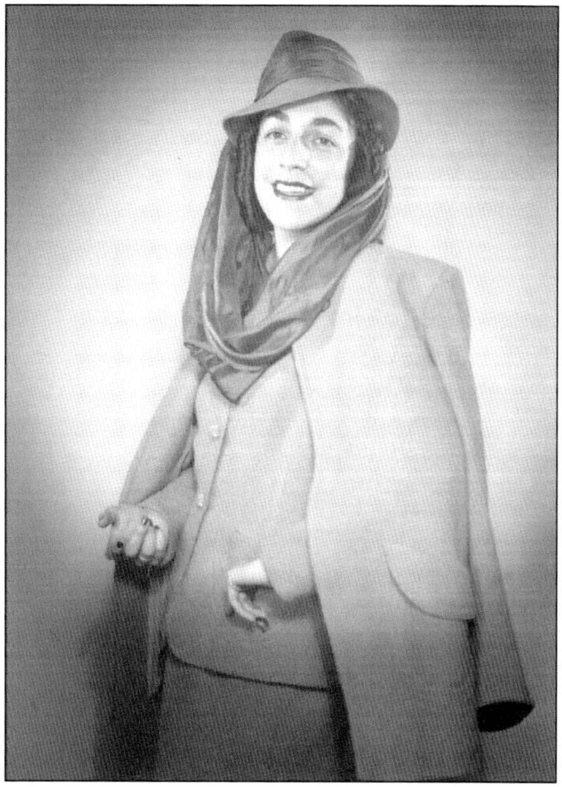

March 12, 1912, is an important date for Girl Scouts because it marks the founding of their organization in the United States by Mrs. Juliette Low. On the 35th anniversary of Girl Scouts in 1947, Winston-Salem could count 1,261 girls in the program, including Brownies, Intermediates, Seniors, and Wing Scouts. Fifty-two troops of girls, ages 7 to 18, were active in the city and county, assisted by over 300 adults.

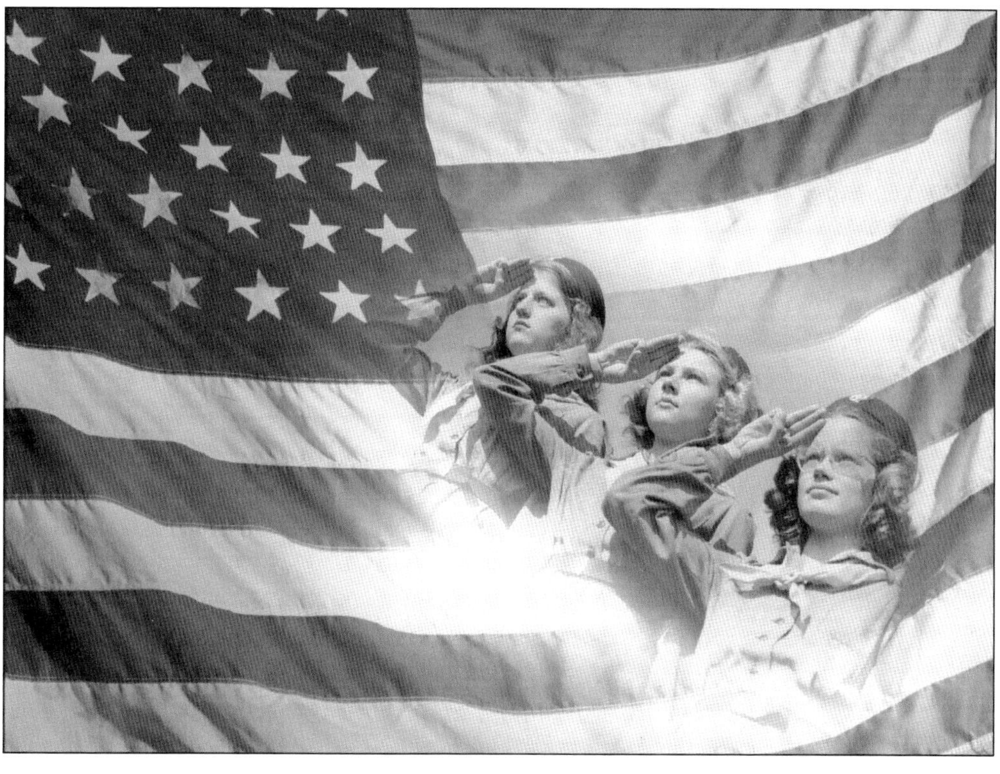

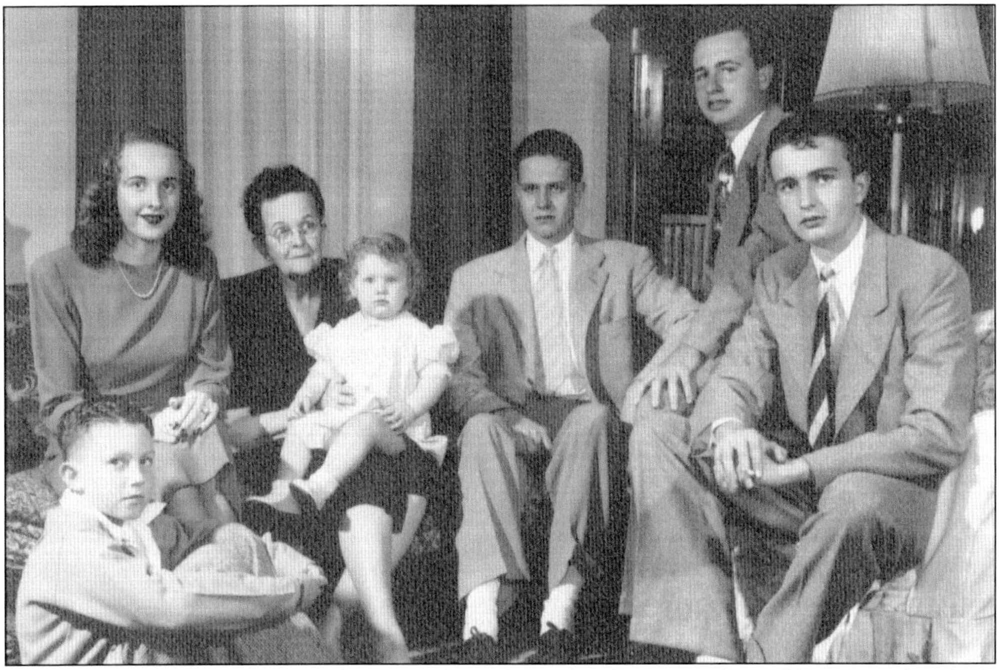

North Carolina governor Gregg Cherry proclaimed that October 12, 1947, would be "Grandmother's Day," a day to honor grandmothers and their contributions in the lives of their grandchildren. Mrs. Mary Kerr Spencer, shown with her grandchildren, was known as "Mother Spencer" in political circles for her work with the Democratic Party. In 1956, she was elected North Carolina Mother of the Year.

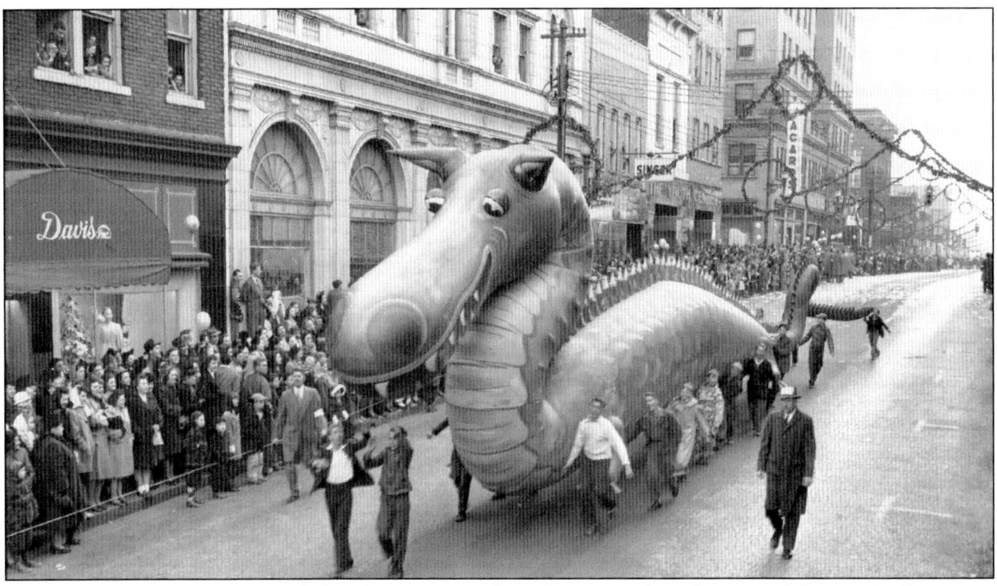

Some 100,000 people jammed the downtown sidewalks to catch a glimpse of the 1947 Christmas parade. They had no trouble seeing the dragon and the largest balloon, Gulliver of *Gulliver's Travels*, even though Gulliver was lying down. Sponsored by the Retail Merchants Association, the parade lasted 30 minutes, with Santa Claus making his appearance at the end. The Christmas lights were turned on, marking the beginning of the Christmas season.

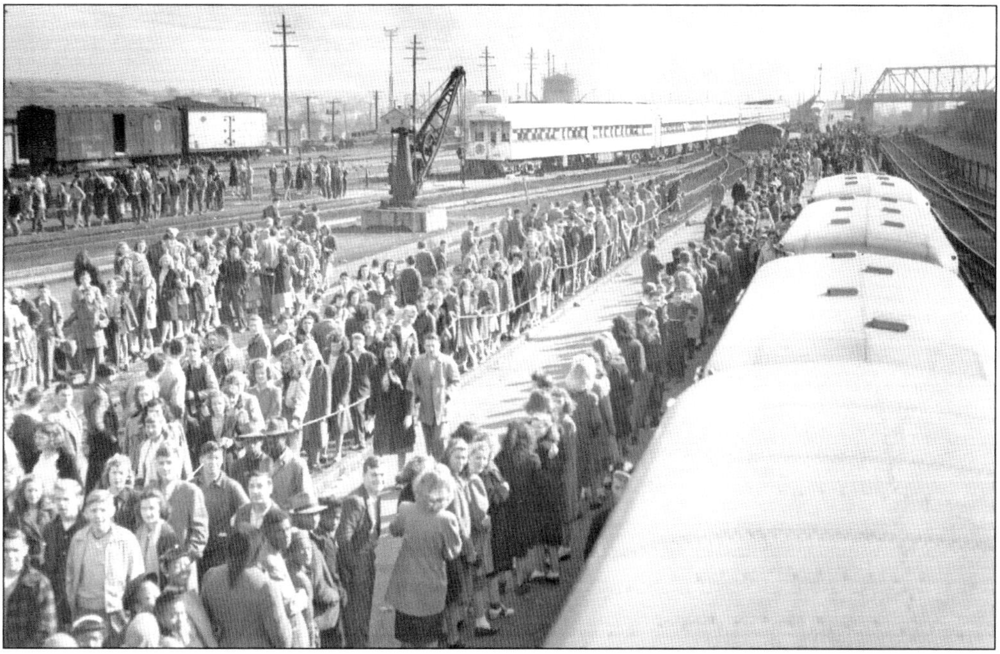

Rededication Week was observed in early December 1947 to awaken citizens to recall how fortunate they are to be Americans. The Freedom Train, sponsored by the American Heritage Foundation, contained documents of democracy. The 11,000 people who passed through the Freedom Train in the 13 hours it was in town marveled at seeing the Magna Carta, the Declaration of Independence, and many other documents they learned about in school.

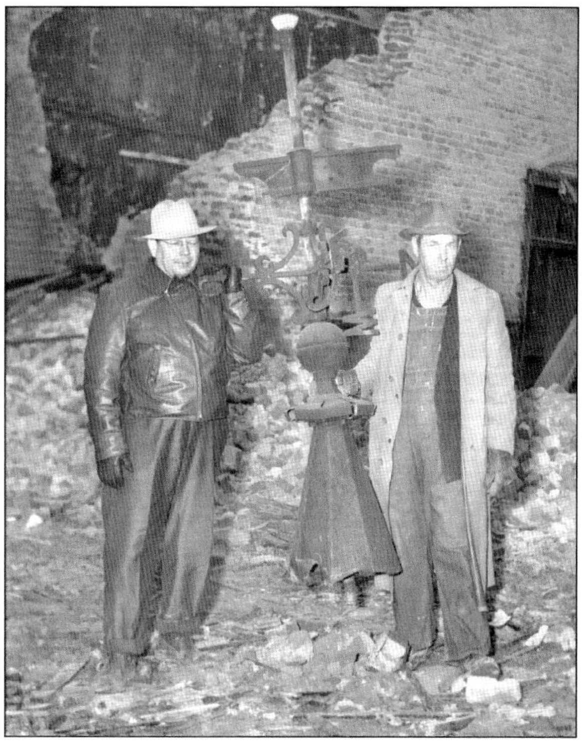

West End School on Fourth Street was demolished in 1947, and the lot was purchased by Sears, Roebuck and Company for the site of its new department store. During the demolition, the six-foot-tall weather vane that stood atop the entrance tower of the school was discovered in the rubble by Frank Jones. Frank purchased the tin weather vane and donated it to the Wachovia Museum in honor of his grandfather, Wiley Keith.

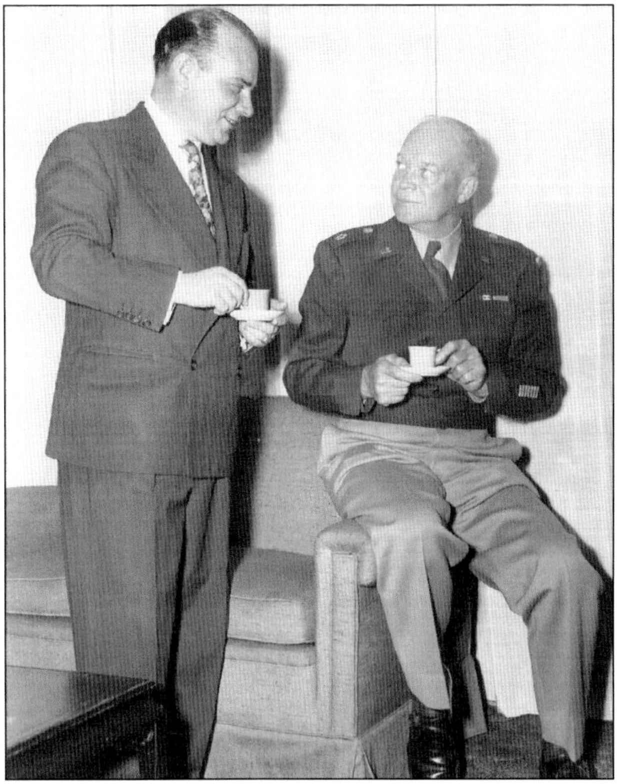

Gen. Dwight Eisenhower (right) stopped in Winston-Salem for a luncheon visit in March 1948 with his friend Frank L. Swadley (left). Eisenhower was returning to Washington after a 14-day tour of major Southern military installations. Swadley was manager of the Hotel Robert E. Lee, and he and Eisenhower knew each other when Swadley worked in Washington. Crowds gathered outside the hotel when word spread about the general's visit.

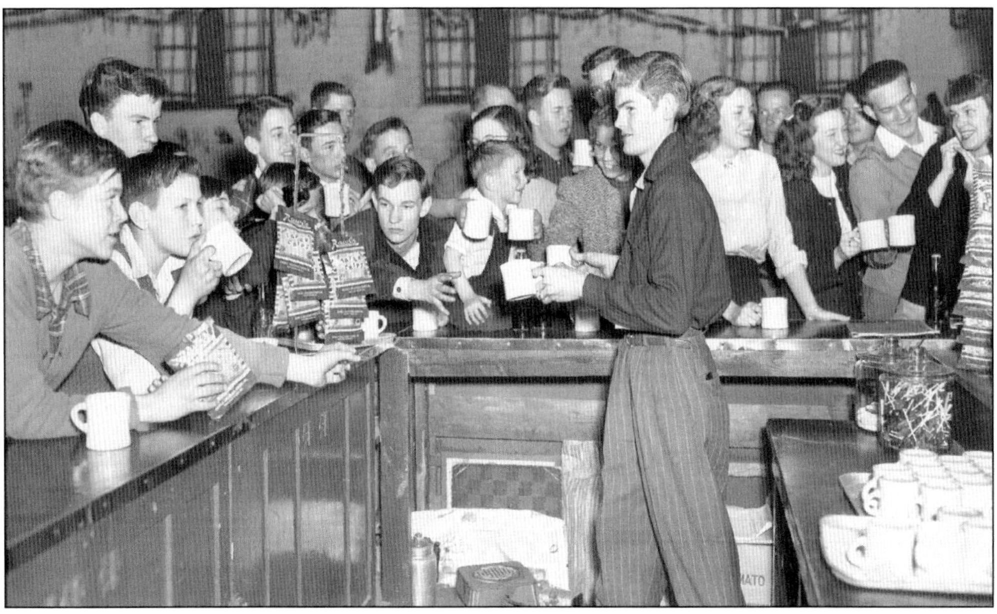

The Friday night crowd at the Granville Teen Town Club kept the snack bar attendant busy handing out snacks and soft drinks. With names like the Gray Gnomes, the Waugh Teen Towners, and the Ardmore Spotlighters, teenage clubs became popular in 1948, sponsored by the City Recreation Department. Clubs were organized with councils that planned events, which included games, dances, roller skating, picnics, hayrides, and movies.

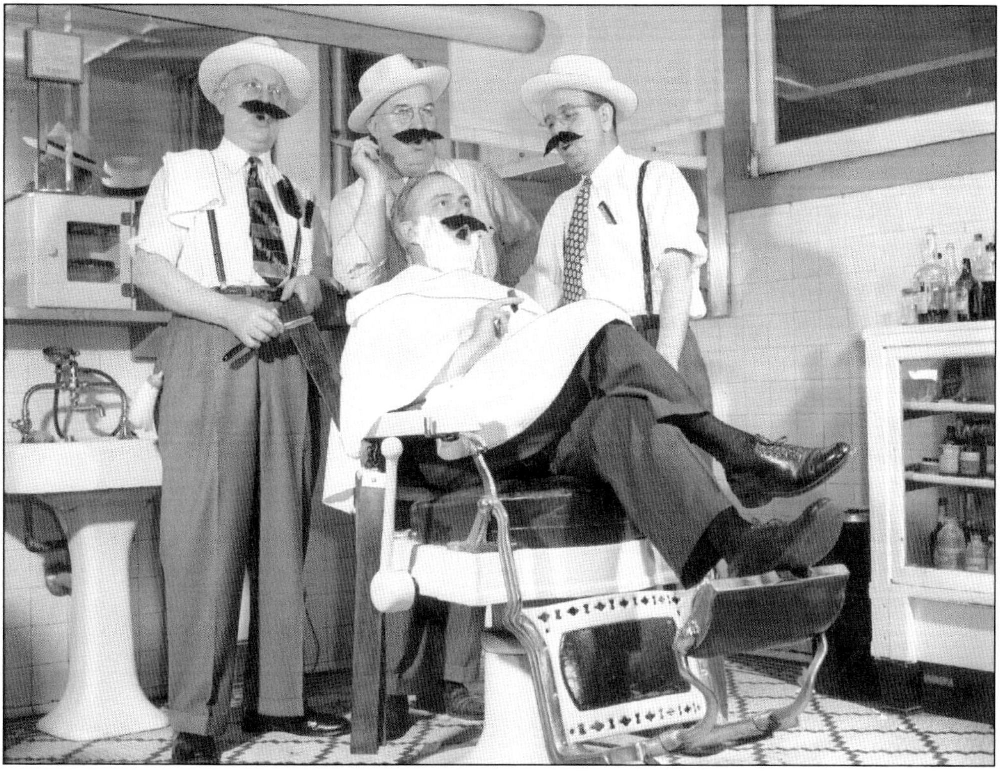

This photograph of the Lions Club Quartet was originally published in an April 1948 newspaper feature about men and their straw hats. The harmonizing men—(standing from left to right) Grady Miller, George Boss, Bourne Hamner, and (seated) Paul Pegram—won third place in the Lions International Convention's singing competition. Frank Jones won first prize in the Cigar Institute's photograph contest because this photograph was judged the best containing a cigar.

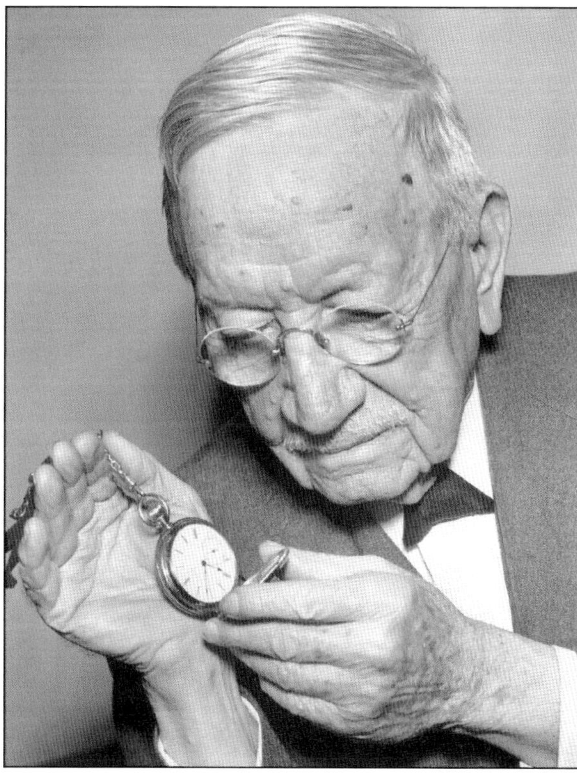

Plans for a Forsyth County industrial fair to be held in Pepper's Warehouse were underway in April 1948. This fair recalled an earlier occasion, in October 1884, when Forsyth County sent an outstanding display to "The Great Exhibition" in Raleigh and won the $100 grand prize. Henry E. Fries, recognized for his contribution to the display, was awarded a gold watch, which he proudly kept for all those years.

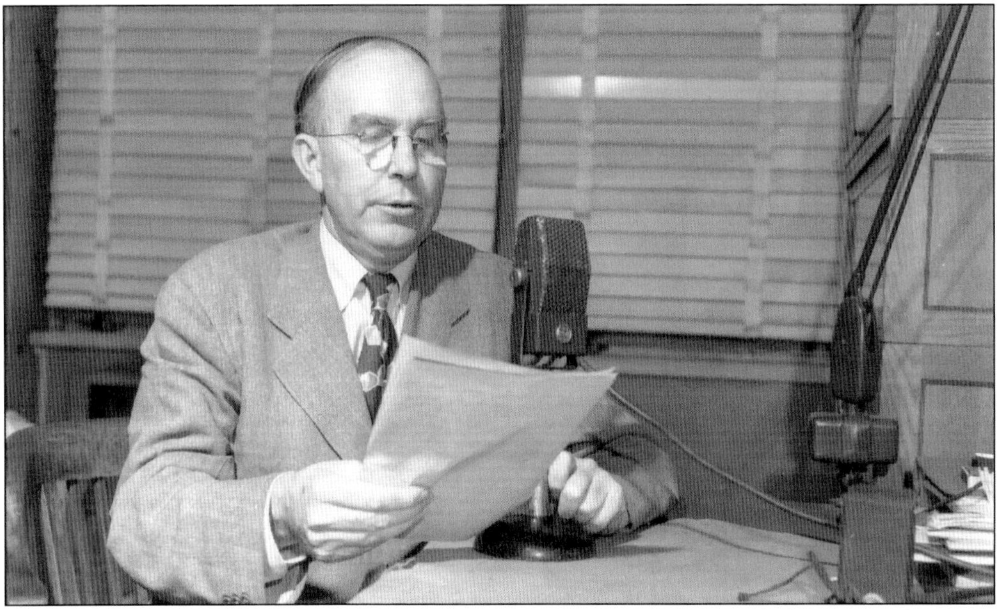

Wiley Sims, shown during a 1948 broadcast, had several jobs before he settled in as "weatherman" for WSJS and WAIR radio stations. One of those jobs, farming, helped him relate to the farmers who listened to his broadcasts and planned their work based upon his forecast. In fact, listeners of all walks of life depended on Wiley to help them dress for the weather and plan their outdoor activities.

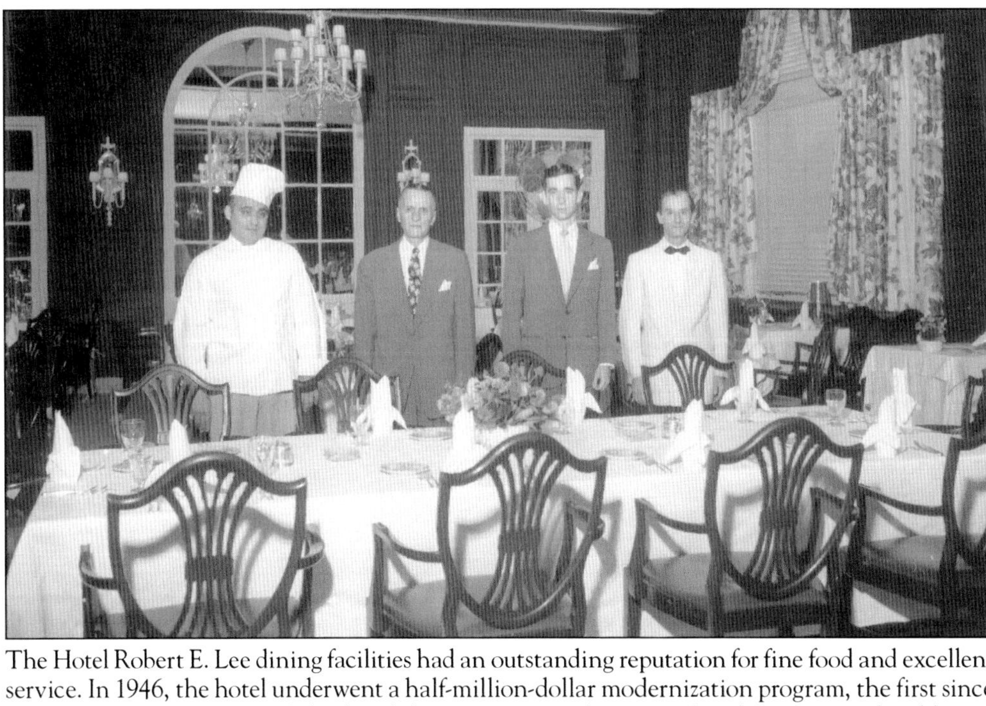

The Hotel Robert E. Lee dining facilities had an outstanding reputation for fine food and excellent service. In 1946, the hotel underwent a half-million-dollar modernization program, the first since it was built in 1921. One of the hotel dining rooms is shown in October 1948, with tables set for a special event. Joe F. Ceruti, second from the left, was maitre d'hotel for nearly nine years, leaving in 1956.

Betsy Dalton Staker often modeled for *Journal* and *Sentinel* photographers, showing new fashion styles for the coming season. In June 1948, fall hat fashions were featured in the fashion pages, and Mrs. Staker modeled a navy felt hat with faille ribbon and draped brim. A full-length fashion photograph of Mrs. Staker, taken by Frank Jones at Old Town Club, appeared in the August 1948 issue of *Vogue* magazine.

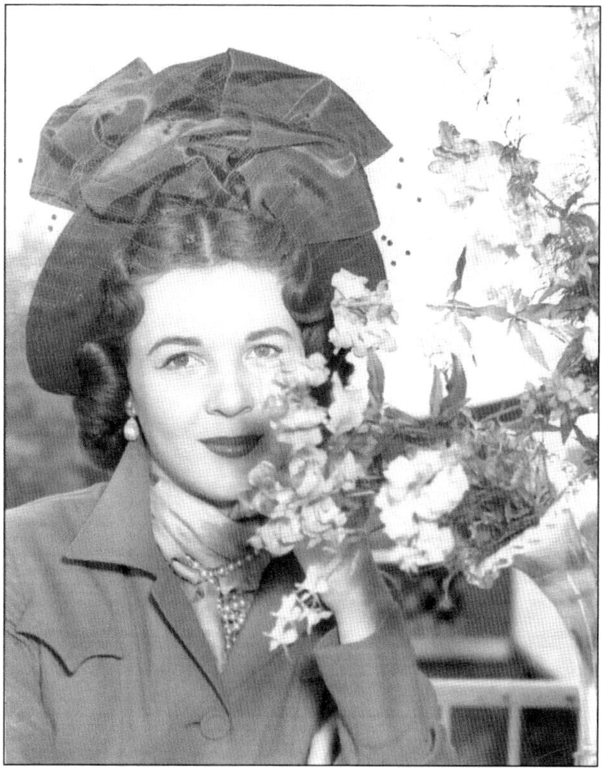

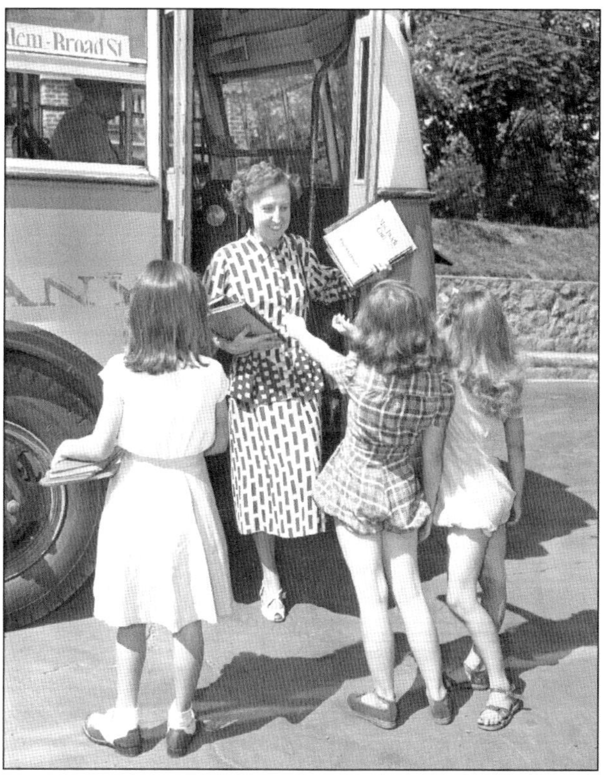

A polio outbreak in August 1948 confined children to their homes. Since the children couldn't get out, Carnegie assistant librarian Mae Kreeger brought the library to them. Neighborhood children asked Miss Kreeger to bring books home, and the requests grew until she brought home an armful of books each evening, selected by the children's librarian. The children were speedy readers and kept Miss Kreeger busy bringing home and returning books.

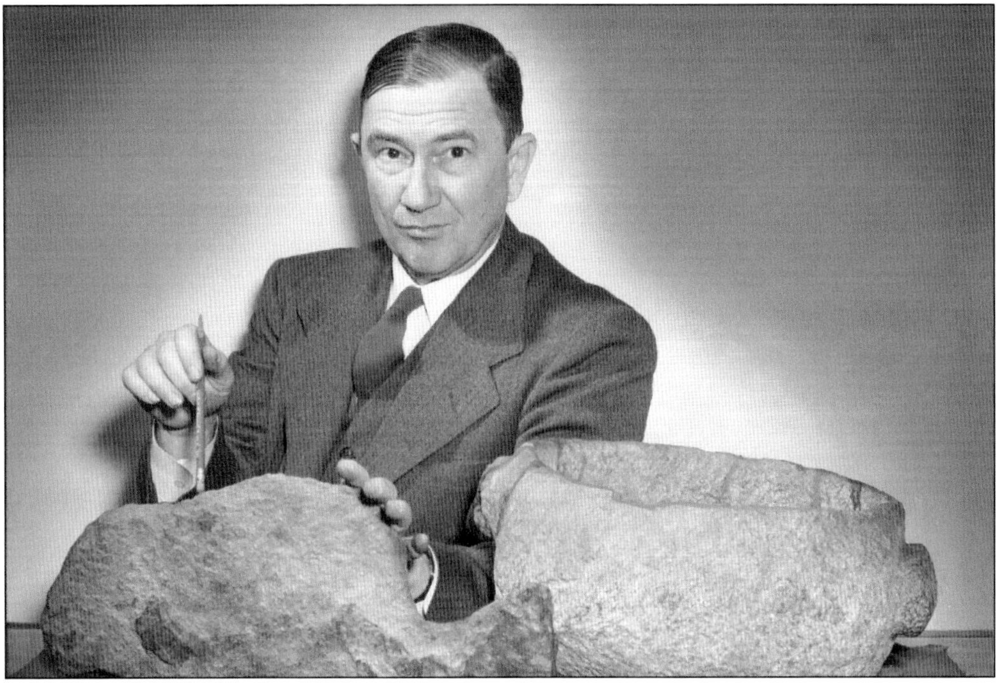

Dr. Douglas L. Rights was a man of varied interests. Professionally he was the pastor of Trinity Moravian Church for 37 years. In the community, he was an active member of the Kiwanis Club and received the Silver Beaver award for his service in Scouting. Dr. Rights is shown in 1948 with archeological relics, just part of his collection that tells the story of how Native Americans lived.

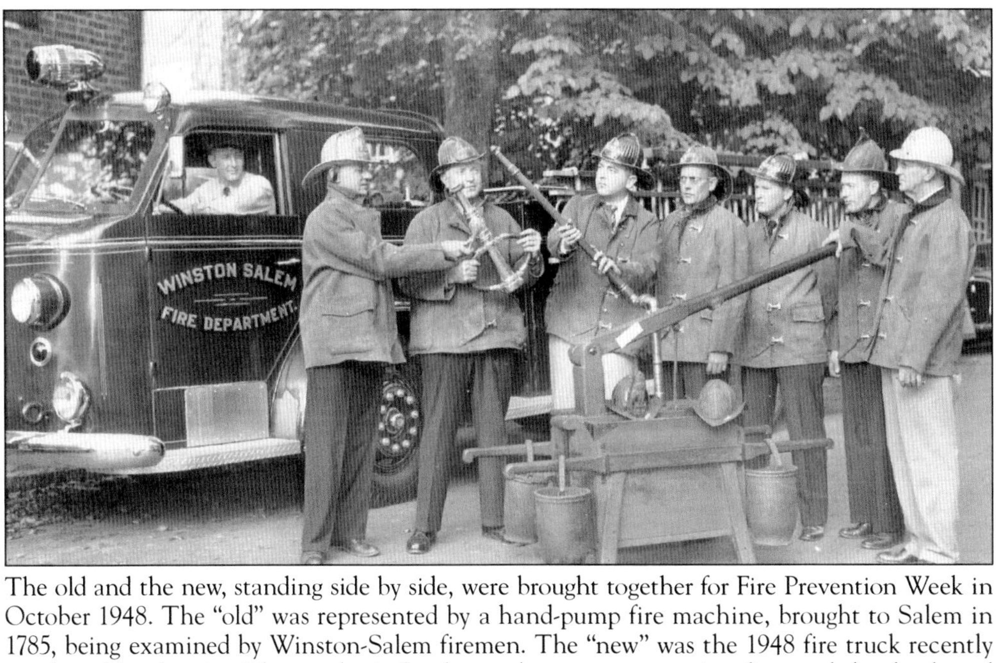

The old and the new, standing side by side, were brought together for Fire Prevention Week in October 1948. The "old" was represented by a hand-pump fire machine, brought to Salem in 1785, being examined by Winston-Salem firemen. The "new" was the 1948 fire truck recently purchased by the city. The emphasis for the week was on preventing fires and the death and destruction they cause.

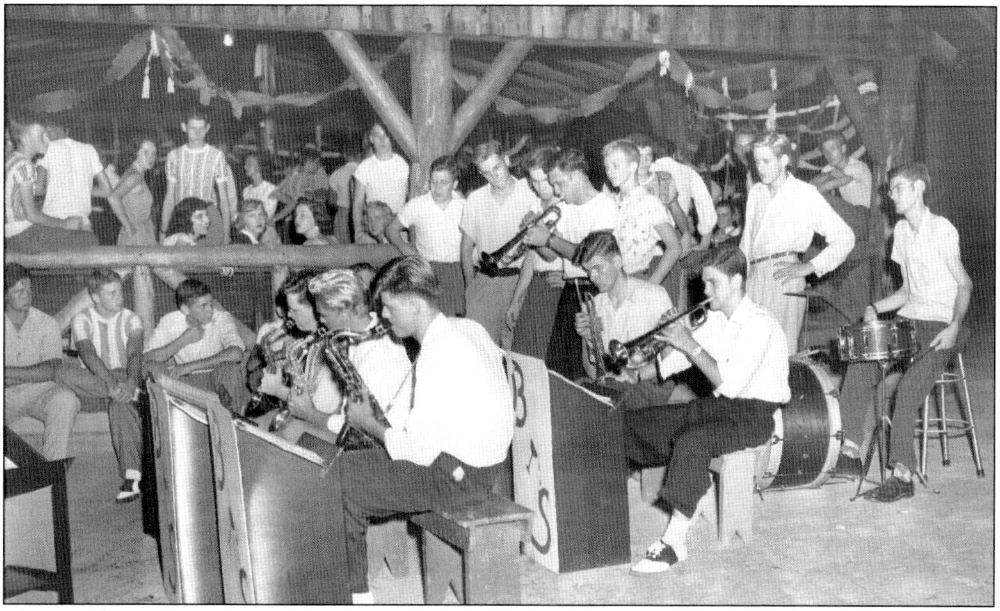

The weekly teenager dance at Miller Park had Bennett Simpson's live orchestra to guide their dance steps in the summer of 1949. The dances were held under the direction of the City Recreation Department and were just part of the summer activities. The 15 city recreation centers planned handicrafts, swimming, tennis tournaments, square dances, softball games, story time for children, and special events all summer.

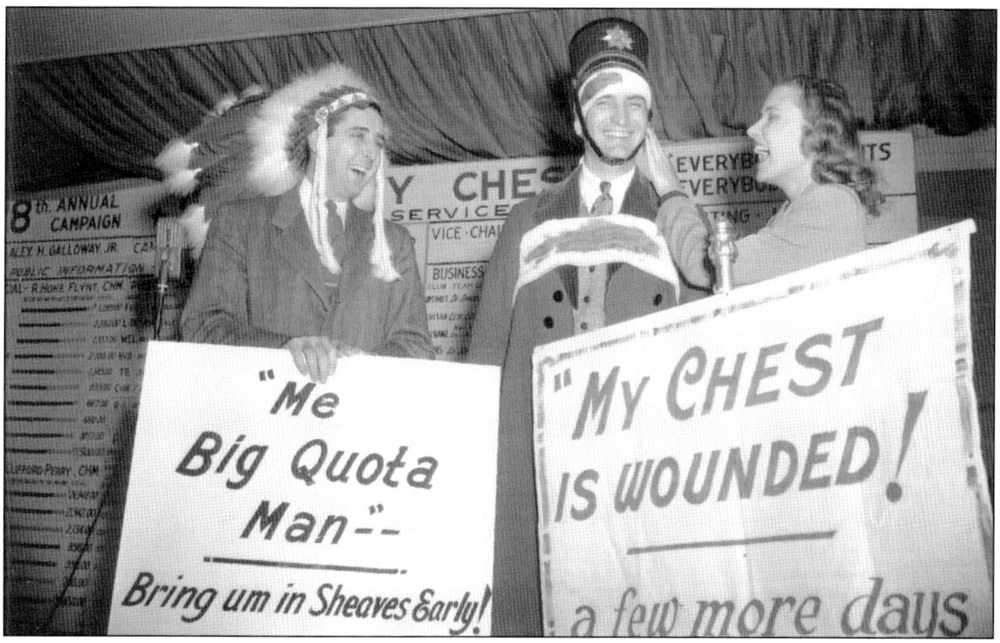

Sometimes fund-raisers need just a little more time to reach their goal. The 1949 Community Chest drive raised 96 percent of the quota but needed extra time to completely fund the 25 Red Feather services that depended on the community's generosity to operate. Reid Holmes (left), Chairman William Womble, and Red Feather girl Ruth Fulk humorously illustrate their point of extending the campaign a few days to reach their goal.

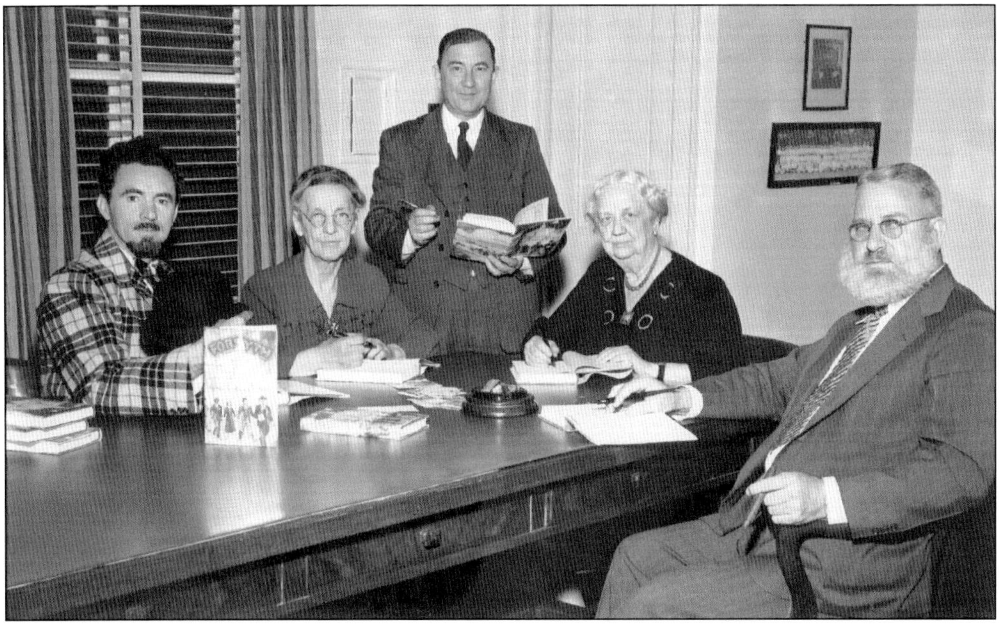

To celebrate Forsyth County's centennial, and to record the county's rich heritage, a history was written, edited, and illustrated in 1949 by local citizens. From left to right, illustrator Joe King, and authors Mary Wiley, Dr. Douglas Rights, Dr. Adelaide Fries, and Harvey Dinkins are shown above at the presentation of the book, *Forsyth: A County on the March*. The two other authors were Flora Ann Lee and Charles N. Siewers. A male group called the "Bushgrowers" had also been making long-term plans for the centennial celebration. They began with abandoning their razors in order to sport mustaches, beards, muttonchops, and any combination of these facial adornments to be counted as a "Bushgrower." Participants are shown below at Wrightsville Beach during their train excursion on the "Bushgrowers' Special," accompanied by their nonbearded female counterparts, all outfitted in 1849-style clothing.

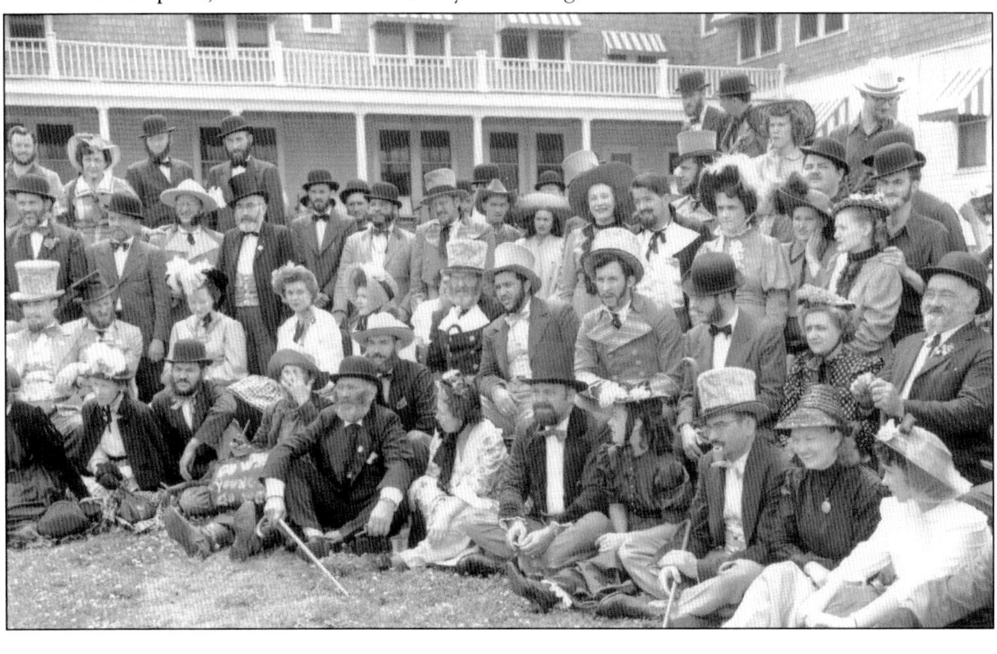

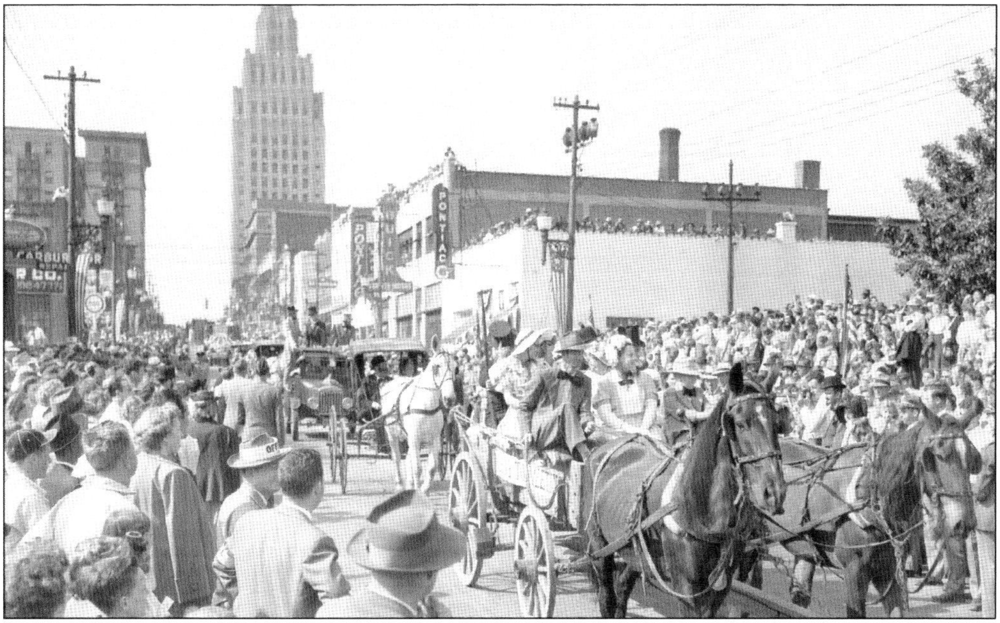

Thousands of spectators lined the streets to catch a glimpse of Forsyth County's Centennial Parade on May 12, 1949. For 1 hour and 15 minutes, the 35 floats, 7 bands, dozens of vehicles, and hundreds of men, women, and children traveled the parade route from Broad Street to Salem College. Jet airplanes flew overhead as parade participants represented the county's history through period clothing, antique and horse-drawn vehicles, and many remembrances of earlier years displayed on the floats. The reviewing stand in front of city hall held distinguished guests, such as Winston-Salem native and movie star Kathryn Grayson (below), flanked by her husband, Johnnie Johnston (left), and North Carolina governor Kerr Scott (right). A time capsule was buried on the courthouse lawn after the parade, to be opened in 2049. The capsule was relocated when the courthouse was expanded in 1960.

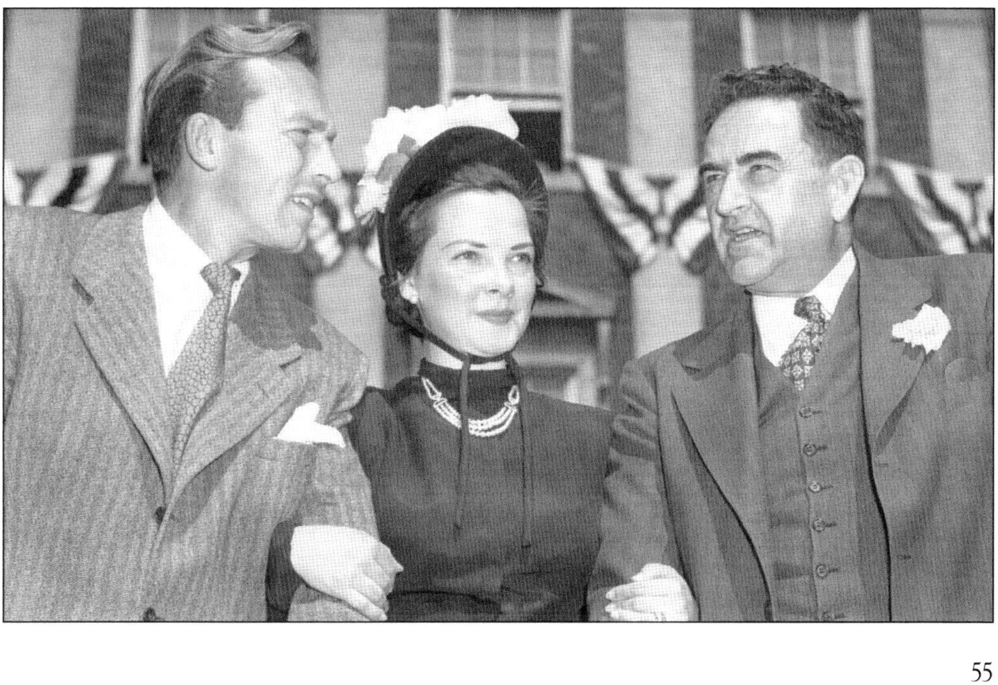

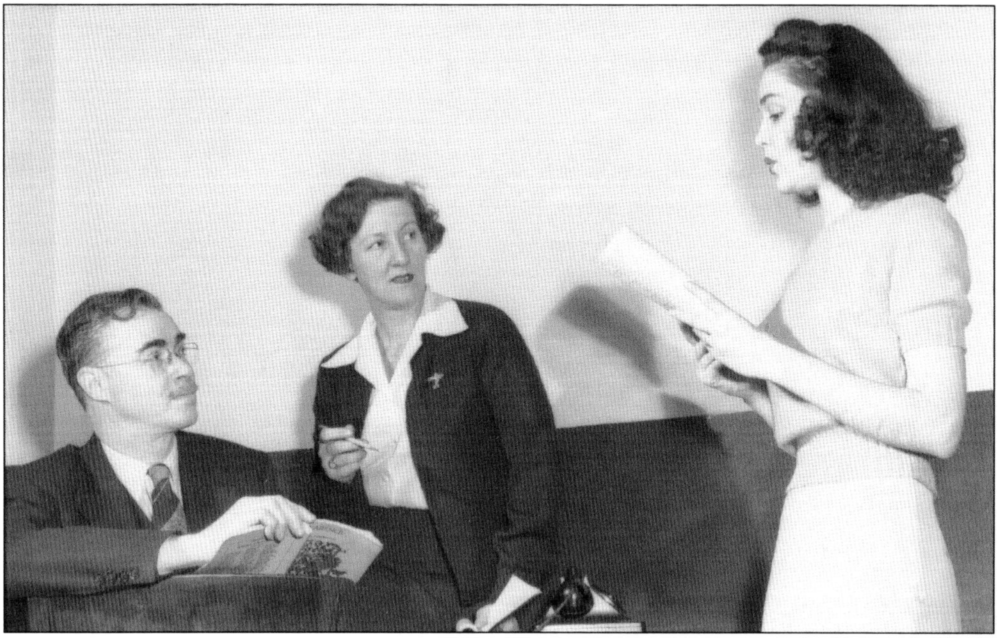

Moving from the basement of a house to a barn may not seem like an improved situation, but when that barn is your first real home, then the move takes on new meaning. The Little Theatre of Winston-Salem moved from its basement home to the second floor of Clyde Shore's barn on Robinhood Road in 1949. Little Theatre members Clarke Billings and Doris Pardington listen as Lee Smith reads for a part in an upcoming play.

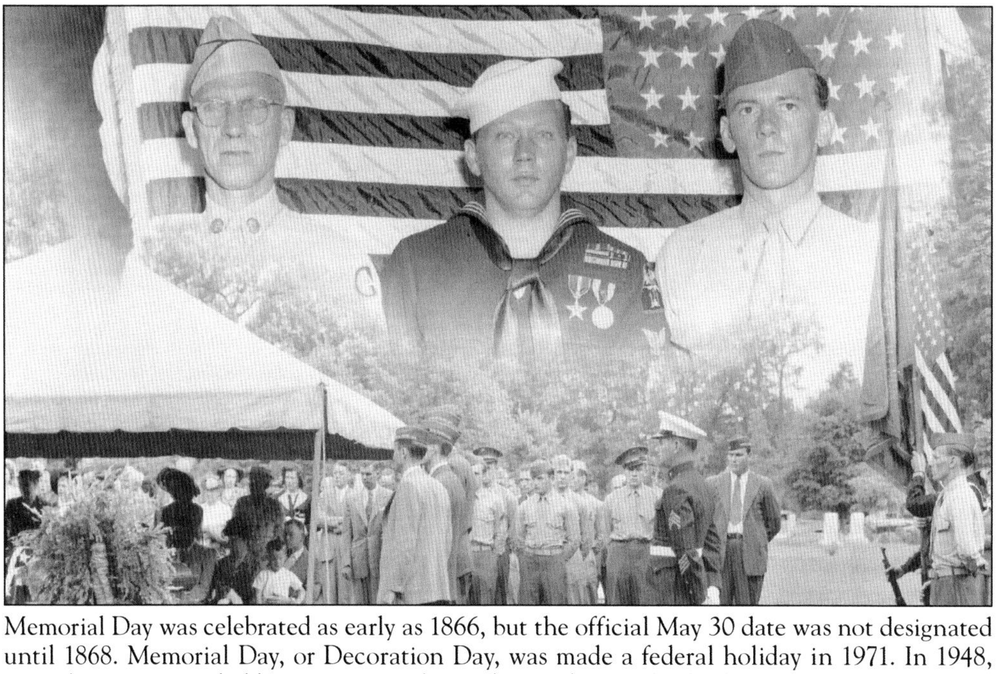

Memorial Day was celebrated as early as 1866, but the official May 30 date was not designated until 1868. Memorial Day, or Decoration Day, was made a federal holiday in 1971. In 1948, special services were held in Winston-Salem to honor the war dead. This composite photograph shows a tribute at the grave of a serviceman attended by an honor guard of the Veterans of Foreign Wars.

Four

THE 1950S

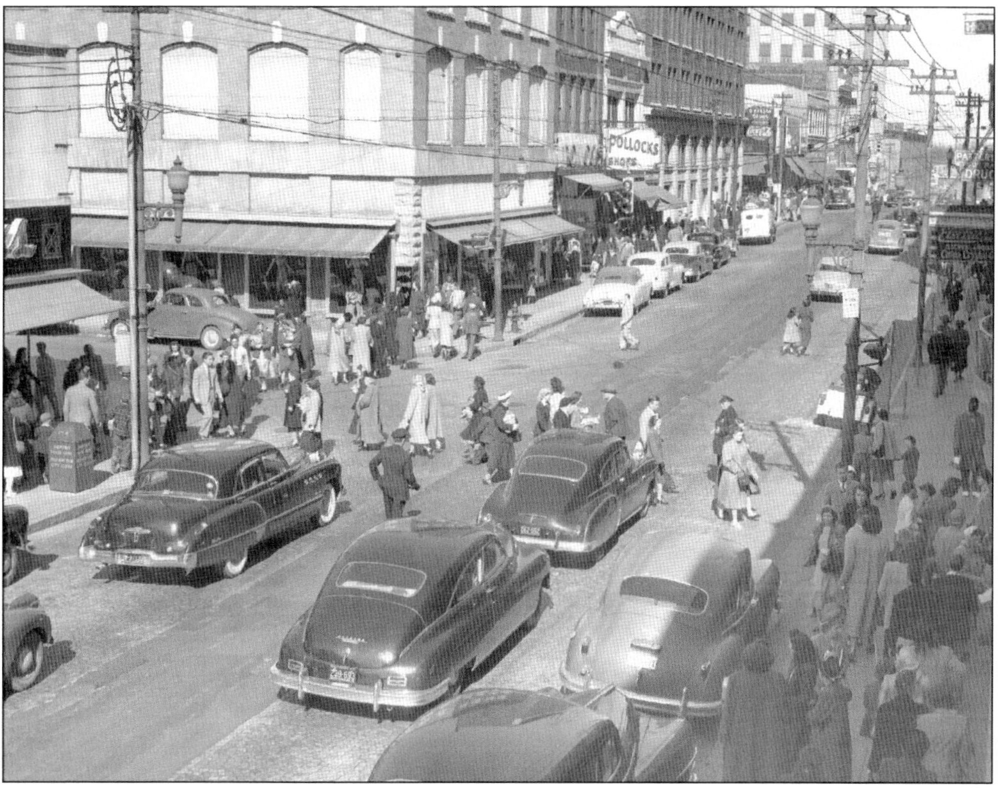

Shoppers on foot and in vehicles crowd the intersection at Fourth and Trade Streets as residents make last-minute preparations for Easter Sunday events the following day. In 1950, as in many years, the city's population swelled with visitors who attended Easter sunrise services at many Moravian churches. On this day before Easter, some of the preparations would include purchasing flowers to adorn the cemeteries throughout the city.

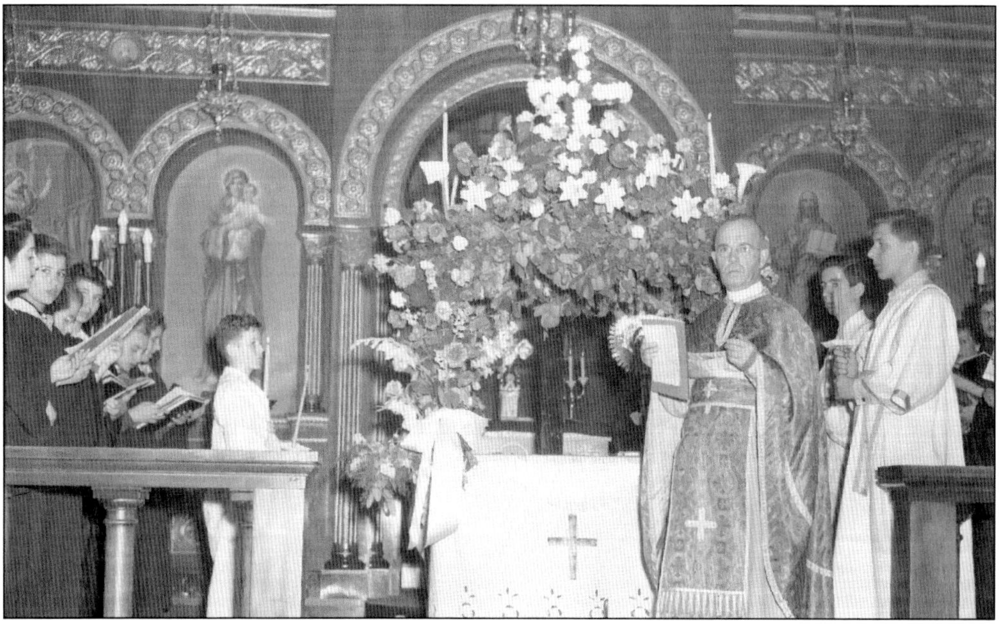

On Good Friday in 1950, the Greek Orthodox Church on West Fourth Street was filled with worshipers to witness the service commemorating Christ's crucifixion. Reverend Thalassinos led the singing during the "Angomia," the funeral service. After the funeral liturgy, each worshipper plucked a flower from the wreath at the altar, to be blessed by the priest. The West Fourth Street church, purchased from the Baptists, was dedicated in 1947.

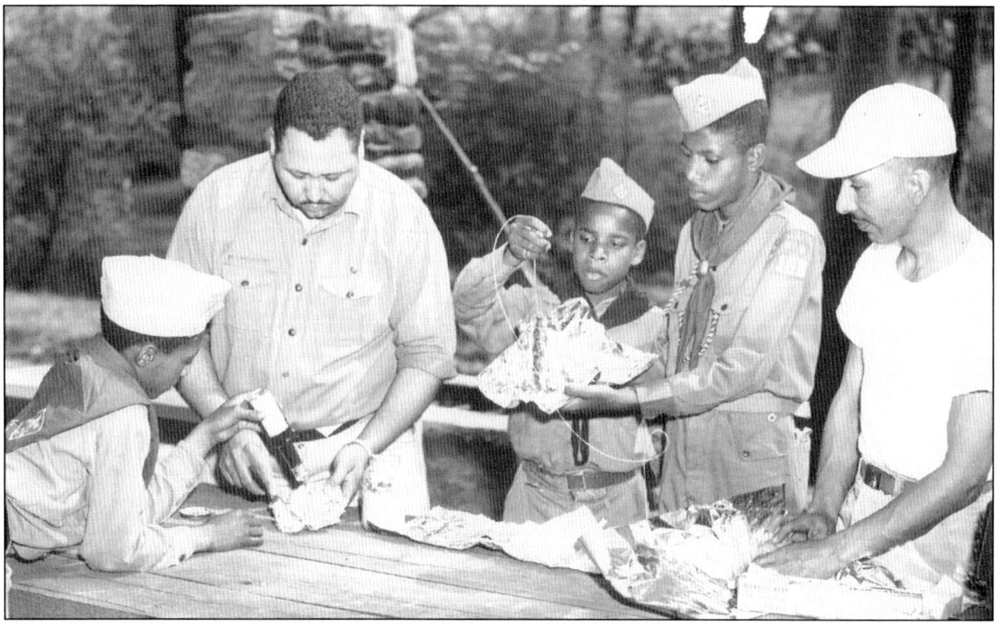

Boy Scout Troop 173 of New Bethel Baptist Church took top honors at the annual Scout rally at Skyland School in the spring of 1950. Seventy-five scouts from 12 Forsyth County troops participated in the rally that tested Scouting skills. Some of the skills tested were knot-tying, fire by friction, compass reading, tent pitching, nature study, and first aid. The Scout leader, shown, demonstrated cooking by wrapping food in aluminum.

Mayor Marshall Kurfees (left) greeted World War I flying ace Eddie Rickenbacker (right) at Smith Reynolds Airport in June 1950. Captain Rickenbacker, president of Eastern Airlines, came to town with an entourage of Eastern Airlines executives on an inspection tour of 88 cities where the airline had branch offices. The purpose of the tour was to hear local problems firsthand, discuss them, and possibly solve them on the spot.

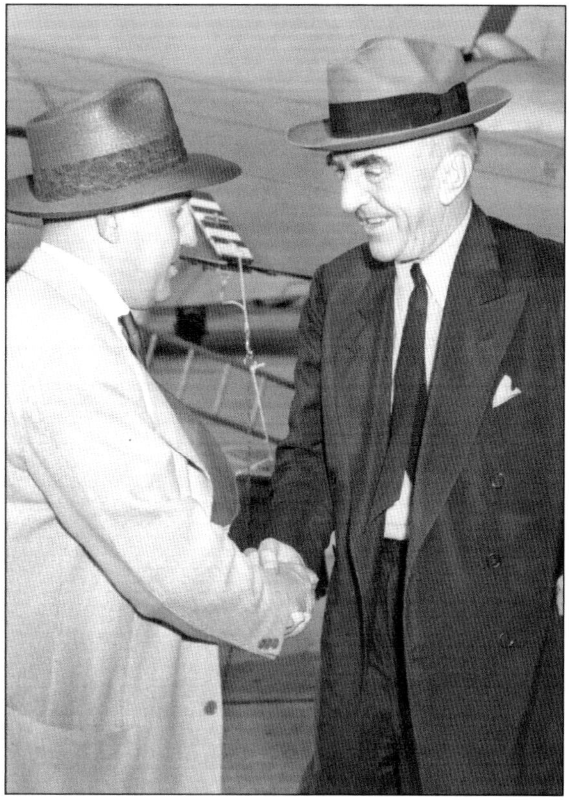

Elizabeth Hedgecock Sparks, known to *Winston-Salem Journal* readers as Beth Tartan, was the home economics editor for many years. In March 1951, as local cooks were baking sugarcake for the Easter season, a controversy arose concerning the true Moravian recipe for sugarcake. Beth Tartan's newspaper columns and cookbooks provided culinary guidance for many years, becoming the last word on preparing and serving food, including Moravian sugarcake.

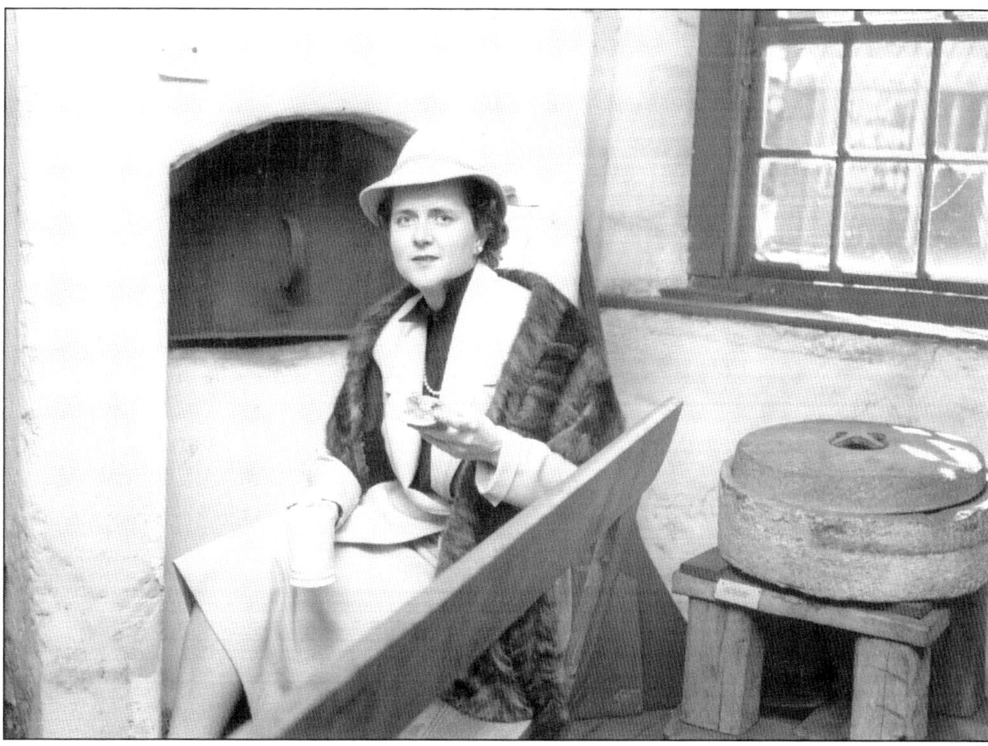

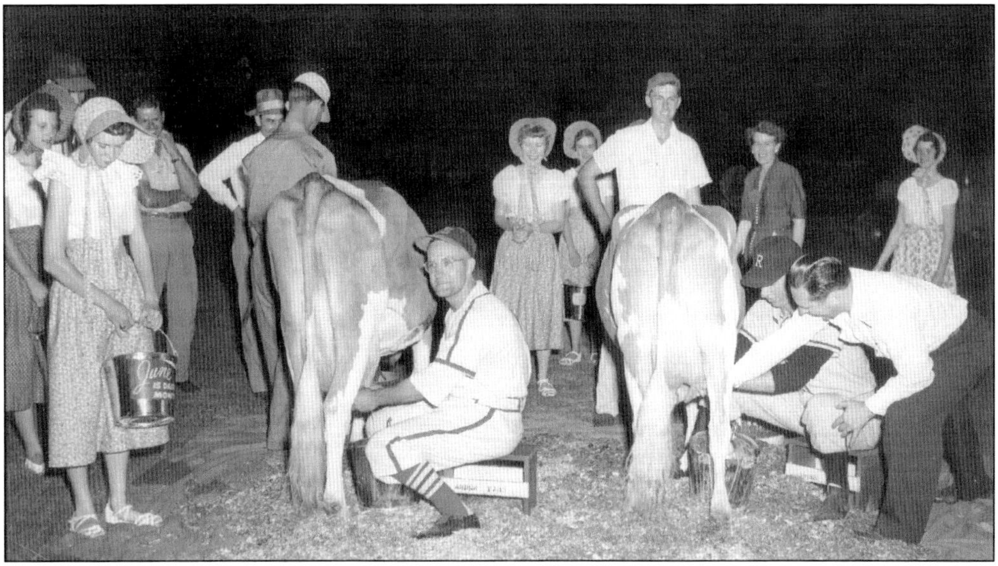

To commemorate Dairy Week in June 1950, a four-man milking contest pitted the Winston-Salem Cardinals' baseball team manager against the Raleigh Caps' manager at Southside Park. The results of the contest went in favor of the Cardinals and might have been an omen for the outcome of the season. On August 30, 1950, the Cardinals defeated Danville to win the Carolina League pennant, the first for Winston-Salem in 22 years.

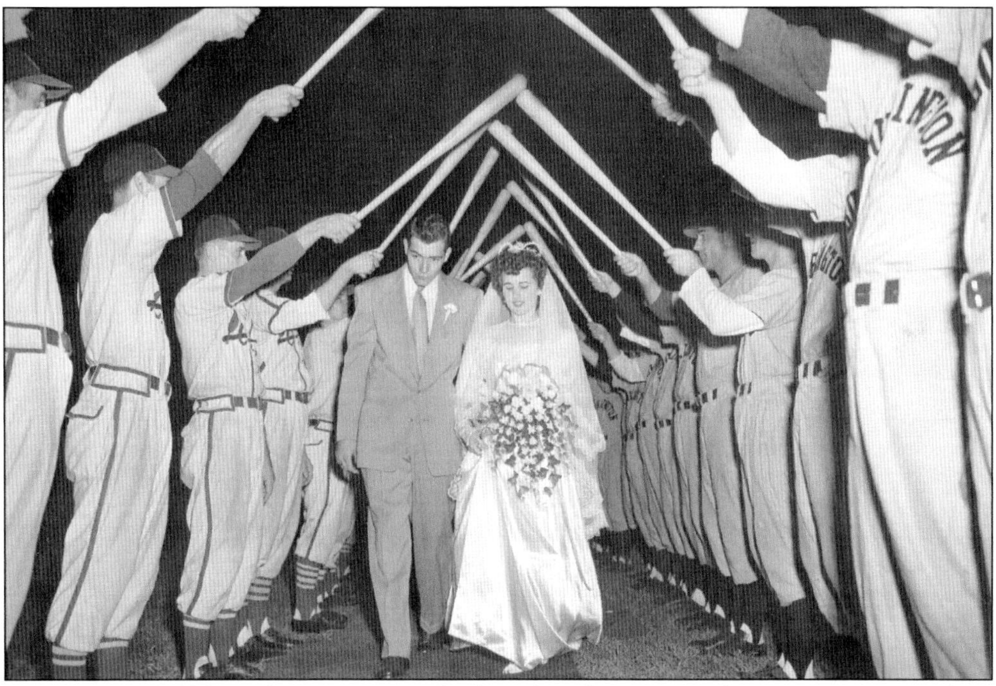

Cardinals baseball fans who came to Southside Park early on September 5, 1950, witnessed the marriage of Rosemarie Henson and Bobby Gene Tiefenauer at home plate. Tiefenauer was the ace relief pitcher for the championship Cardinals. After the wedding, the couple walked under an archway of bats held by the Cardinals and the opposing team members of the Burlington Bees. The Cardinals lost to the Bees, 12 to 4.

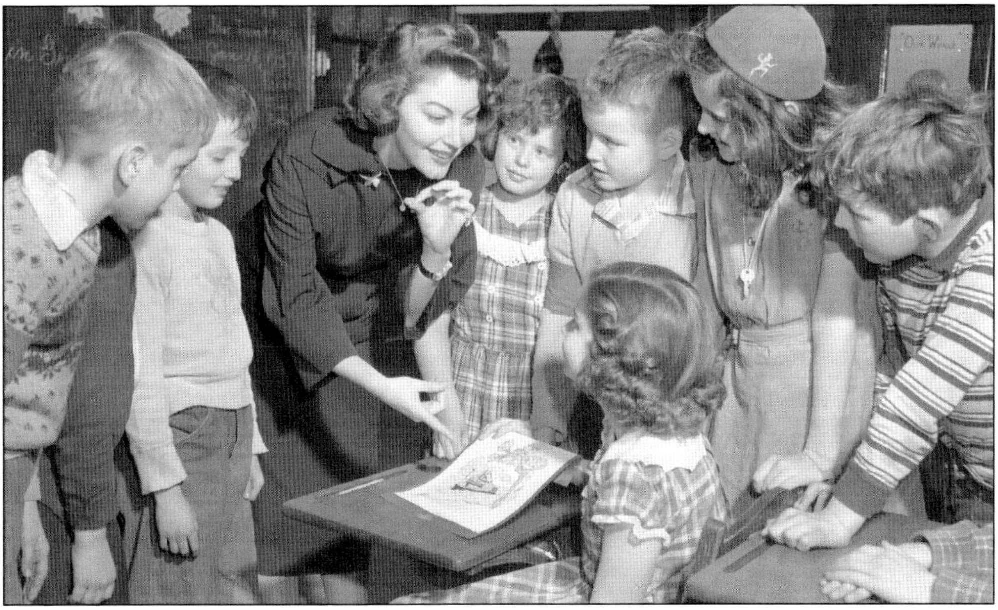

Fourth graders at Wiley School had stars in their eyes when Ava Gardner visited their classroom on January 16, 1951, at the request of her niece, Jean Pearce (seated). The students enthusiastically asked questions about motion pictures and their favorite movie stars, and Ava graciously answered their questions and signed autographs. When asked about the small boat on her necklace, Ava said it was a memento of her recent movie, *Showboat.*

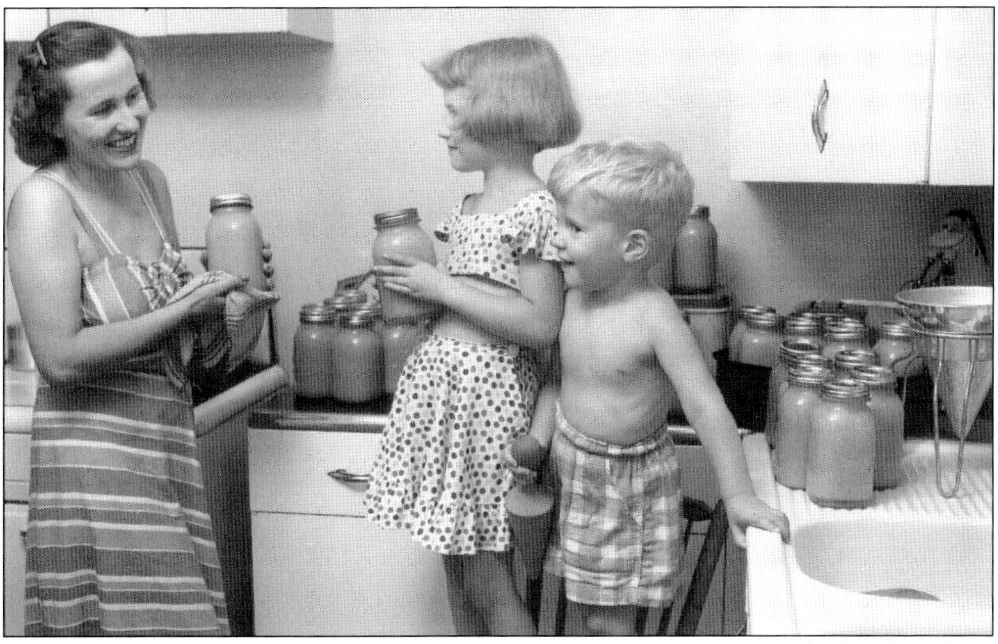

Freezing and canning make the great flavors of summertime fruits and vegetables last throughout the winter. In July 1951, *Winston-Salem Journal* home economics editor, Beth Tartan, wrote a feature article on the dos and don'ts of freezing and canning methods. One of the article photographs showed Mrs. Hiram Cody Jr. getting help from her children, Harriet and Chip, in wiping the 46 jars of golden applesauce she prepared.

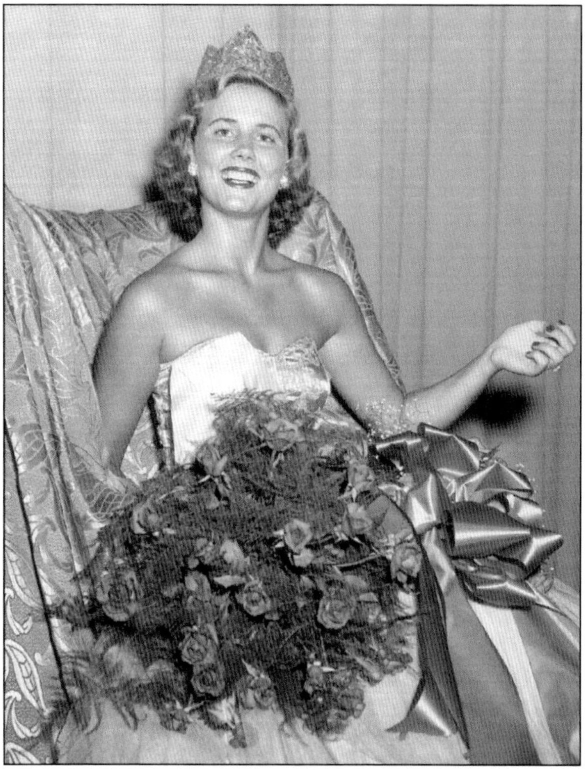

LuLong Ogburn was crowned Miss North Carolina 1951 at the state beauty pageant in Burlington. Originally from Smithfield, Miss Ogburn won third place in the Miss America pageant held in September 1951. Crowned when she was a rising sophomore at Salem College, Miss Ogburn was an outstanding musician, honor student, athlete, and student leader during her years at Salem.

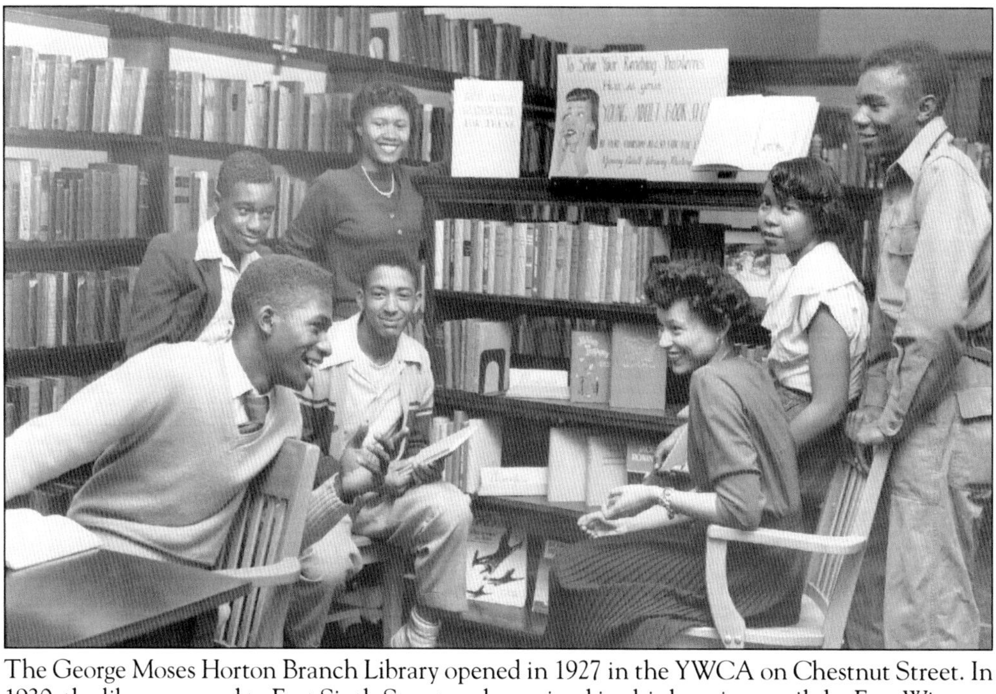

The George Moses Horton Branch Library opened in 1927 in the YWCA on Chestnut Street. In 1930, the library moved to East Sixth Street and remained in this location until the East Winston Branch Library opened in 1954. Mrs. Mary Henry, seated right, was the librarian for the new section for young people that opened in 1951 at the Horton Library.

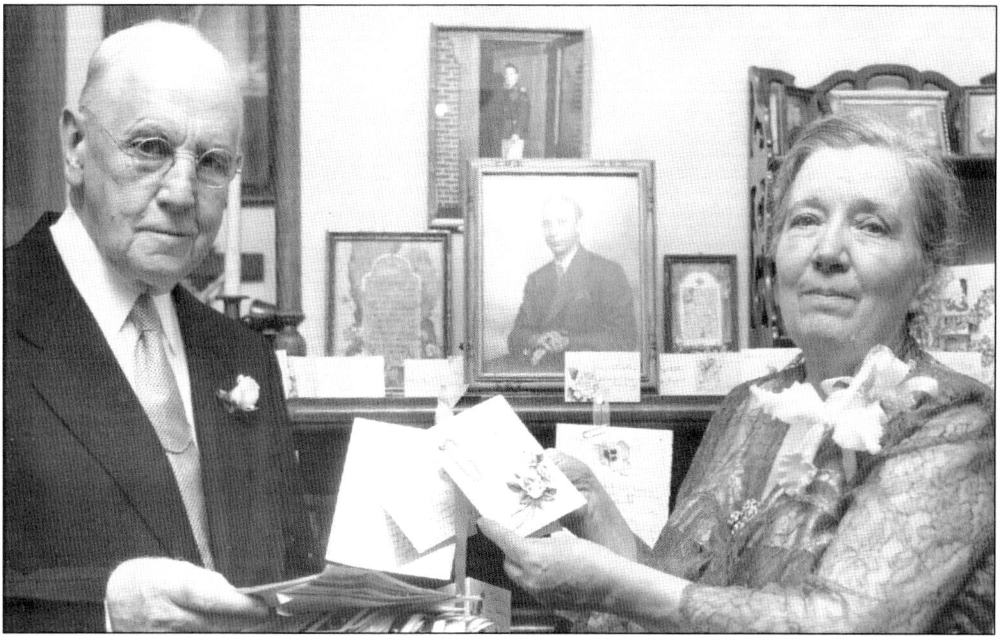

John Kenneth Pfohl and Bessie Whittington were married August 21, 1901, and celebrated their golden wedding anniversary in 1951, surrounded by family and friends at their home on South Church Street. Bishop and Mrs. Pfohl spent the day receiving words of congratulations and best wishes through telephone calls and greeting cards. Among their many gifts was a special musical arrangement of the Twenty-third Psalm sent from a friend in Germany.

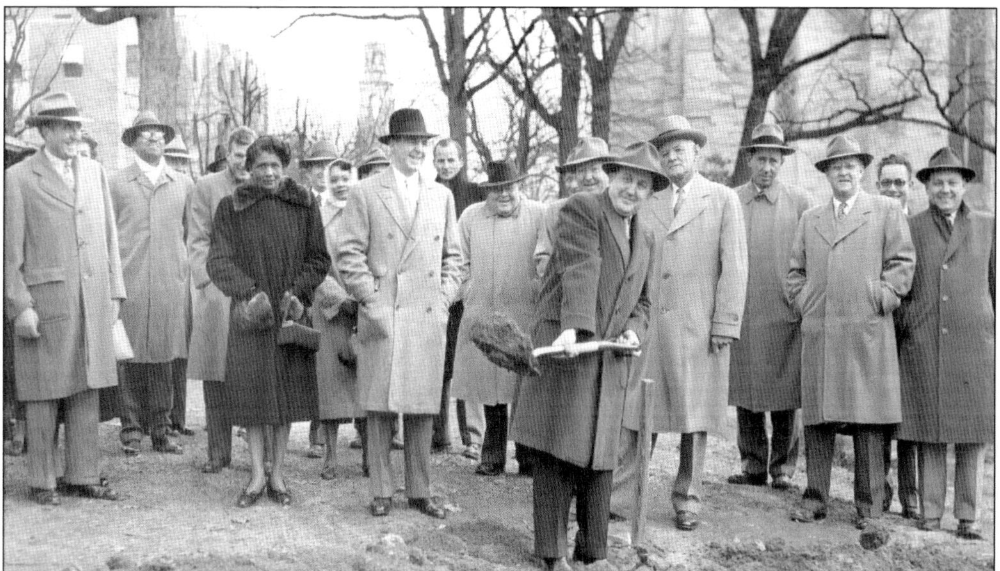

Surrounded by community leaders and library personnel, Mayor Marshall Kurfees lifted the first shovelful of dirt for the new Fifth Street Library on a cold day in December 1951. The ground was being prepared for digging the foundation when officials met to commemorate the start of construction. The second shovelful of dirt was tossed into the air by Ralph Hanes, primary fund-raiser for the building and for the book fund.

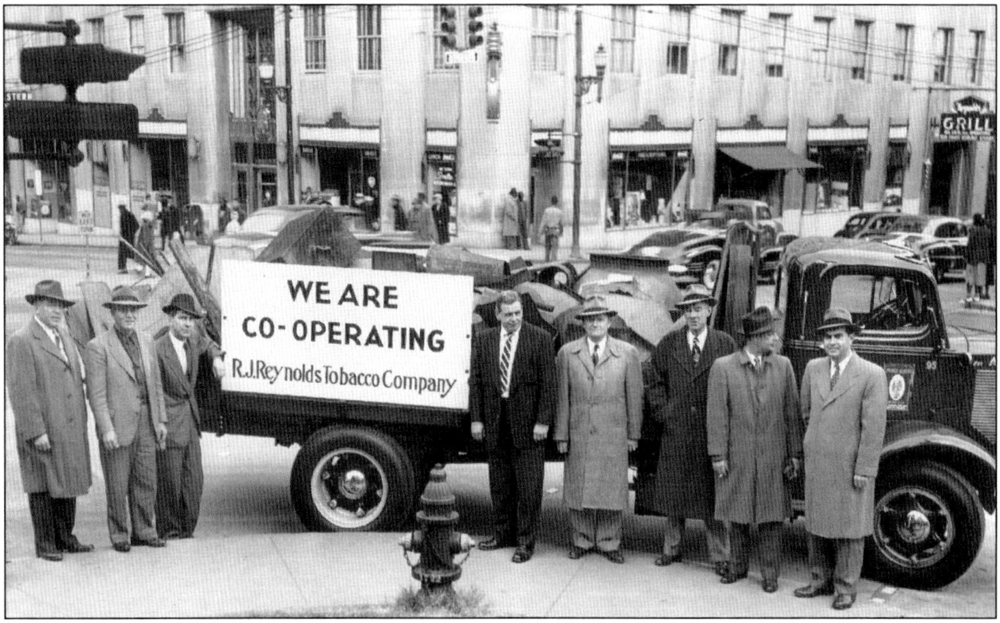

Most parades are given to show off the finest and the best. But the used household items and dilapidated vehicles in the parade held in January 1952 were headed straight for the junk yard. The scrap metal parade was held to remind citizens that everyone can help in easing the country's metal shortage. Parade organizers gathered for a photograph in front of a truck carrying scrap metal from R. J. Reynolds Tobacco Company.

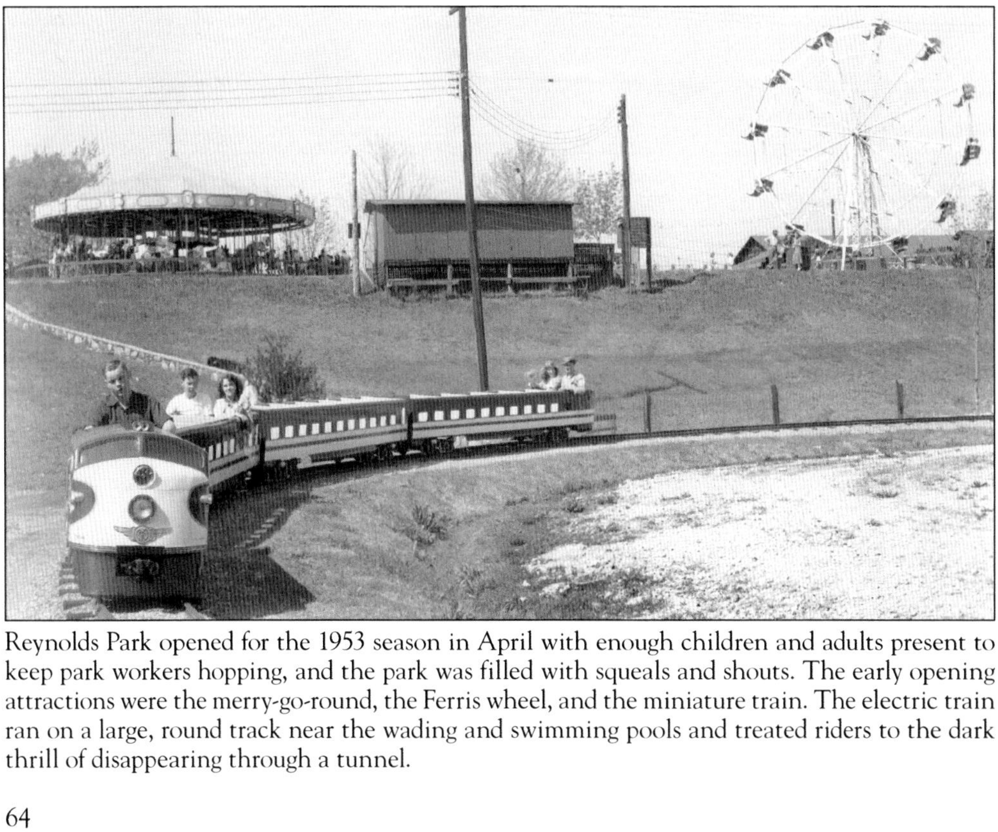

Reynolds Park opened for the 1953 season in April with enough children and adults present to keep park workers hopping, and the park was filled with squeals and shouts. The early opening attractions were the merry-go-round, the Ferris wheel, and the miniature train. The electric train ran on a large, round track near the wading and swimming pools and treated riders to the dark thrill of disappearing through a tunnel.

Reynolds Auditorium rocked with a packed crowd of 2,000 arts patrons for the 1953 Arts Follies. The show featured fast-paced acts of singing, dancing, acting, and comedy, all with the purpose of raising money to fund Winston-Salem's 17 cultural organizations for the coming year. In one of the acts, three lovely ladies were dressed in red and covered with diamonds to interpret the song "Diamonds Are a Girl's Best Friend."

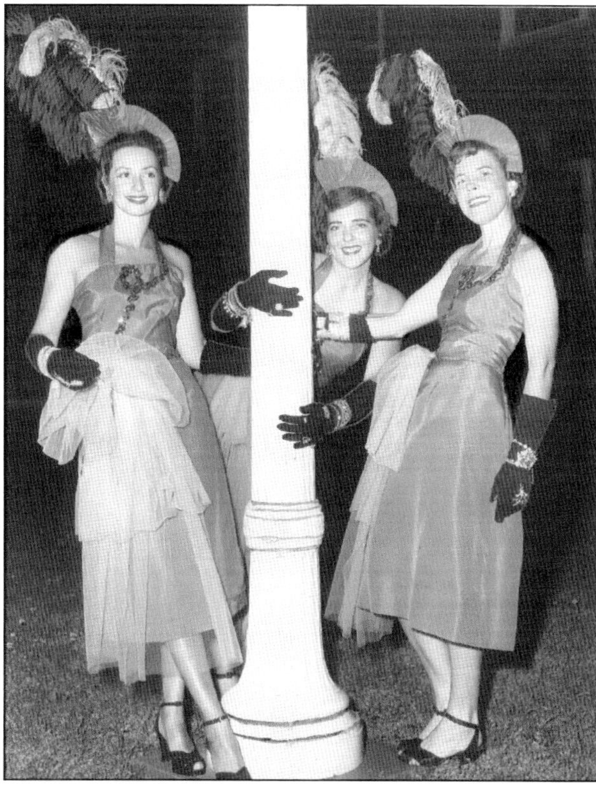

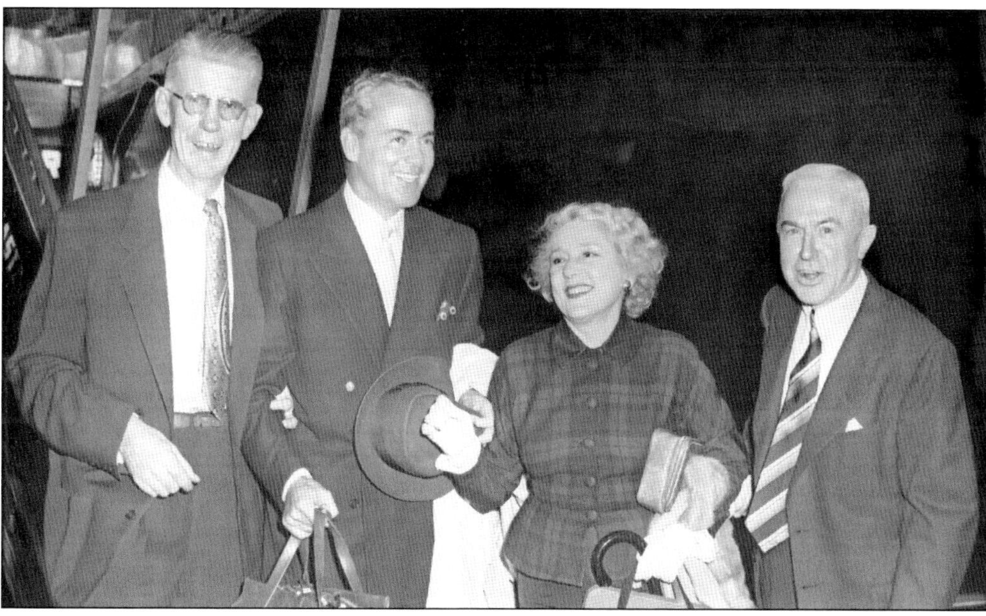

Television was in its infancy in October 1953 when Mary Pickford and her husband, Buddy Rogers, visited Winston-Salem as stockholders of WSJS Television. Mary Pickford, known as America's first sweetheart of the movies, was enthusiastic about the future of television. On this visit, Mr. and Mrs. Rogers were greeted by Harold Essex (left), director of WSJS, and W. K. Hoyt (right), publisher of the *Winston-Salem Journal*.

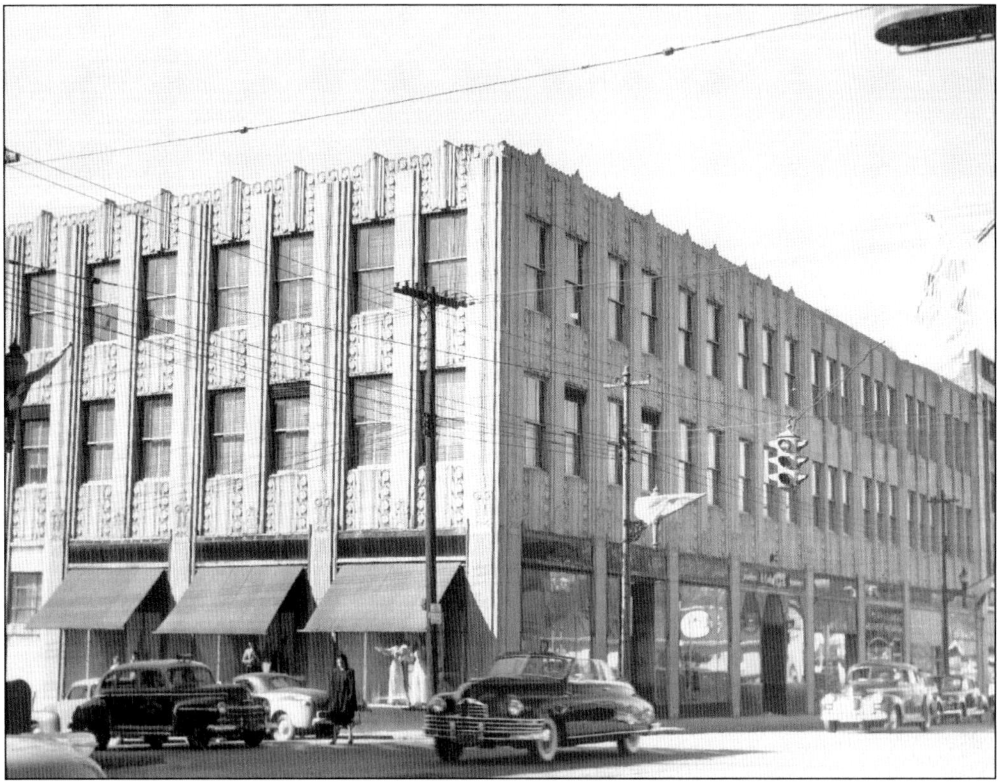

People referred to the business at the corner of Fourth and Spruce Streets as Sosnik's for years after the name was formally changed to Thalhimers in 1953. Morris Sosnik and his brother-in-law, Samuel Sosnik, established the ladies' ready-to-wear store in 1920 on Liberty Street. Ten years later, the business moved to 500 West Fourth Street. In 1949, Sosnik's merged with Thalhimers of Richmond to become Sosnik-Thalhimers, and the building, designed by Raymond Loewy, was enlarged and expanded in 1950. Thalhimers carried clothing for all members of the family, plus home furnishings, fine china, and silver. A beauty salon was located on the third floor, and the basement level featured candy and budget departments. Brides found their dream wedding gowns on the second floor, shown below in 1959, with the shoe department (right) and the Salem Shop (left).

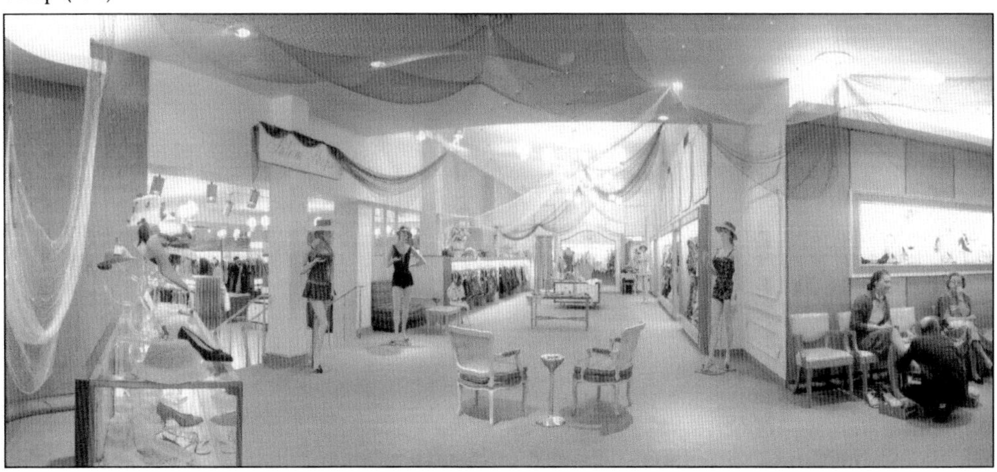

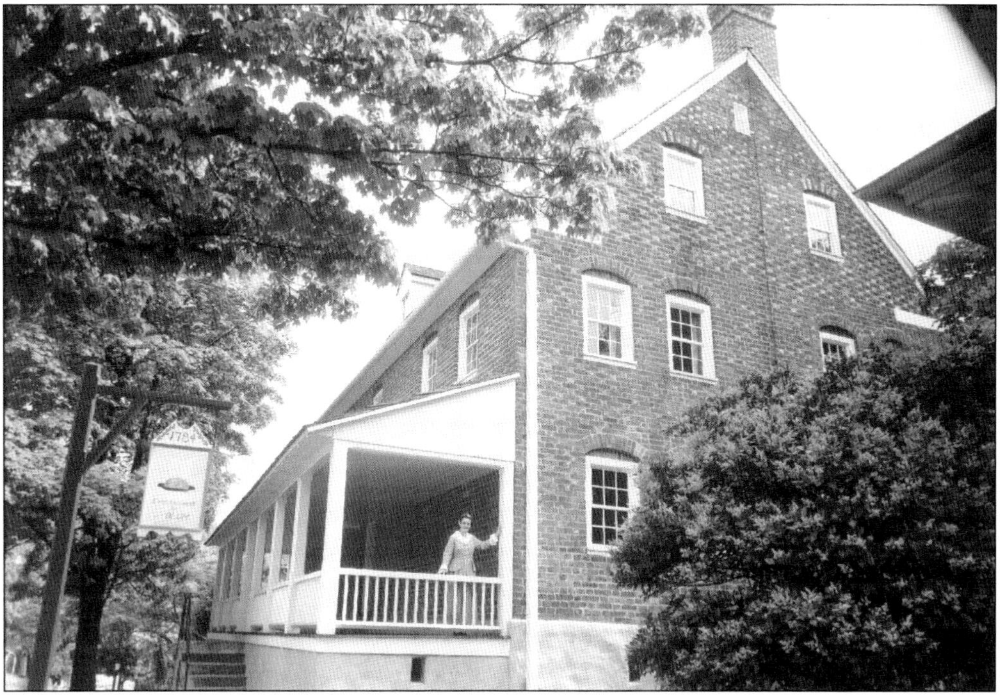

George Washington visited Salem on May 31, 1791, and enjoyed the town's hospitality and the accommodations of the Salem Tavern. One hundred and sixty-five years later, restored to its original appearance, the tavern opened as a symbol of hospitality to the weary and friendship to the stranger. The ceremonies held in 1956 marked the completion of phase one for the Old Salem restoration project. The Wachovia Museum and the John Vogler House were the other two exhibit buildings open at that time to the public. The Wachovia Museum was dedicated in September 1954, housed in the former Salem Boys School on the corner of Main and Academy Streets. Many dignitaries and former students of the school attended the festivities and admired the treasures collected and maintained by the Wachovia Historical Society, which was organized in 1895. P. H. Hanes (left), R. Arthur Spaugh (middle), and Dr. Frank Albright gather for the unveiling ceremony.

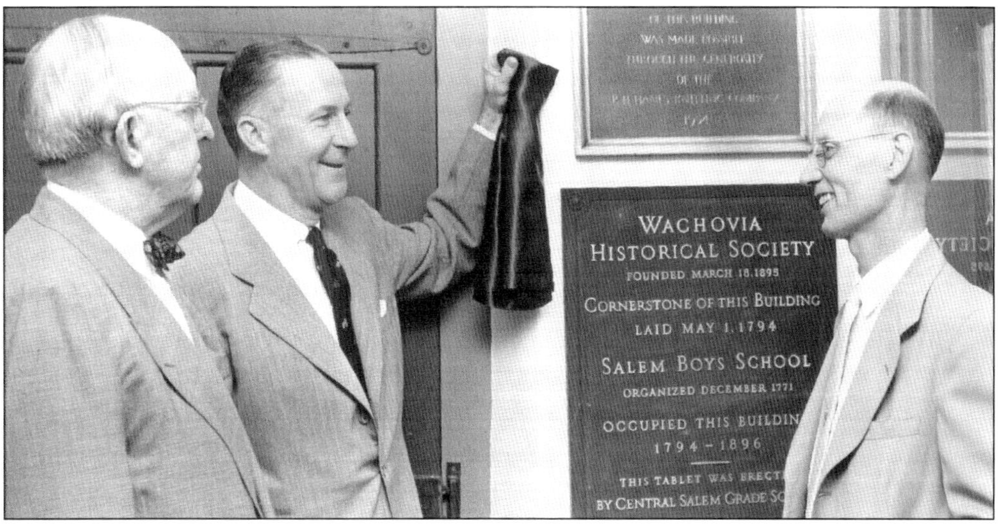

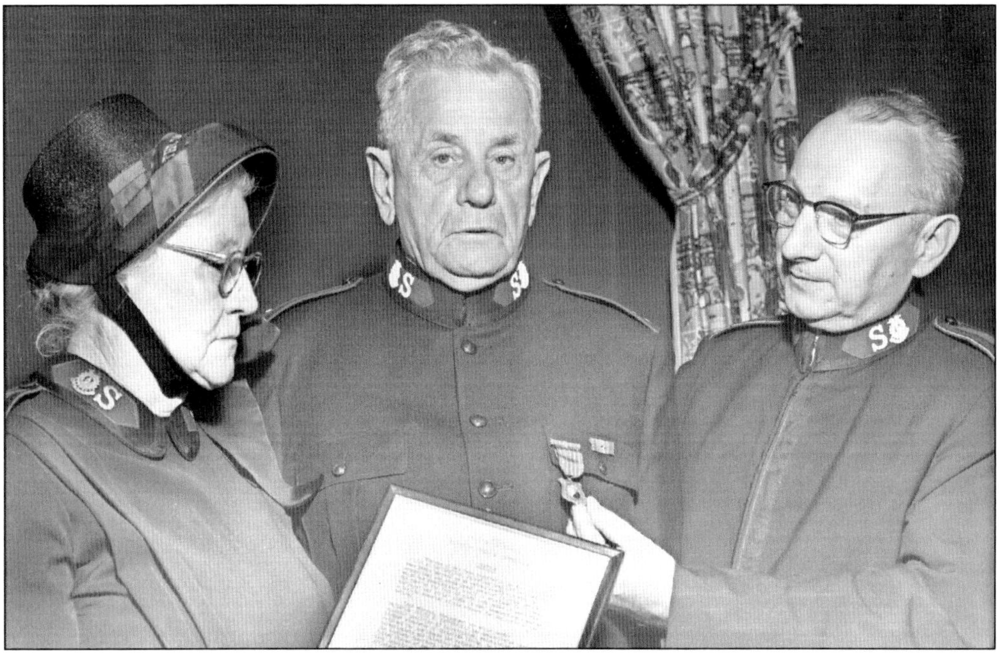

Brigadiers August (left) and Julius Satterfield (center) were awarded the Salvation Army's highest award, the Order of the Founder, by Lt. Col. G. A. Stephan (right) in 1954. The couple officially retired in 1952 but continued to serve as city commanders until 1963. Having served nearly 60 years as an officer, one of Brig. Julius Satterfield's dreams came true a few .days before his death in March 1971, when a new citadel was dedicated on South Marshall Street.

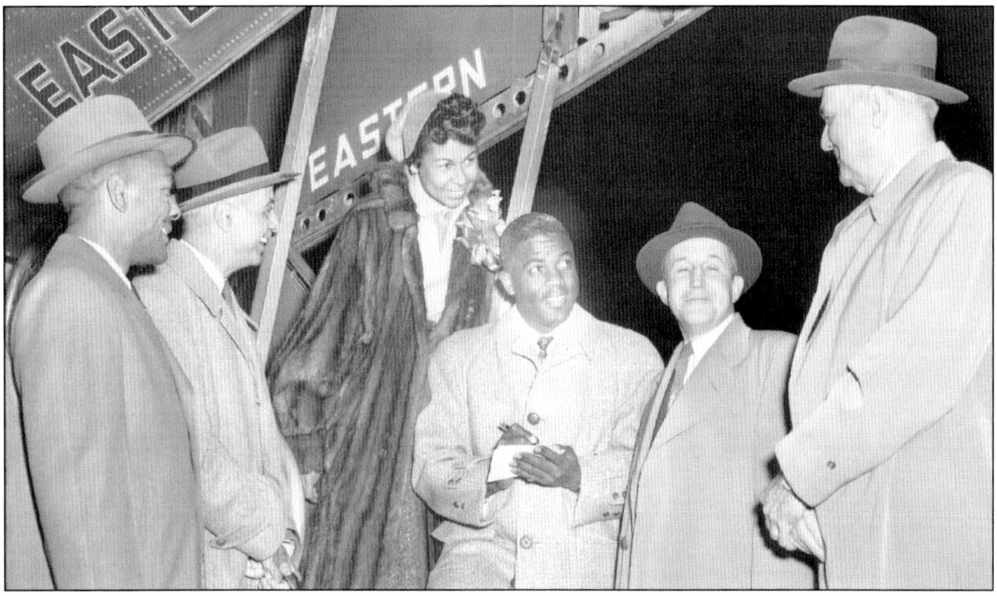

Baseball star Jackie Robinson arrived at Smith Reynolds Airport as the honored guest for Winston-Salem State College's homecoming weekend in November 1954. Greeting Mr. and Mrs. Robinson (center) from left to right were E. L. Patterson, Dr. F. L. Atkins, Mayor Marshall Kurfees, and Sheriff Ernie Shore. The Dodgers' star left-fielder signed an autograph for Mayor Kurfees to kick off the weekend festivities, which included a dance, a downtown parade, and the football game.

The beginning of Girl Scout Week in March 1955 was the occasion for a newspaper feature on the many activities of Girl Scouts of all ages. Intermediate Scouts learned to properly bathe a baby under the supervision of Girl Scout leader Mrs. Charles Robinson (right). Nearly 3,000 girls and women took part in this special week by wearing their brown (Brownies) and green (Scouts and leaders) uniforms to Sunday church services.

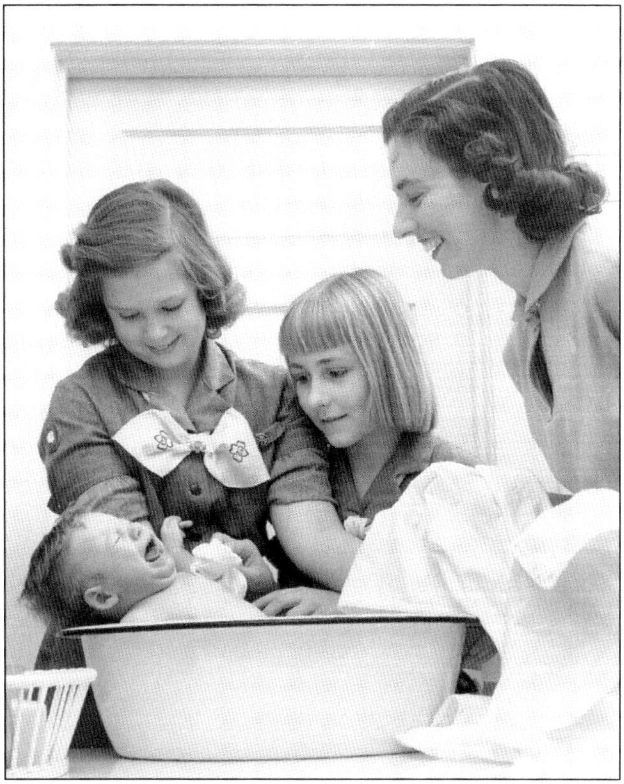

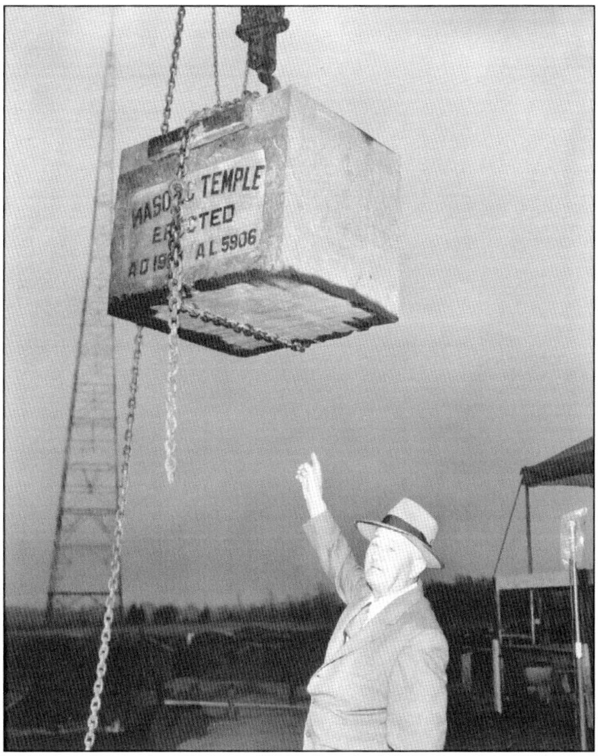

Irvin W. Grogan Sr. points to the cornerstone that was installed at the new Masonic Temple on Miller Street from the former temple at the corner of Fourth and Trade Streets. The cornerstone laying took place on March 19, 1955, with Gov. Luther Hodges as guest speaker. A contractor by profession, Irvin Grogan was master of Salem Lodge in 1926, a 32nd-degree Mason, and grandfather of the author.

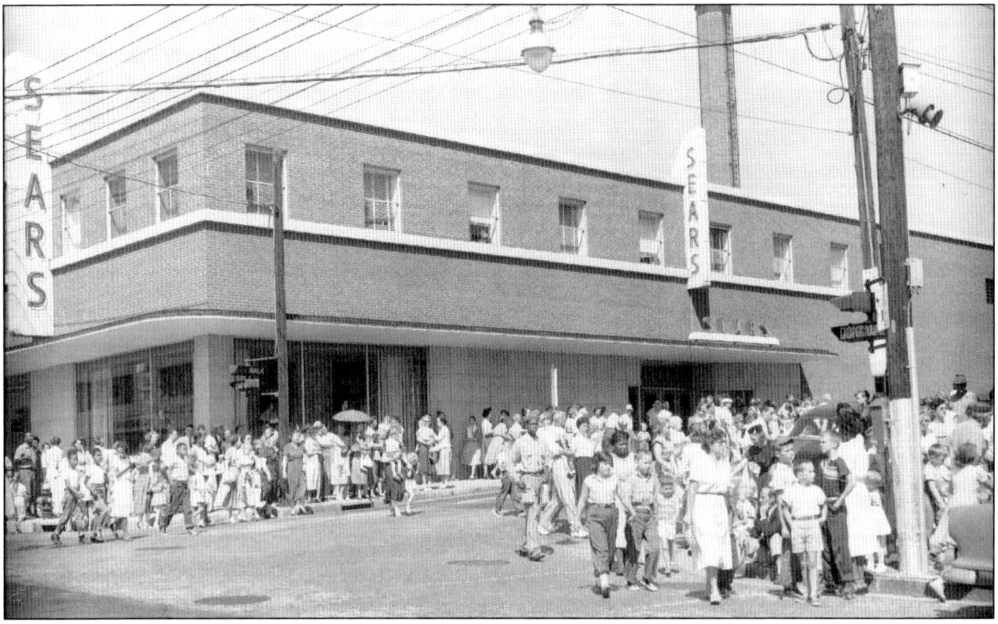

Sears, Roebuck and Company moved from its 416 North Trade Street location to a new building on the corner of Fourth and Broad Streets about 1949. On this day in September 1954, the streets around Sears were crowded with back-to-school shoppers. Some of the shoppers may have parked on the roof-top parking lot and, if they planned it right, descended into the store at the fragrant candy and peanut counter.

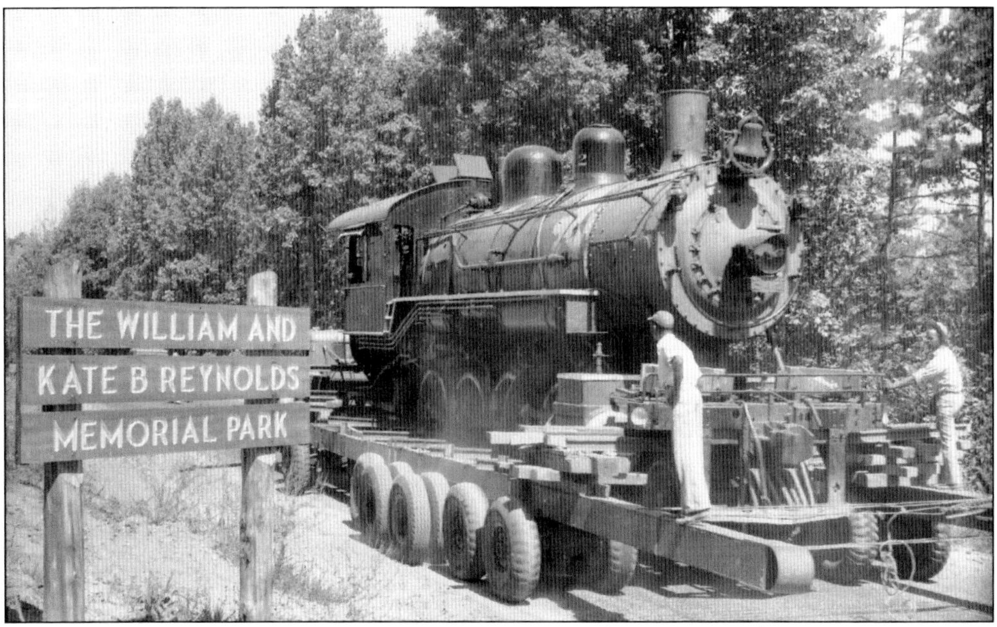

Where do old train engines go for retirement? They probably dream of going to a nice park, sitting on a strip of track, and listening to the sounds of children having a good time. "Old 542," the 1903 Southern Railway locomotive, wasn't dreaming when it was moved to Tanglewood Park in September 1954, where it lived until 1991, when it was replaced by Southern locomotive number 1894.

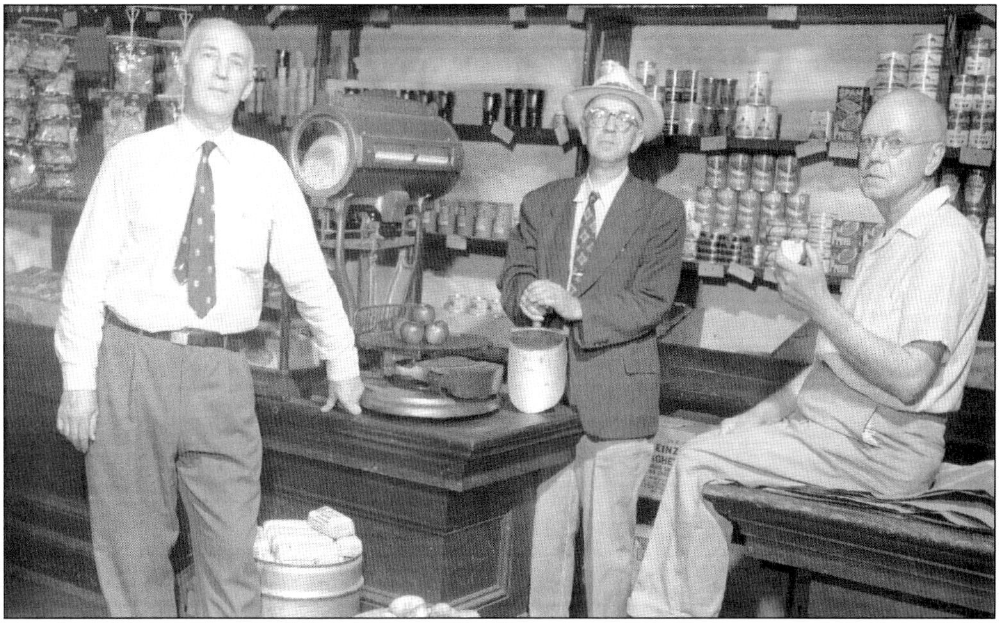

Efird Brothers was founded by Francis B. Efird Sr. in 1885 and, for the next 70 years, served the city as a grocery and fruit business. From left to right, owners A. Bahnson Efird and Francis B. Efird Jr., with clerk J. E. Hepler, prepare to close the store, which was located on the corner of Liberty and Sixth Streets. At the time the business closed in 1955, it was known as the city's oldest grocery store.

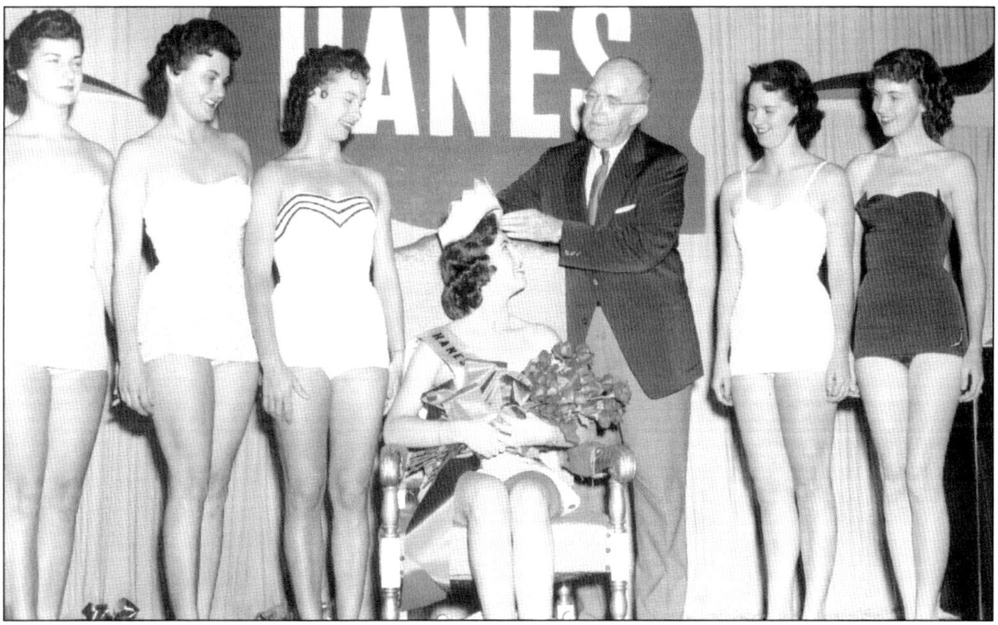

The annual Hanes Family Day in June 1955 attracted 10,000 people at the Hanes Recreation Park. The activities included two beauty contests, "Miss Hanes Knitter" and "Miss Hanes Teenette," the winners crowned by P. H. Hanes Sr. During the day, prizes were given for field events for children, employee handiwork, and special drawings. Other events included a carnival, games and refreshments, family picnic, and shows featuring Minnie Pearl and "Little" Jimmy Dickens.

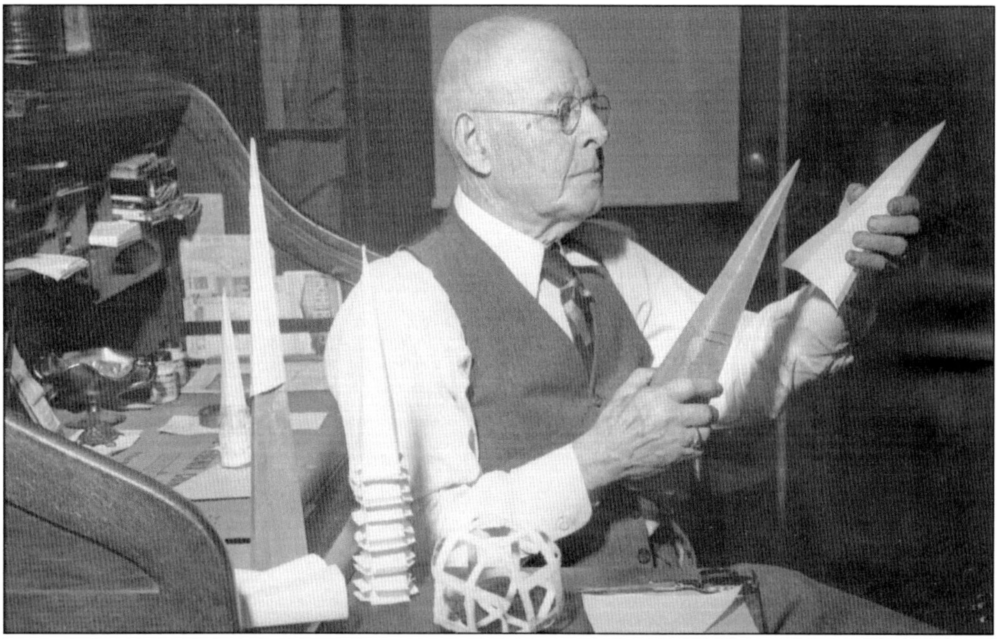

Moravian, or Advent, stars are identified with Winston-Salem and are frequently seen in home and downtown Christmas decorations. The handmade stars were originally made in Germany, but local history credits Julius Lineback with making the first stars in Salem. Julius, called "the star-maker," found two wooden star molds in his office and experimented with them until the result was a star with 26 rays. Julius's son, Harry (above), inherited his father's fascination with the stars and continued the tedious tradition. A letter to the editor of the *Winston-Salem Journal* prompted city officials to consider using the Moravian star in the city's Christmas decorations. On November 27, 1959, sixty-four large Plexiglas Moravian stars were lighted downtown to begin the Advent season, reminding citizens of Winston-Salem's unique heritage and of the timeless message embodied in the Advent star.

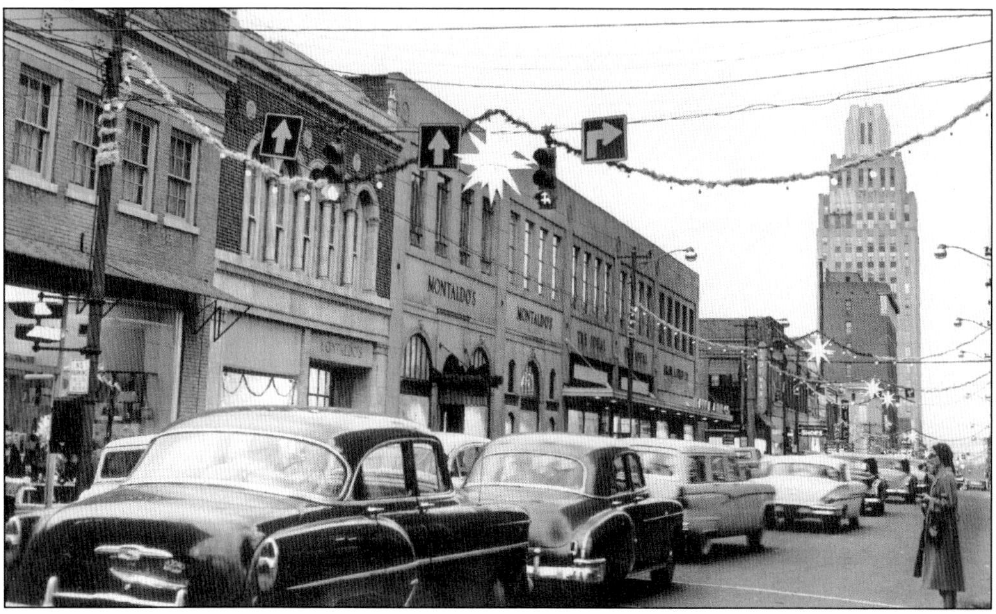

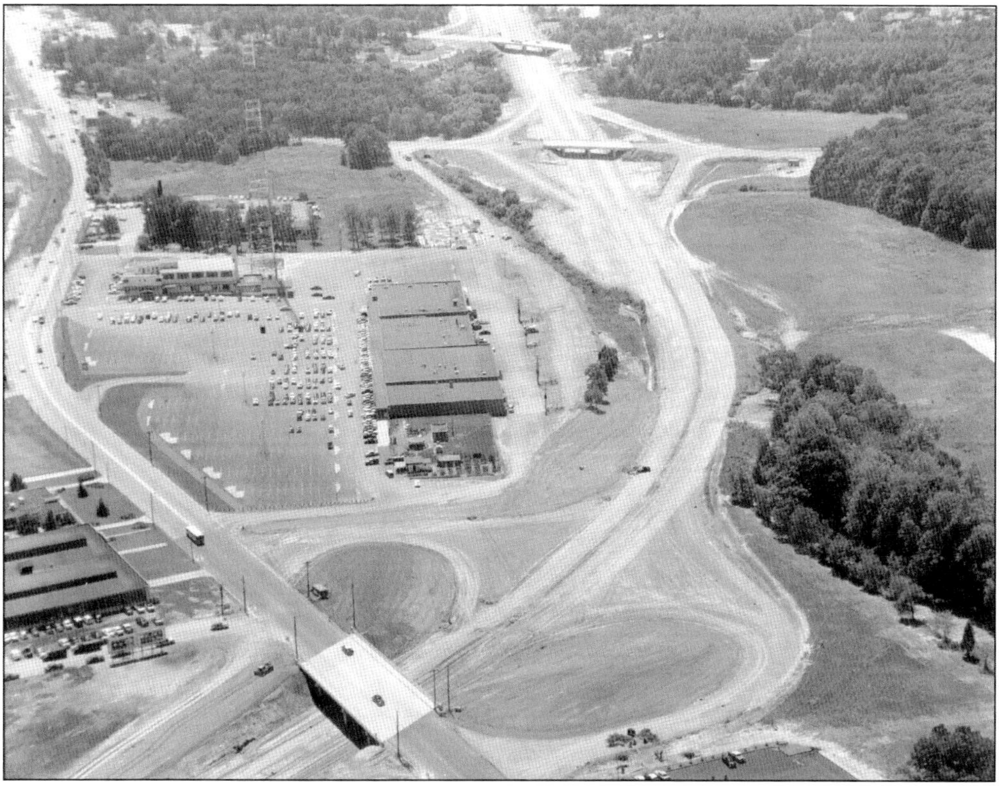

Construction of Interstate 40 in the mid-1950s opened new areas for retail growth and provided a fast route for getting there. Shopping centers began springing up near these superhighways, called "thruways" in their early days. Developers of the new shopping center near the East-West superhighway called their center "Thruway" even though the highway name was later changed. Thruway Shopping Center opened October 13, 1955, on a former dairy farm site.

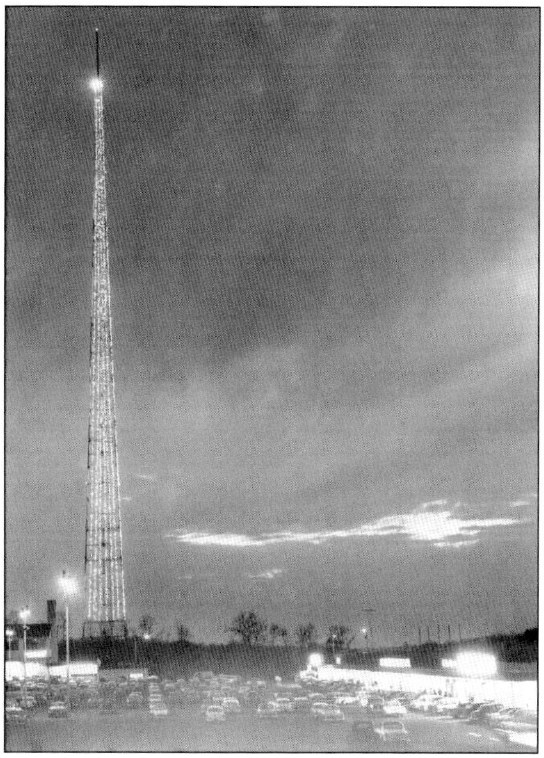

Among Thruway's original 15 stores and services were Artistic Flowers, Dewey's Bakery, McPhail's, Woolworth, Tiny Town, Marken's, Lamberti's, Food Fair, Stanley's Shoes, and Eckerd's. The most visible feature of the shopping center was the 586-foot-tall WTOB radio tower built by a Texas rigging company. The tower was particularly visible at Christmas when 3,000 colored bulbs were lighted, brightening the night sky above the shopping center.

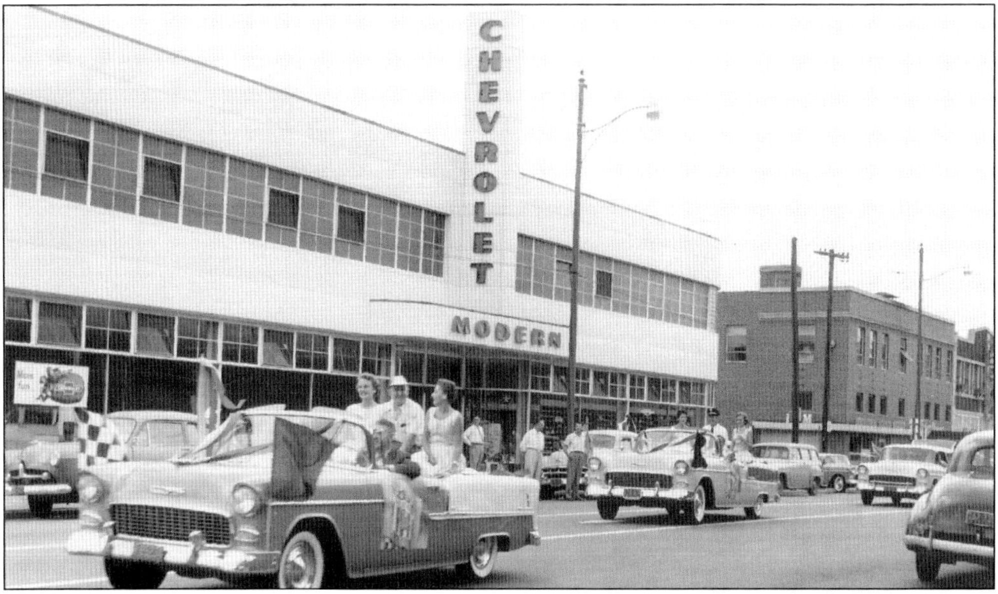

The Baseball Week parade carried on in 1955 with the noticeable absence of the Winston-Salem Twins baseball team. The team boycotted the parade because the team manager was released the previous week. Participating were the American Legion Little League team and the Hanes Hosiery softball team. Riding in the convertibles, past the Modern Chevrolet Building at Fourth and Broad Streets, were local officials and Miss Winston-Salem.

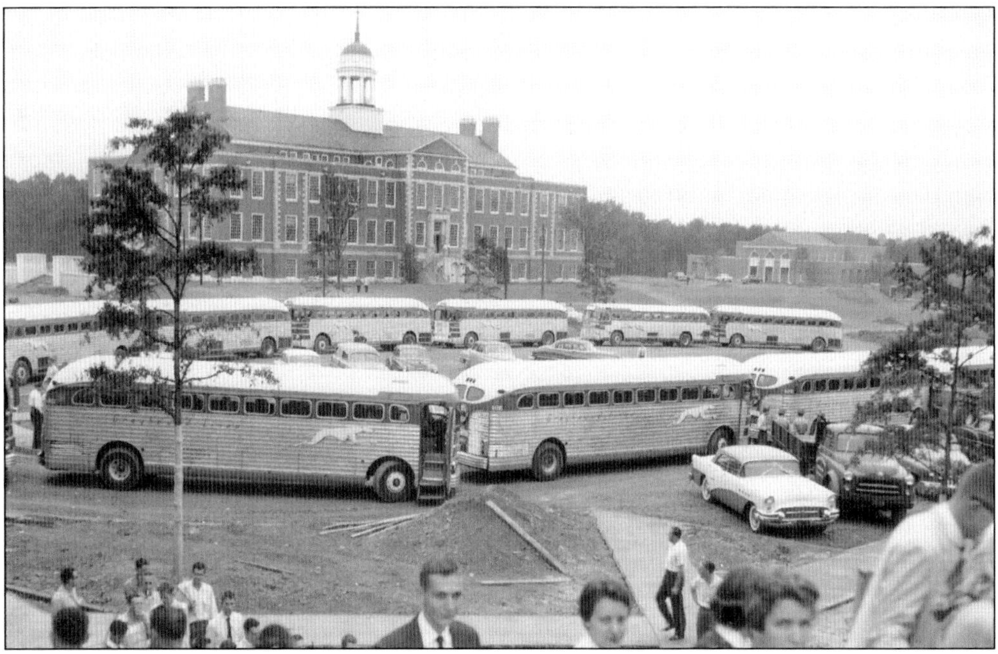

More than 600 Wake Forest College students and alumni toured the new campus on a rainy day in September 1955. Guests were able to tour many classroom buildings and dormitories, as well as the Z. Smith Reynolds Library, which is shown in the photograph. After the campus tour, students were treated to a barbecue supper and then headed to Bowman Gray Stadium to see the Wake Forest versus South Carolina football game.

An April 1956 newspaper article featured parents and children that bore a striking resemblance to each other. Jane Pepper Masich and her husband, Tony, each had a child who resembled them and are shown with fraternal twins David and Mark. The boys were almost nine months old when the photograph was taken, before their brother, Kent, made it a young male threesome about four years later.

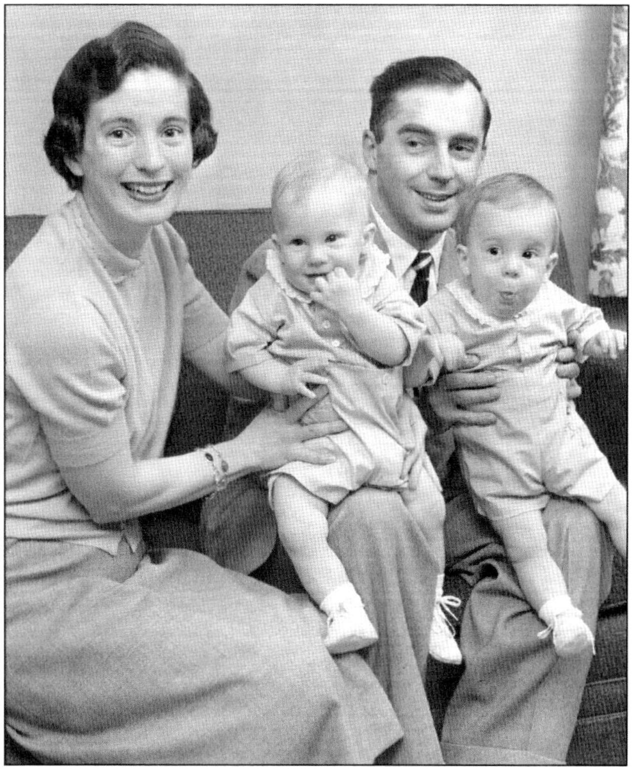

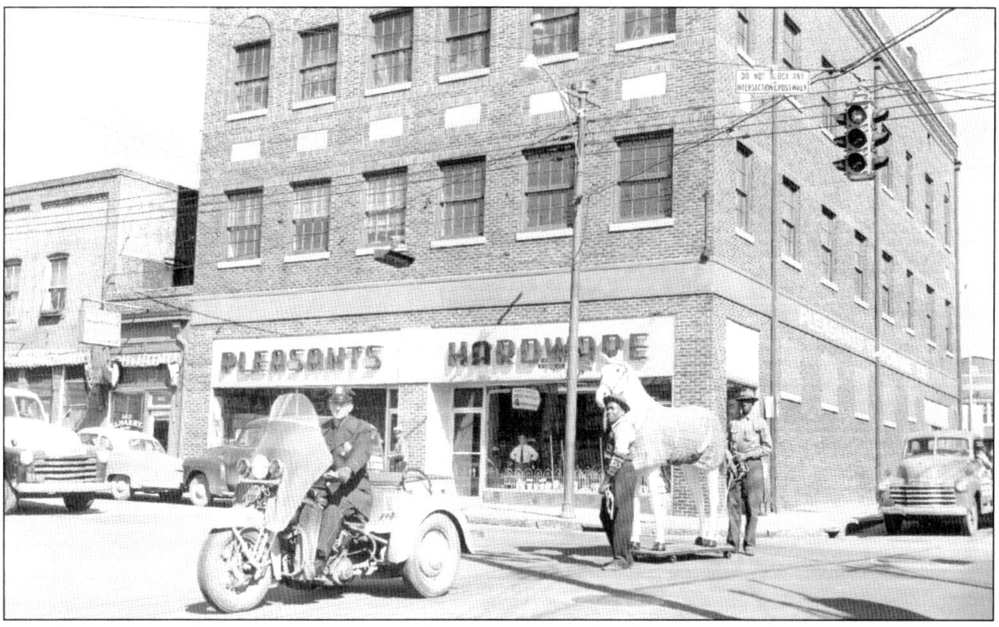

A police escort and two grooms were needed to escort Dobbin from his comfy stall in the Pleasants Hardware store at Liberty and Sixth Street to his new home at Ragland Harness Shop. The February 1956 move was not the first for Dobbin, who had traveled several times in his nearly 100 years as a wooden landmark. In 1971, Dobbin moved again, to the Pleasants Hardware store on Northwest Boulevard.

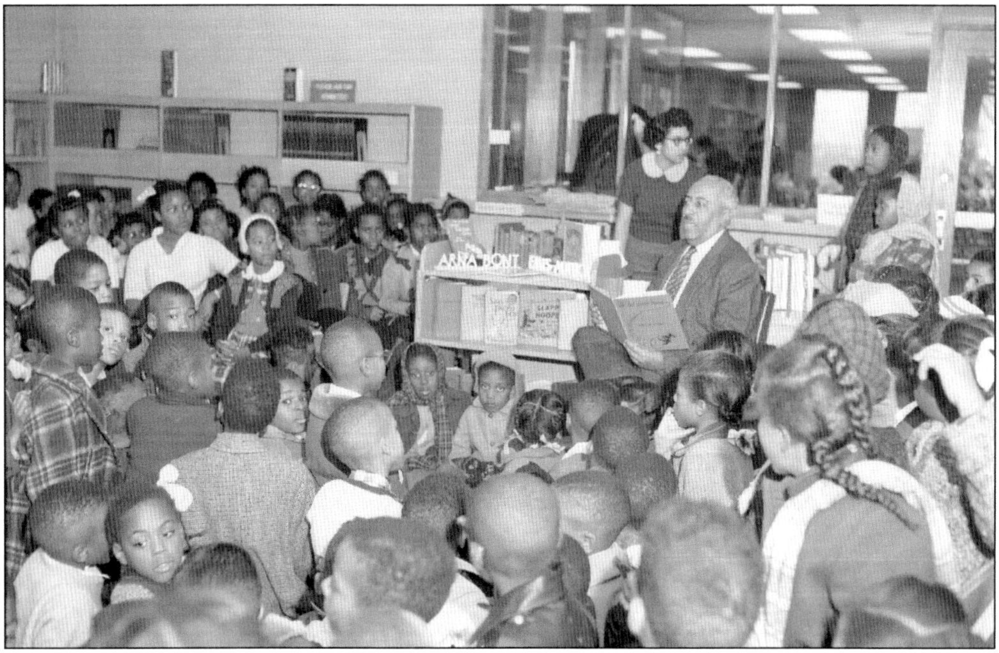

Author Arna Bontemps spent a day at the East Winston Branch Library as the feature attraction of Children's Book Week in November 1956. As librarian of Fisk University in Nashville, Tennessee, Arna had authored 11 books at the time of his visit. During the day, he read stories to overflow groups of children and high-school students and spoke with adults who work with children on the importance of reading.

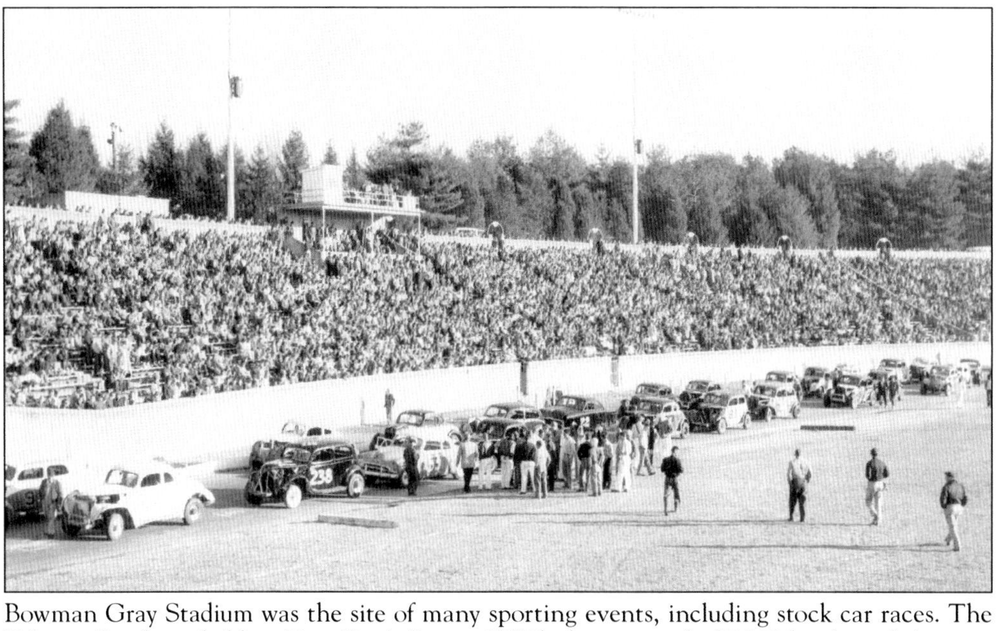

Bowman Gray Stadium was the site of many sporting events, including stock car races. The Tobacco Bowl was held on New Year's Day in 1957 before a crowd of 7,000 hardy souls braving overcast skies and cool temperatures. Carl Burris of Leaksville won the race, with Phillip (Pee Wee) Jones of Winston-Salem the runner-up for the third straight time. Jones won the Bowman Gray Stadium track championship in 1956.

Ernie G. Shore was born in Yadkin County and pitched baseball at his East Bend high school and at Guilford College. When he played professional baseball, he roomed with Babe Ruth and was later named to the North Carolina Hall of Fame. In 1936, he was elected sheriff of Forsyth County and served until he retired in 1970. The city's new baseball stadium opened in 1956, named for Ernie Shore.

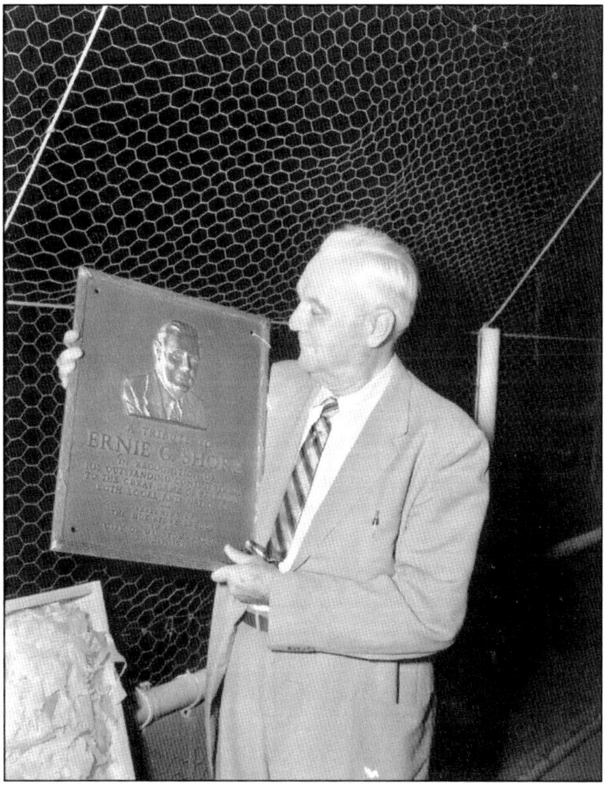

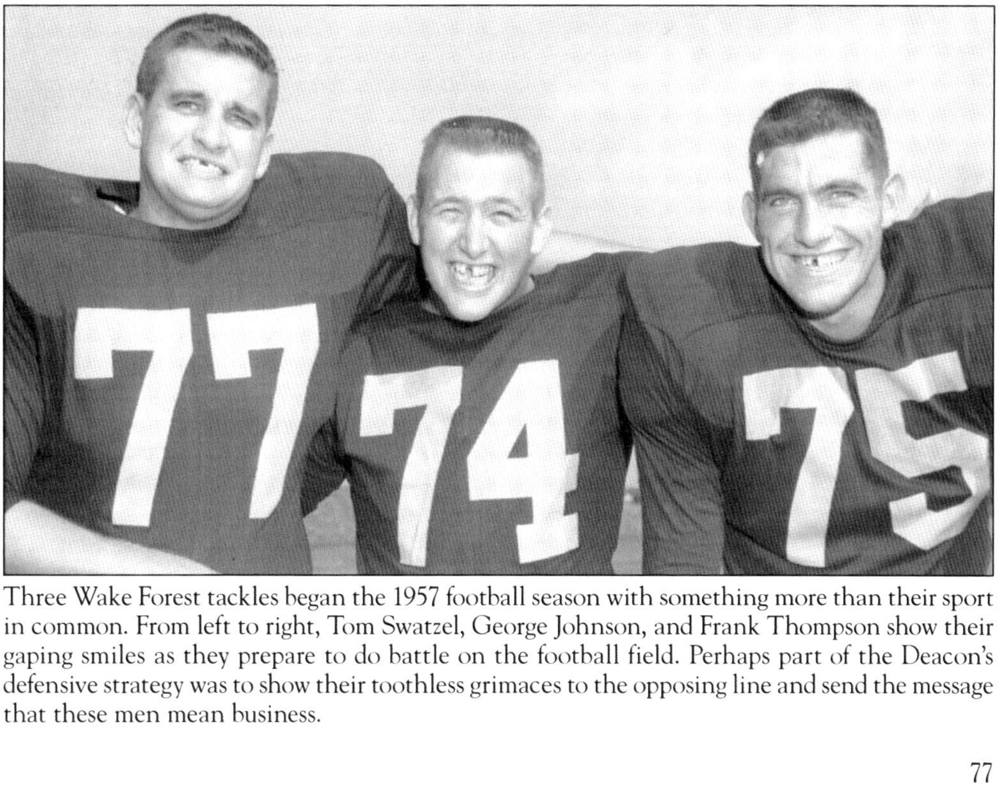

Three Wake Forest tackles began the 1957 football season with something more than their sport in common. From left to right, Tom Swatzel, George Johnson, and Frank Thompson show their gaping smiles as they prepare to do battle on the football field. Perhaps part of the Deacon's defensive strategy was to show their toothless grimaces to the opposing line and send the message that these men mean business.

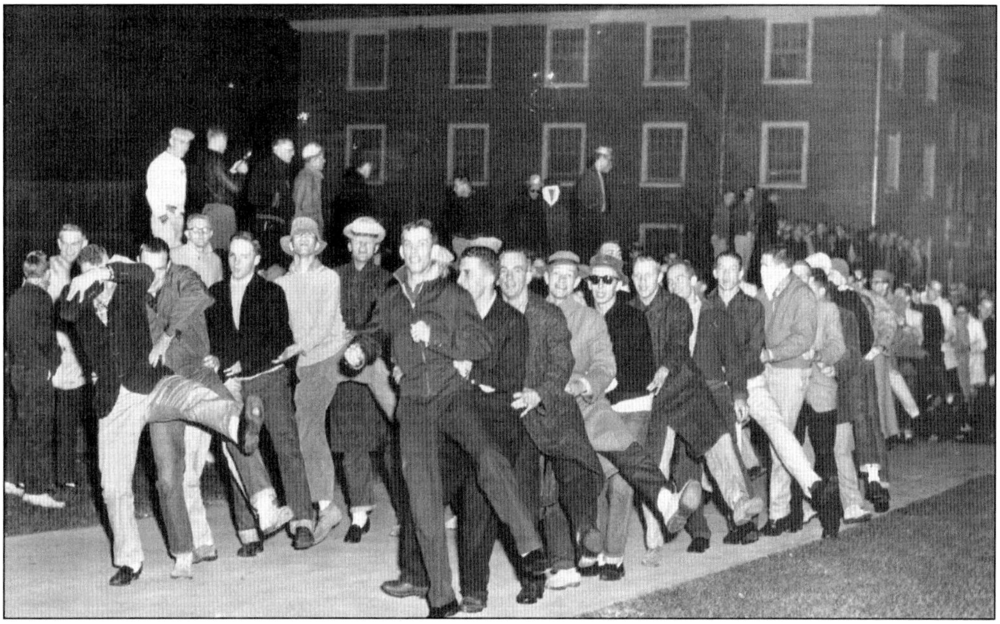

Wake Forest College students, many wearing dark glasses and handkerchiefs over their faces, danced the bunny hop across campus in November 1957. The demonstration was to protest the Baptist State Convention's vote to uphold the 1937 ruling that banned dancing on campus for Baptist educational institutions. School administrators maintained that the school trustees should make the decision and supported on-campus dancing.

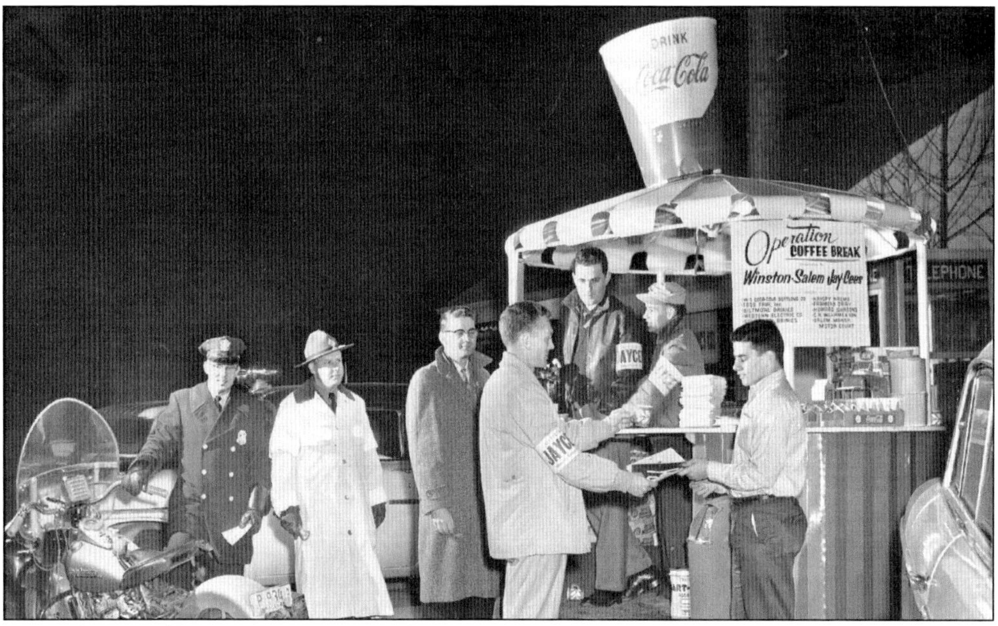

"Slow down and live" was the message the Jaycees conveyed during their 1957 Thanksgiving eve campaign to reduce highway accidents. The Jaycees joined with state and local law enforcement officers to flag down motorists and offer safety advice. The Jaycees, represented in the refreshment stand by Martin M. Mackie (left) and Jimmie Roberson, expected to give away more than 30,000 doughnuts, soft drinks, and coffee in the 12-hour period.

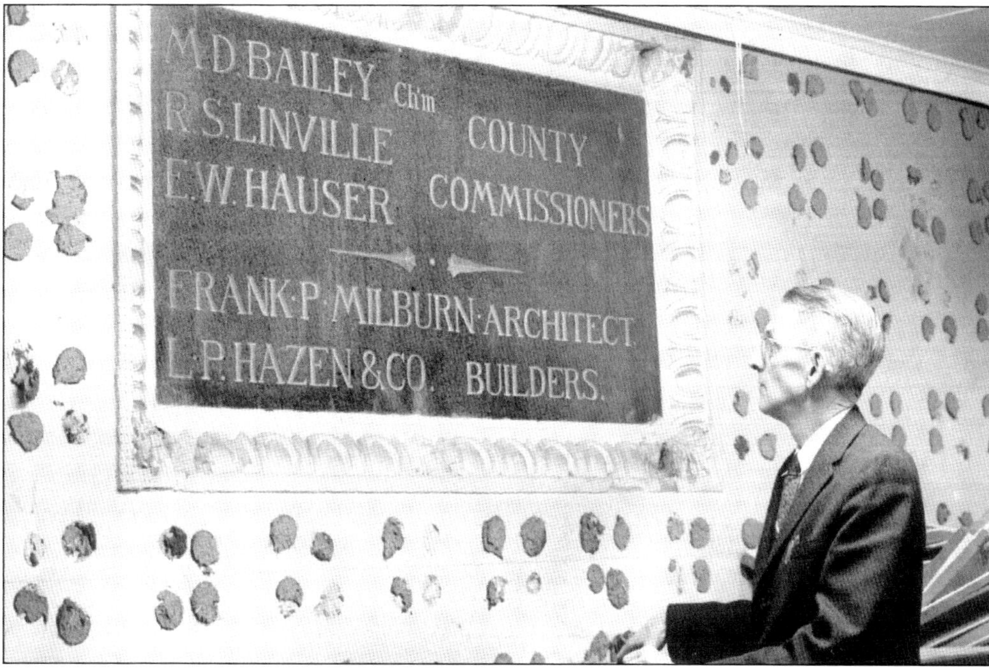

William E. Church, Forsyth Superior Court clerk, identified the mysterious marker exposed during the 1959 Forsyth County Courthouse expansion. The marker was located on the original exterior wall of the 1897 courthouse, listing the names of the board of commissioners, the architect, and the builder. In 1927, the courthouse was expanded, enclosing the older structure and covering the marker. Mr. Church was employed by the county during the 1927 remodeling.

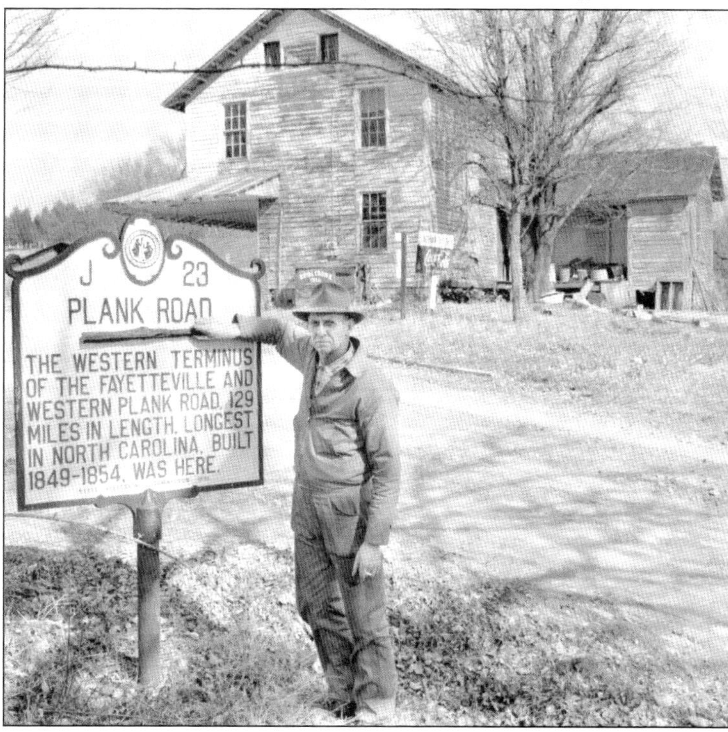

A settlement called Bethania was established on June 12, 1759. A 200th anniversary celebration began in March 1959 and included a homecoming, several religious services, and an outdoor drama written by Kermit Hunter. J. A Shore owned the general store shown in the background of the photograph. He holds a piece of the plank road that ran from Bethania to Salem, which he unearthed while plowing his field.

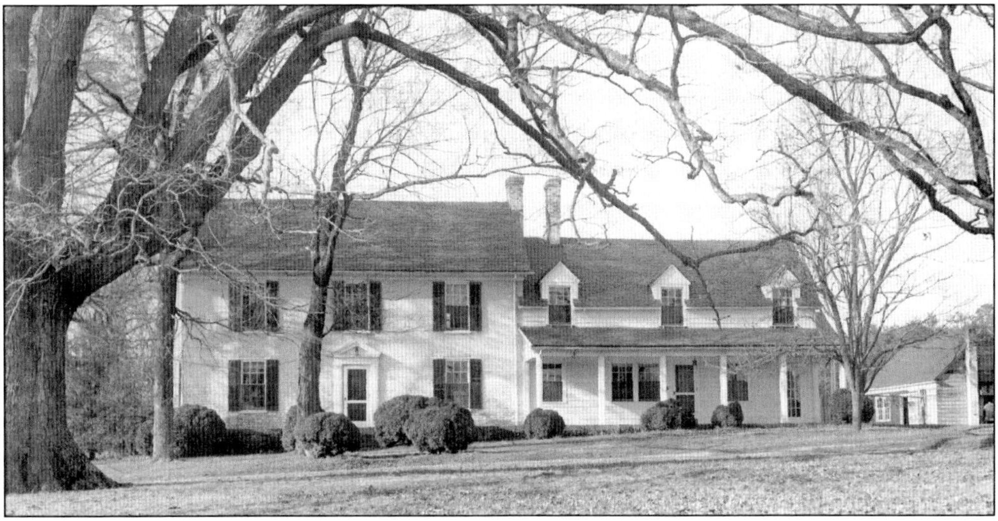

Pine Brook Country Club opened near Germanton on May 14, 1955, with 327 members. The 12 charter members selected the 100-year-old Cox house and farm for the new clubhouse and 18-hole golf course. Parts of the house were expanded and renovated to accommodate the many social functions planned for the new club. In the years that followed the opening, a ballroom was added, plus a swimming pool and locker rooms.

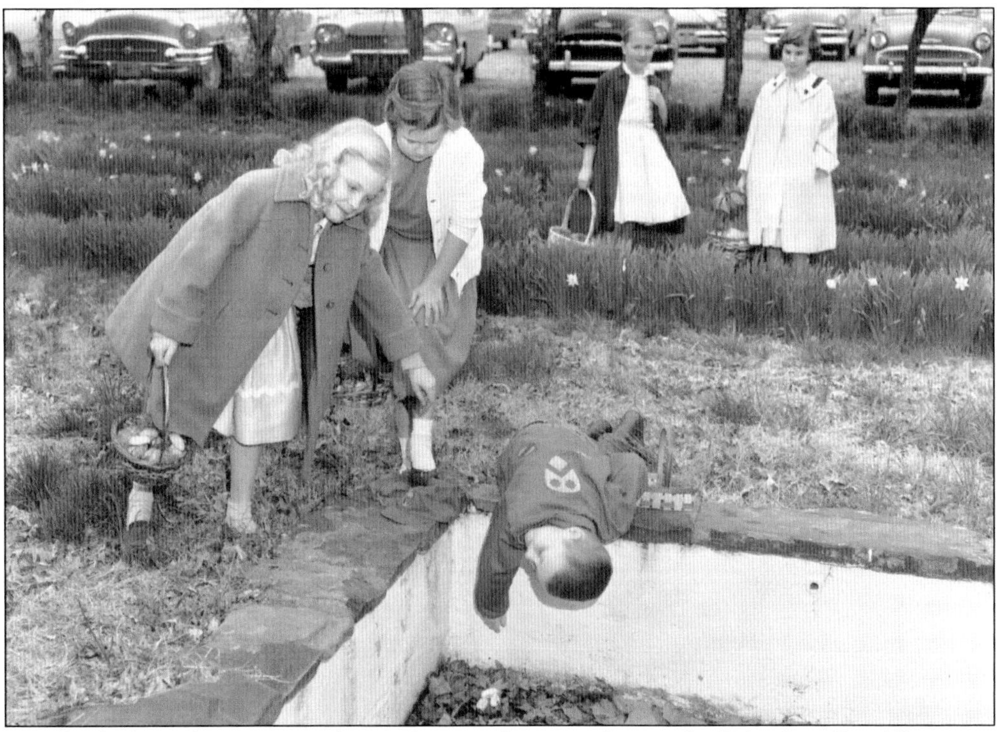

Fourth of July pool parties complete with greased watermelons and a "Miss Pine Brook" contest, golf championships, teen dances, and many special events took place at Pine Brook. An Easter egg hunt in 1958 attracted 100 children who searched for eggs on the club grounds. From left to right in the foreground of the photograph above, Debbie Gibson, Carolyn Moran, and Burt Smith discuss who will get the egg just out of reach.

“What do you want for Christmas?” Chances are that Bob Newsom of Bethania did not answer “ties, and plenty of them.” This newspaper feature for the day after Christmas in 1957 shows what would have been a common Christmas Day scene in many homes. Bob was able to make use of his ties when he dressed for his job in the Industrial Engineering Department at R. J. Reynolds Tobacco Company.

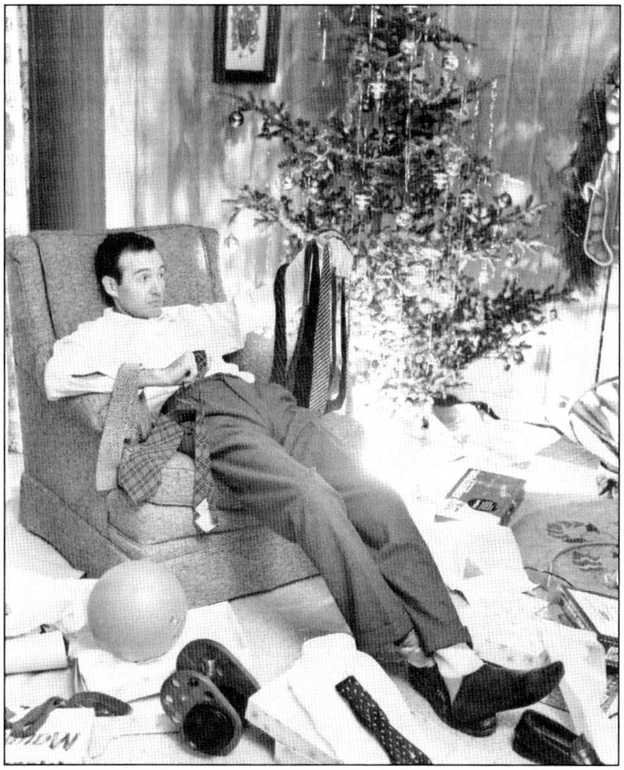

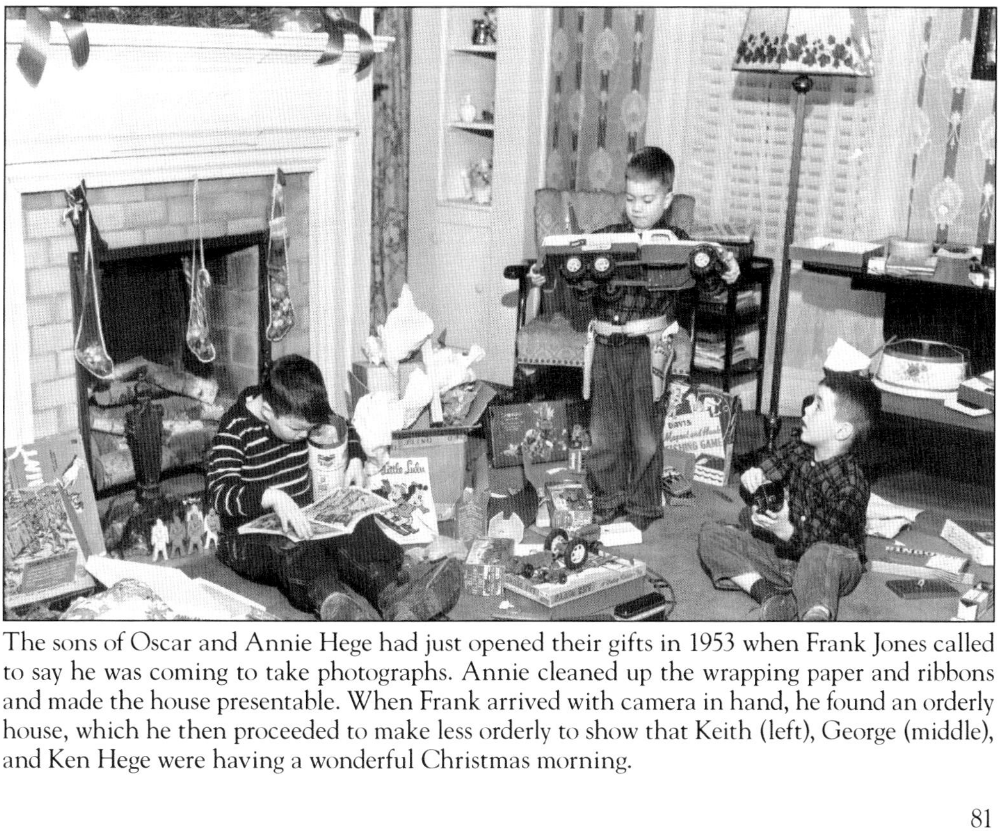

The sons of Oscar and Annie Hege had just opened their gifts in 1953 when Frank Jones called to say he was coming to take photographs. Annie cleaned up the wrapping paper and ribbons and made the house presentable. When Frank arrived with camera in hand, he found an orderly house, which he then proceeded to make less orderly to show that Keith (left), George (middle), and Ken Hege were having a wonderful Christmas morning.

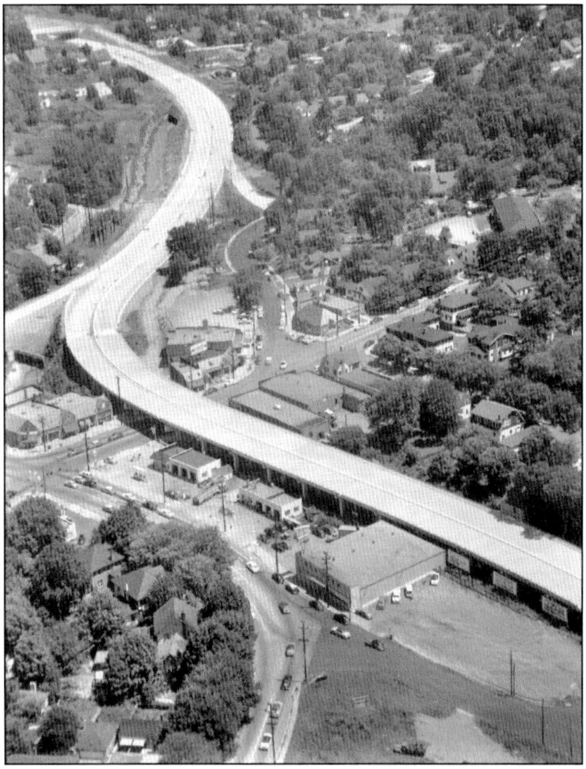

The new interstate highway, referred to as I-40, snaked its way through town, as shown in this 1957 aerial. This section of the highway was called the "Hawthorne Curve" because of the abrupt curve in the road just over and past Hawthorne Road. Most of the curve has been straightened in the last few years, causing the removal of several buildings that were located to the right of the curve.

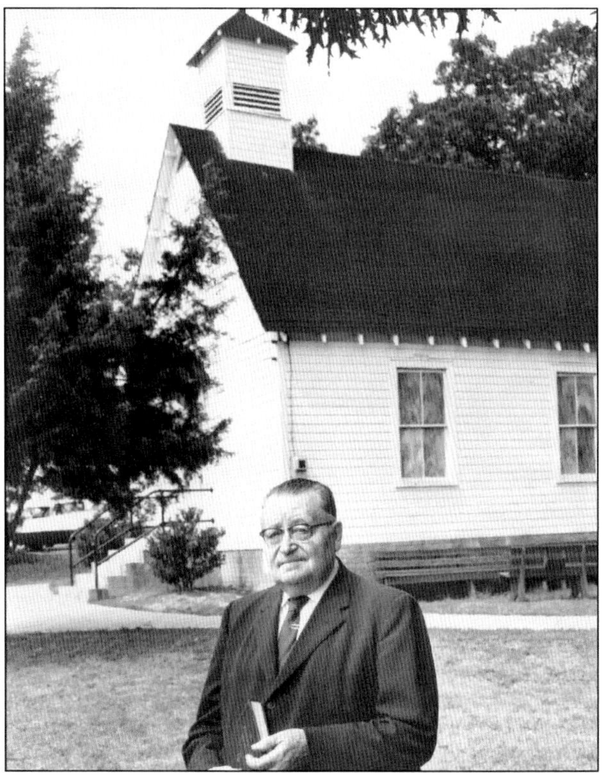

Rev. George Bruner stood outside the Wachovia Arbor Moravian Church on June 26, 1959, as he prepared to perform the church's first wedding ceremony in 43 years. Organized in 1893 and built first in 1894, the church was located off Twenty-fifth Street. The little white structure was attended by about 30 people on Sundays and had a cemetery that dated to 1894. Tragically the church burned on December 26, 1989.

Five

The 1960s

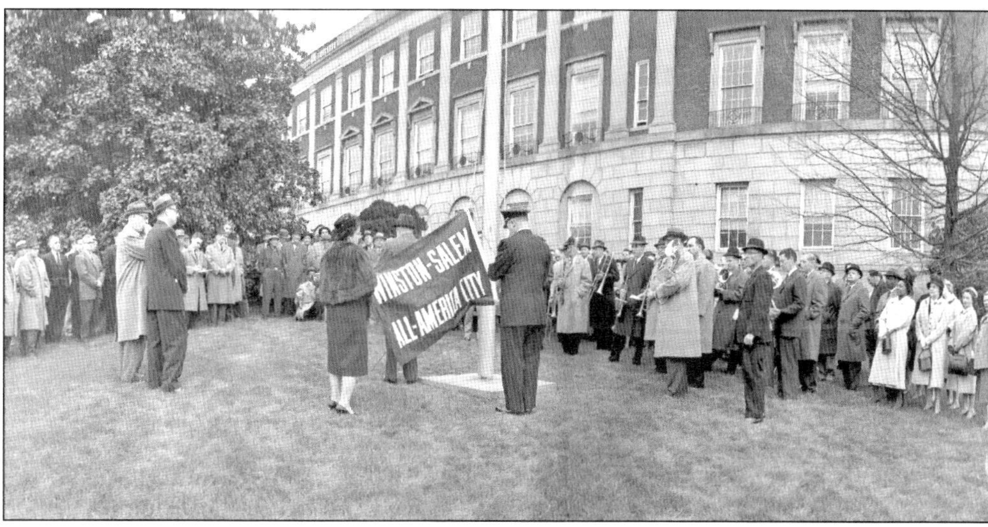

A special flag-raising was held on the city hall lawn on February 4, 1960. Mayor Marshall Kurfees raised the purple-and-white flag, proclaiming Winston-Salem to be an All-America City. Emphasizing teamwork in eight current city projects, the award application reflected the city's motto, "City founded upon cooperation." Dr. Dale Gramley added his speaking skills to the city's presentation and earned the city its first All-America City award.

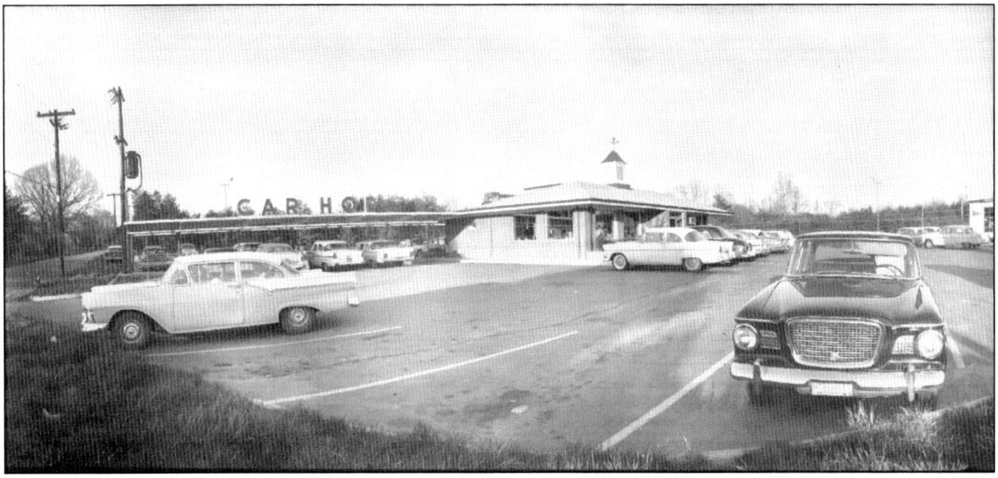

Staley's Drive-in at Reynolda and Oldtown Roads was built in 1959, replacing the earlier drive-in restaurant and gas station combination built by Lawrence Staley. The restaurant offered seating inside, plus 50 car spaces for patrons to park and order from the menu with the push of a button. An addition was built on the left side of the building in 1963, called the Open Hearth Room, which would seat 130 people.

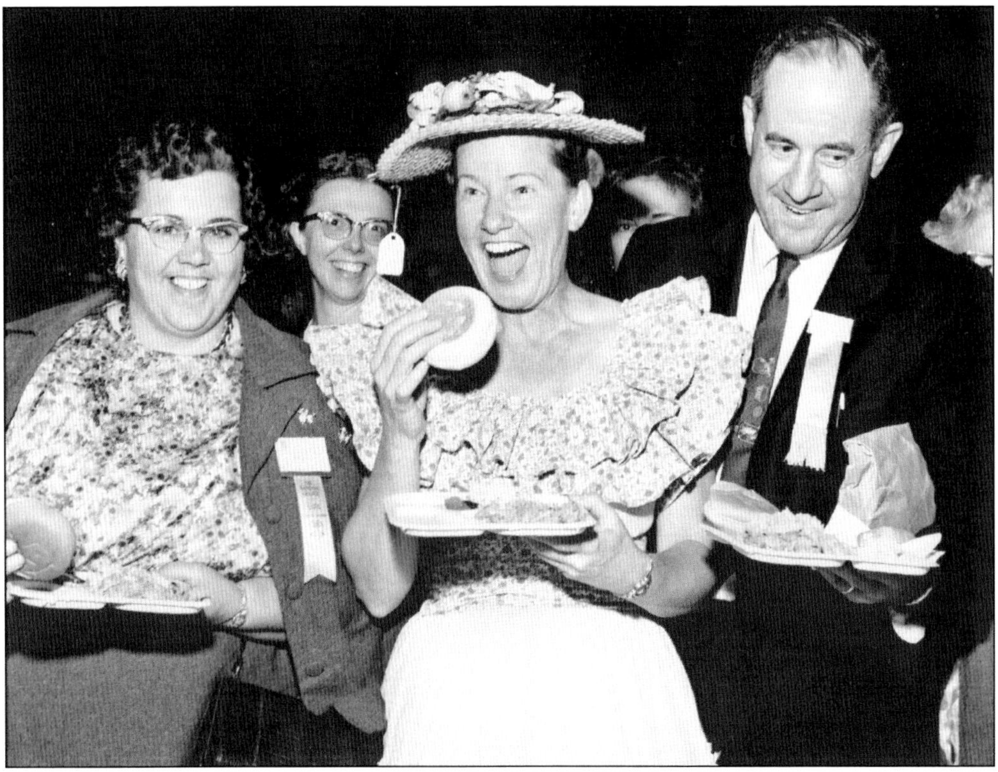

How-dy! Grand Old Opry performer Minnie Pearl was the featured attraction for the National Grange Convention held in Winston-Salem in November 1960. She entertained over 2,000 fans at the barbecue supper in the Memorial Coliseum. Don Gibson, originally from Cleveland County, also performed with Minnie Pearl. The entire show rested on their shoulders because the Nashville band didn't show, and her sidekick, Grandpa Jones, had new baby duty in Nashville.

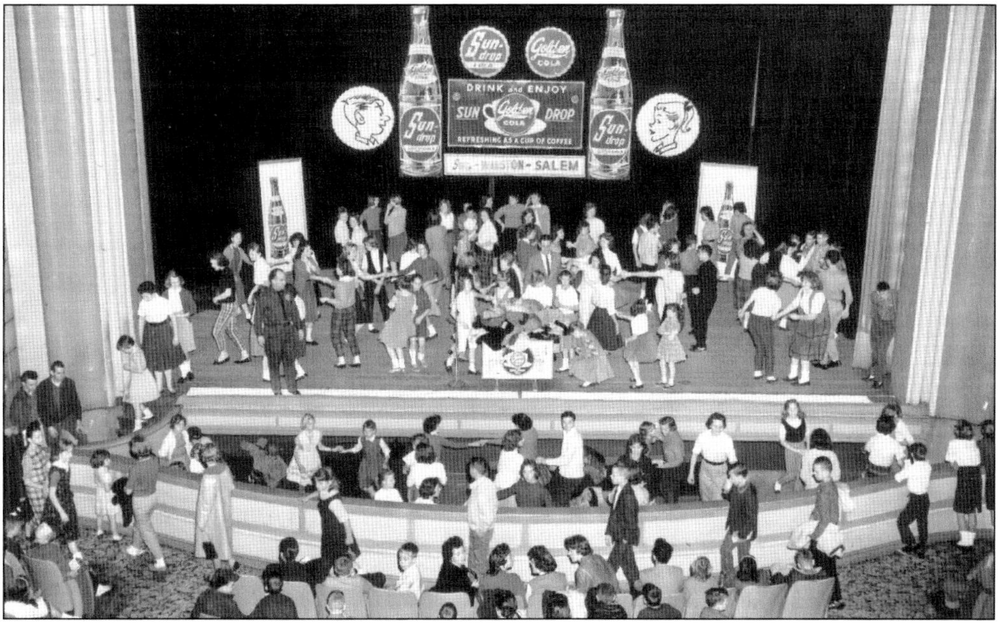

One of the popular features at the Carolina Theatre was the Saturday Morning Kiddie Show. For the price of five Sun-Drop Cola bottle caps or a quarter, children were entertained from 9 to 12 every Saturday morning with cartoons, bingo, a feature movie, and a dance party with a live band. In March 1961, attendees could see *Snowfire the Horse* and hear the Monotones, with Dick Bennick as host.

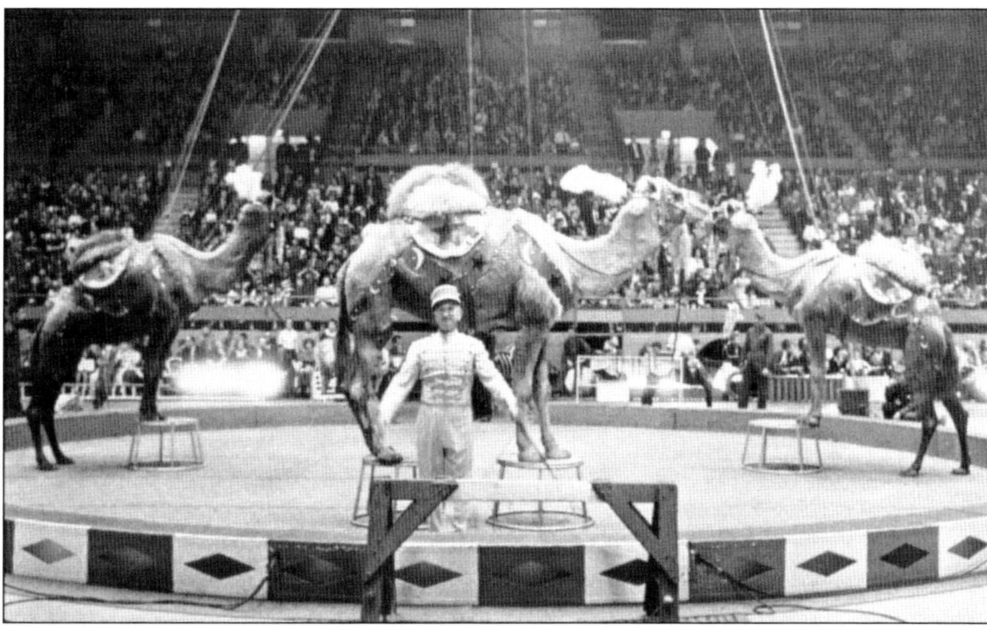

In 1956, the Ringling Brothers and Barnum and Bailey Circus had abandoned performing in their big outdoor tent and moved indoors. The "Greatest Show on Earth" arrived in mid-February 1961 in the 15 red-and-silver railroad cars that carried all performers, animals, tractors, properties, floats, and wardrobe for the show. Proclaimed as the show for all ages, the circus entertained for three days at the Memorial Coliseum.

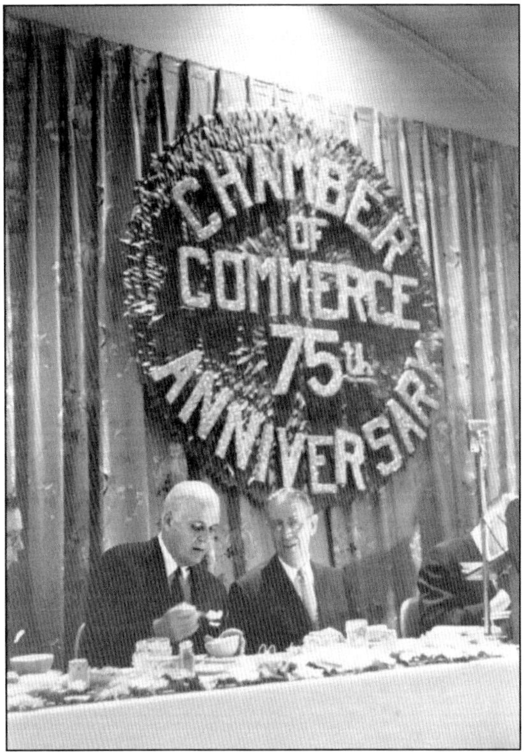

The Winston-Salem Chamber of Commerce marked its diamond anniversary in May 1960 with a dinner at the Hotel Robert E. Lee. The 300 chamber members heard speeches commenting on the city's progress over the years. They also witnessed the "Parade of Diamonds," over $1 million worth of diamonds modeled by Winston-Salem women. A giant ice sculpture of the numerals "75," surrounded by sparklers, was rolled in for the evening's finale.

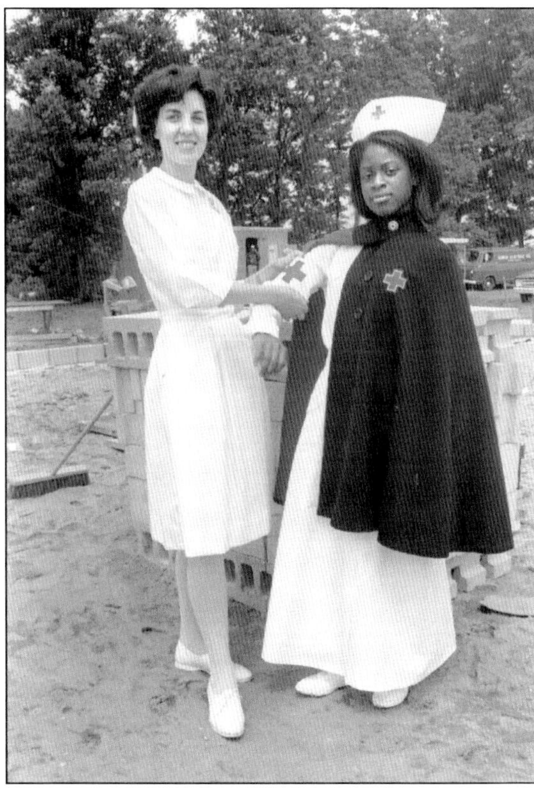

Fifty years after the Winston-Salem chapter of the American Red Cross received its charter on May 9, 1917, chapter members gathered to celebrate their past, present, and future. Volunteers modeled the variety of uniforms worn by Red Cross nurses during the past 50 years. The chapter's first disaster call was to set up two emergency hospitals to handle the large numbers of October 1918 flu epidemic patients.

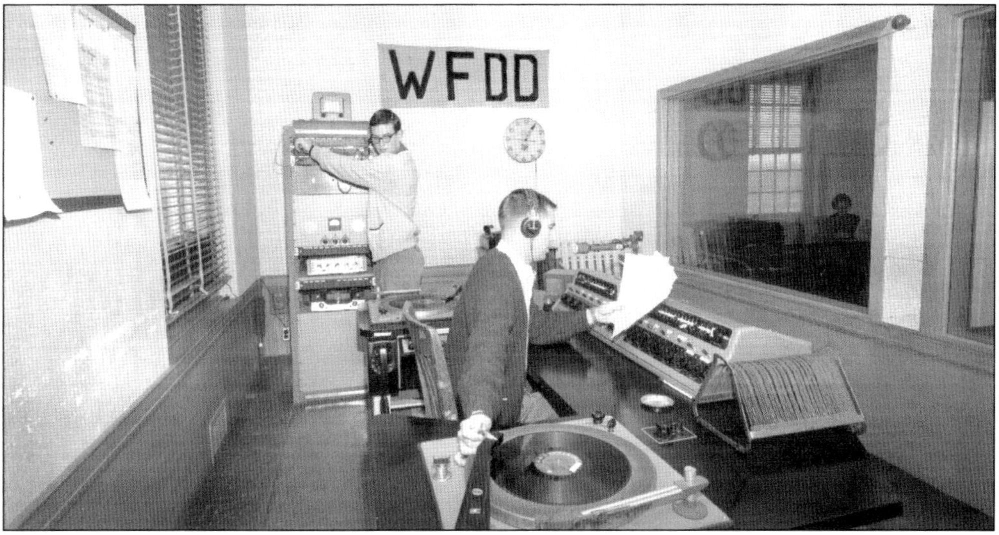

WFDD (Wake Forest Demon Deacons) radio was one of the Pub Row residents in Reynolda Hall at Wake Forest College, along with offices for the student newspaper, *The Student*, and the college annual, *The Howler*. WFDD radio station was on the air for 11 hours in 1956, with 20 student announcers handling the programs. Each dormitory on campus had a small transmitter, which relayed the programs throughout the dormitory.

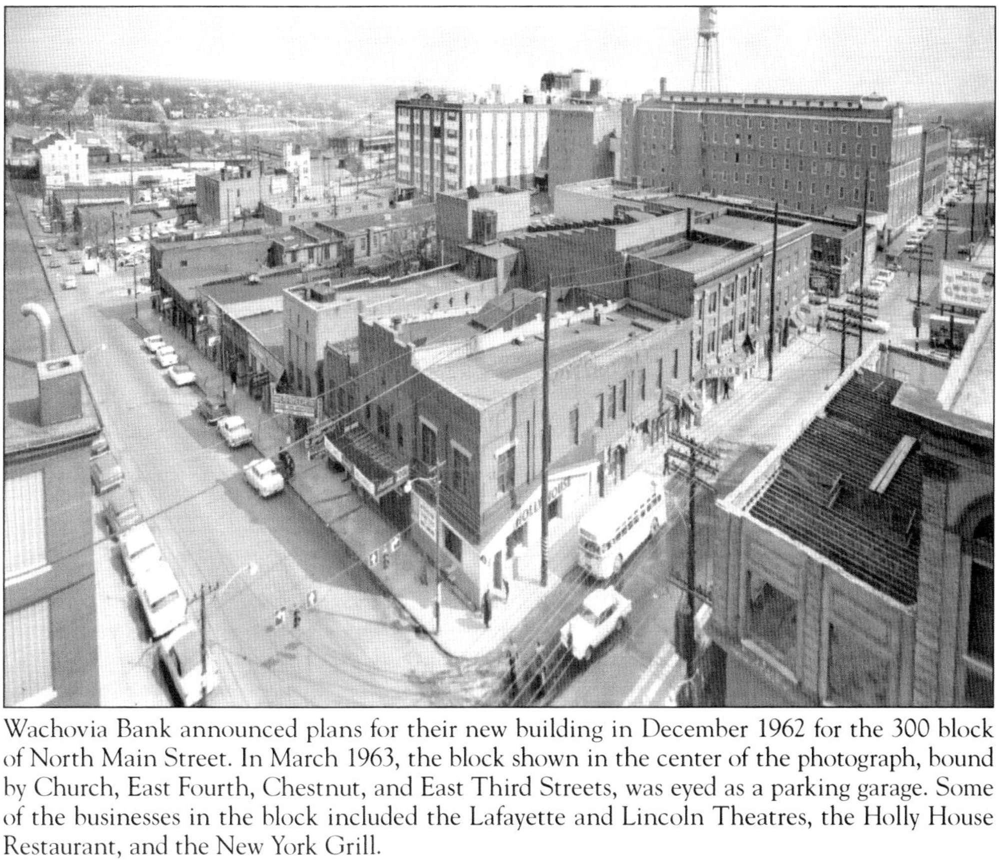

Wachovia Bank announced plans for their new building in December 1962 for the 300 block of North Main Street. In March 1963, the block shown in the center of the photograph, bound by Church, East Fourth, Chestnut, and East Third Streets, was eyed as a parking garage. Some of the businesses in the block included the Lafayette and Lincoln Theatres, the Holly House Restaurant, and the New York Grill.

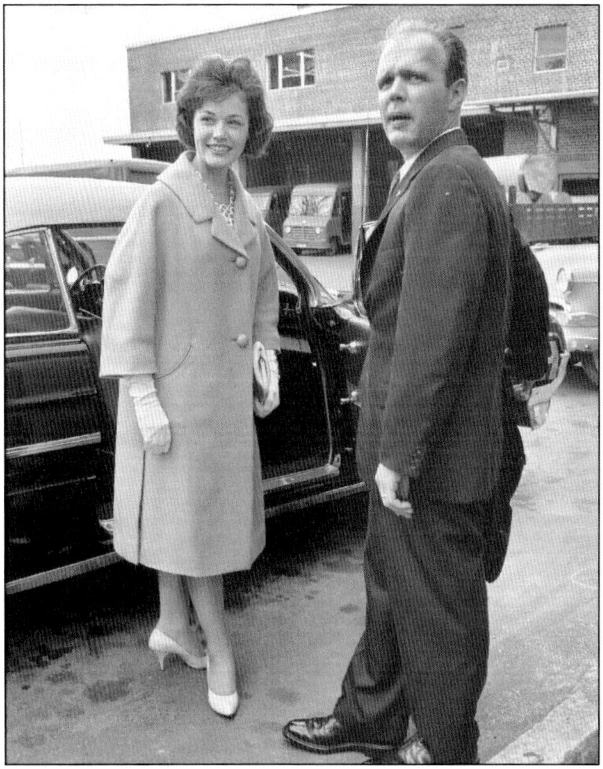

Nancy Anne Fleming, Miss America 1961, was welcomed to Winston-Salem by J. T. Greene Jr., president of the Junior Chamber of Commerce. Miss Fleming was in town for the crowning of a new Miss Winston-Salem and was the honored guest in a parade down Fourth Street. Just one year out of high school, Miss Fleming held a press conference for newspaper writers from the local high schools.

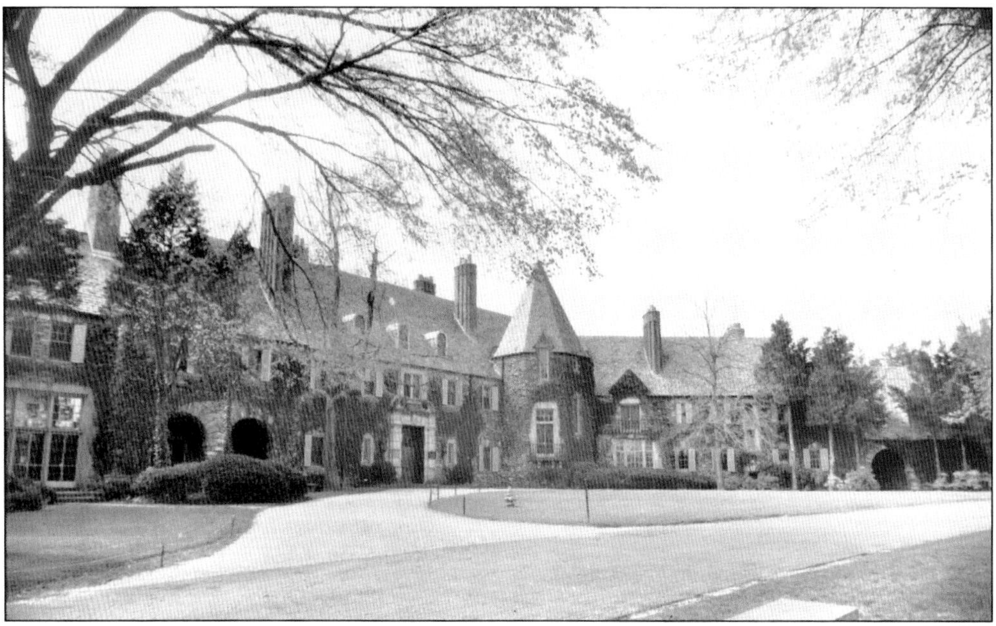

It takes a lot of flowers to fill a 70-room mansion, so the Winston-Salem Council of Garden Clubs limited their arrangements to selected rooms in the Graylyn Manor House for their flower show. "Symphony of Flowers" was the theme for the flower show at Graylyn in 1961. The council was organized in 1932 and held its first show in 1934 at the new Norman Stockton store on Cherry Street.

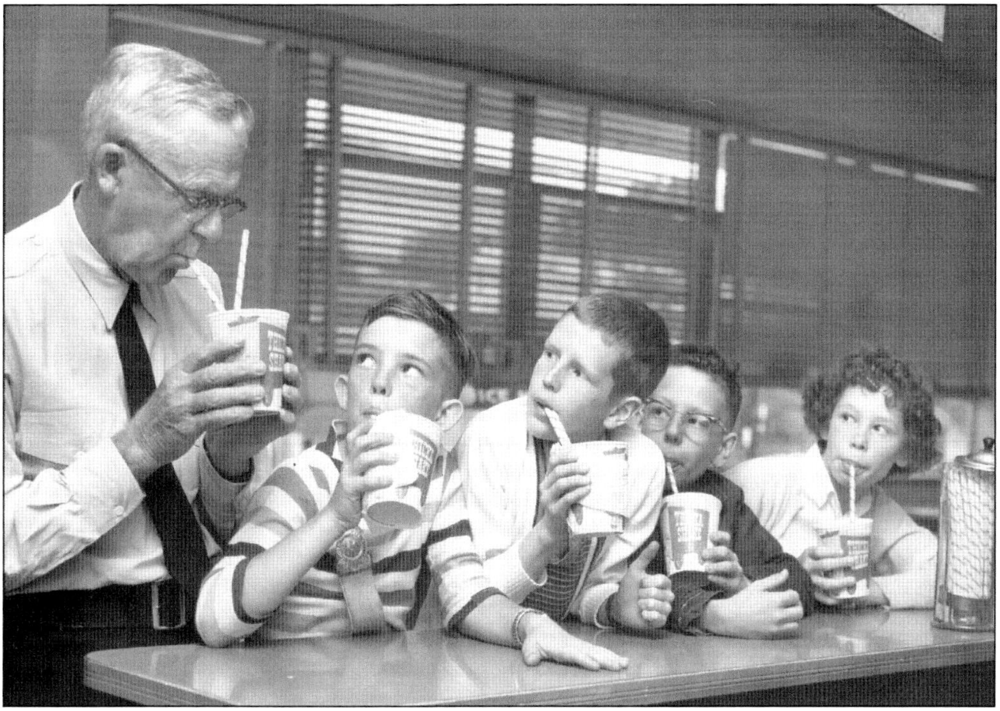

John Thomas Flynn retired from two long-term careers. He worked for the Winston-Salem Fire Department for 33 years and then began a 21-year career as one of the first school guards in the city. Mr. Flynn (left) is treating his sixth-grade safety patrol officers from North Elementary School to milk shakes near the end of the school year in 1961, rewarding them for a job well done.

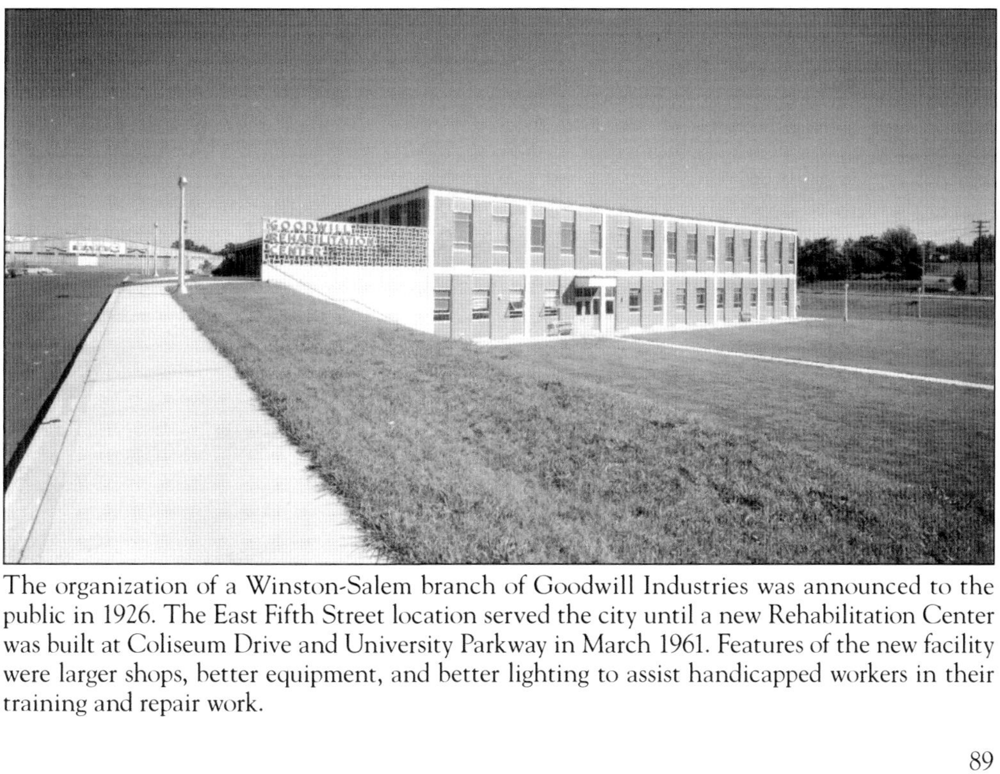

The organization of a Winston-Salem branch of Goodwill Industries was announced to the public in 1926. The East Fifth Street location served the city until a new Rehabilitation Center was built at Coliseum Drive and University Parkway in March 1961. Features of the new facility were larger shops, better equipment, and better lighting to assist handicapped workers in their training and repair work.

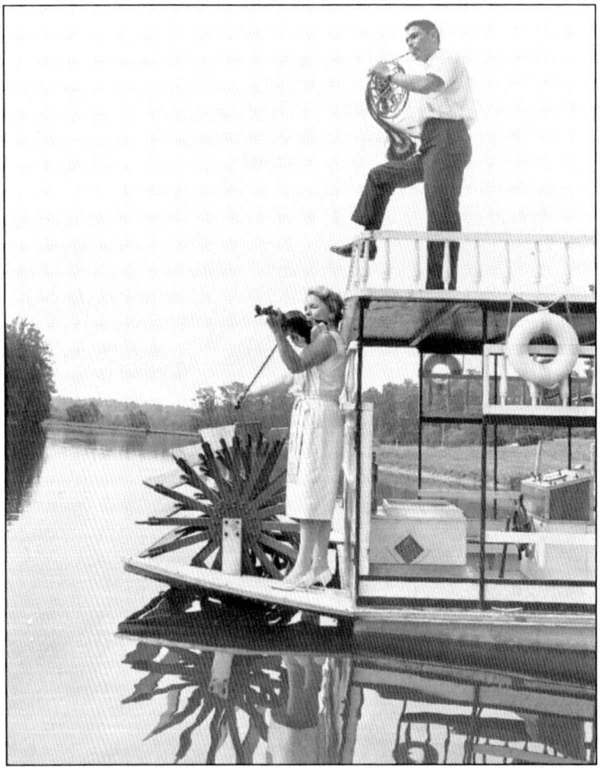

A joint membership drive was just beginning in September 1961 for the Winston-Salem Symphony Association and the Little Theatre. Symphony musicians Marjorie Angell, violin, and Richard Saylor, French horn, are advertising an upcoming pops concert that will feature musical excerpts from Jerome Kern's *Showboat*. The showboat in the photograph was on Mallard Lake at Tanglewood Park.

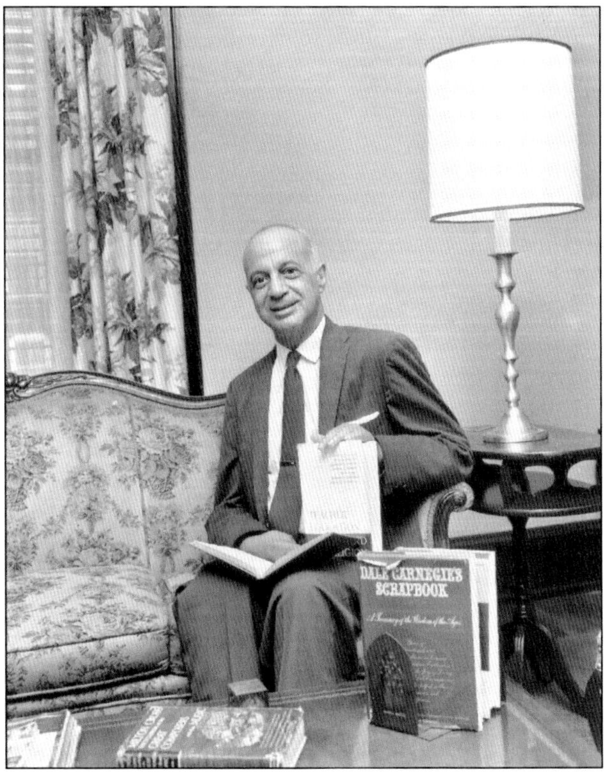

Dr. Francis L. Atkins followed his father, Simon G. Atkins, as president of Winston-Salem Teachers College in 1934. Dr. Atkins was a student at the school his father founded, Slater School, and returned as a teacher in 1920. Shortly after Dr. Atkins's retirement in 1961, the name of the school was changed to Winston-Salem State College. When he was named president emeritus in 1974, the school had reached university status.

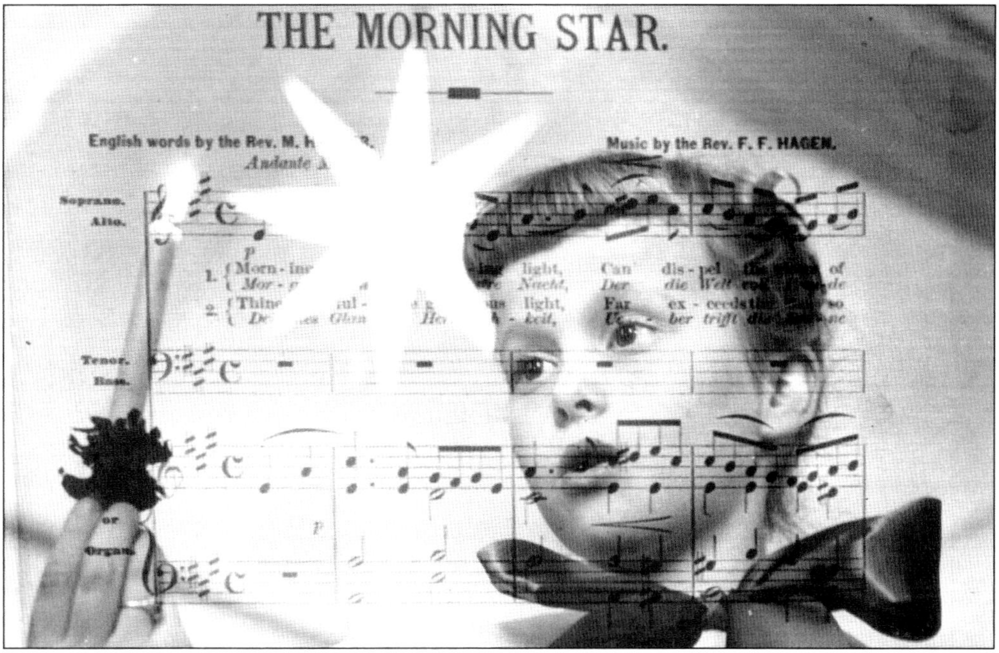

When Winston-Salem residents opened their newspapers on Christmas morning in 1961, the front page featured this composite photograph of a young girl dressed in a white choir robe with black bow holding a lighted Moravian candle. Also in the photograph is the outline of a Moravian star and sheet music to the hymn, "The Morning Star." Composite photographs such as this take time and creativity but make a memorable impression.

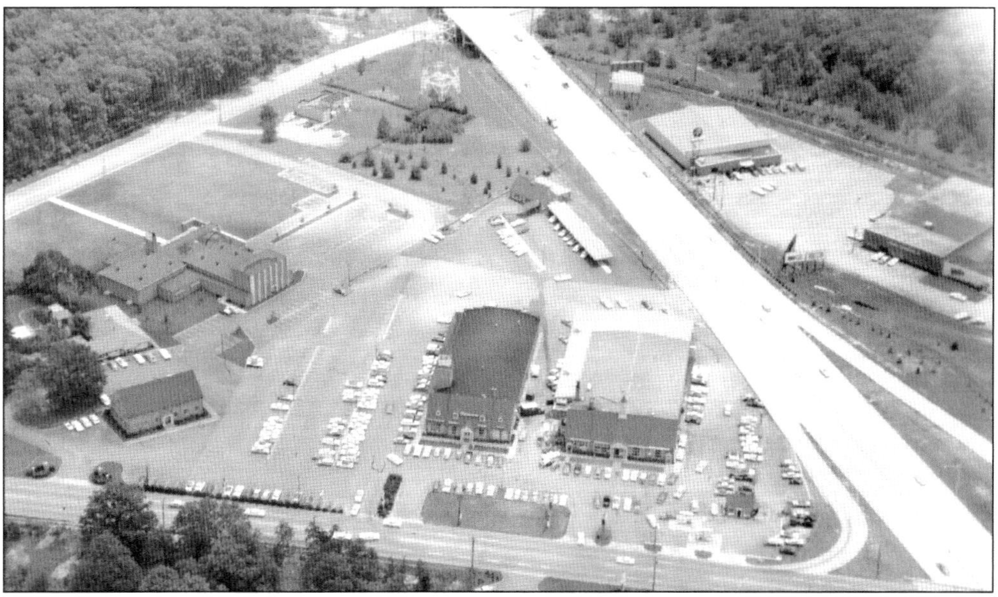

The interior of the triangle formed by Miller Street, Stratford Road, and Interstate 40 has changed from its look in 1961. The two large buildings to the right in the triangle are the Farmer's Dairy Bar (left) with the A&P Food Store behind. Offices occupied the building at right, with Major League Bowling Lanes in the rear. The Triangle Drive-In Restaurant, a popular eating and cruising destination, sat behind the two buildings.

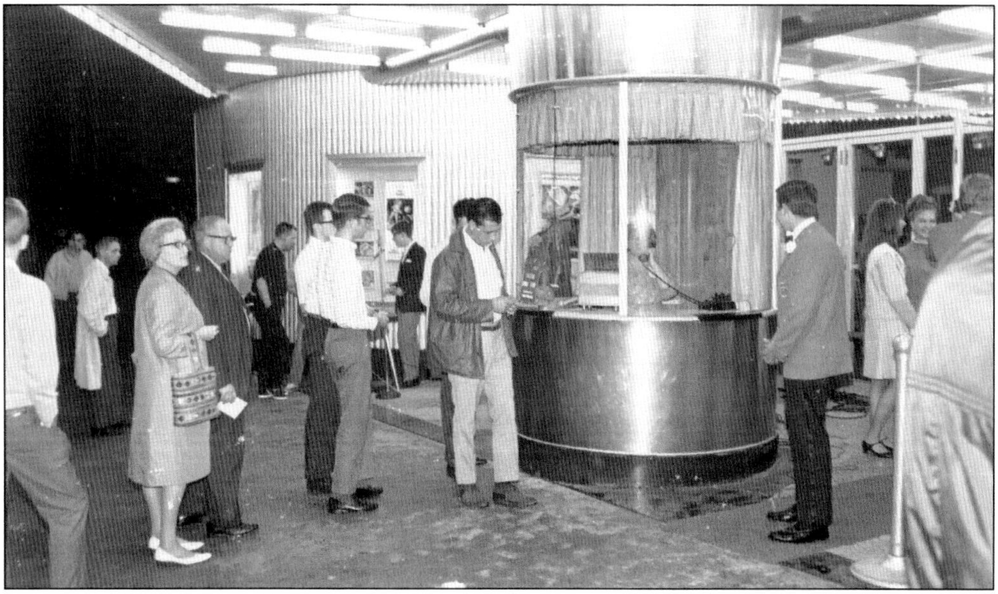

The Winston Theatre opened on West Fourth Street in April 1949, designed by well-known theater architect Earle Stillwell of Hendersonville. Jane Wyman starred in the opening attraction, *Kiss in the Dark*. The modern theater seated 1,000 people and featured the latest look in carpeting and lighting. This photograph shows the remodeled theater in 1968, with a new projection system and screen, new furnishings, and opening with the movie *Barbarella*.

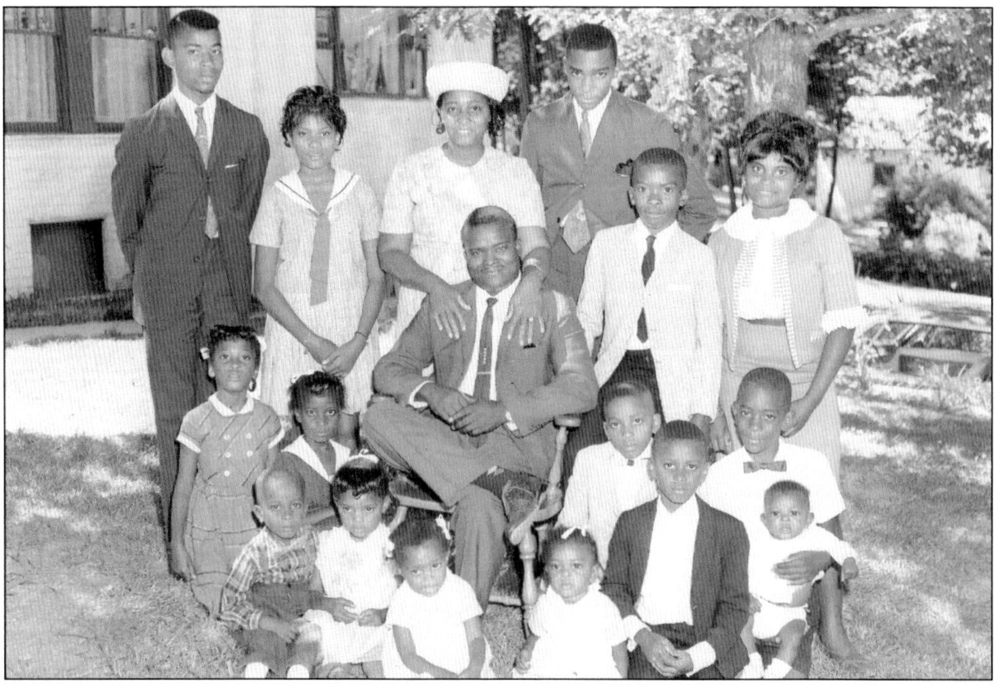

It's Father's Day, and Milton Hughes has 16 reasons to smile and be proud. Fifteen of his 16 children, all dressed in their Sunday best, surround him and Mrs. Hughes. The children range in age from 4 months to 20 years of age. The photograph of the Hughes family was the Father's Day newspaper feature in June 1966.

Eight-year-old Nancy Jane Turner wanted a pair of gold hoop earrings. Promised a pair by an aunt, she pierced her ears and kept the holes in place with tiny straws inserted through the holes. Her aunt's promise to give Nancy the earrings was forgotten upon the aunt's death in 1880. Then Nancy bought a pair from a mail-order catalog, which she later lost. In 1898, her husband, Charlie Gentle, bought her the pair she was still wearing in 1962, 64 years later.

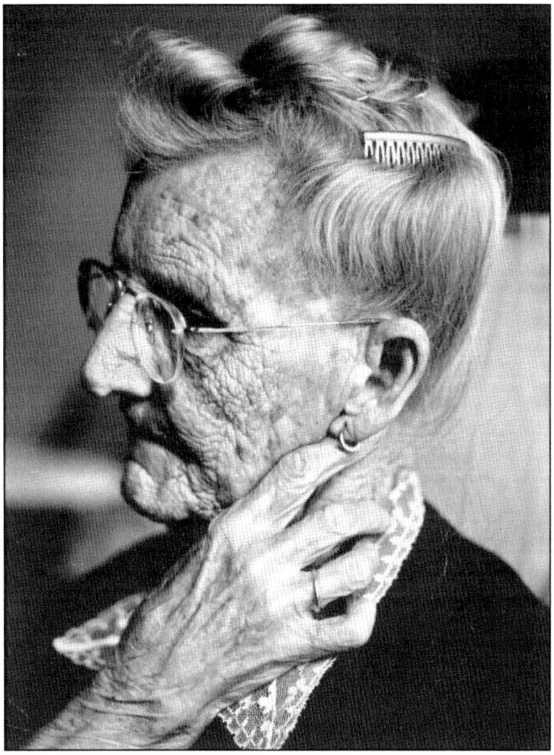

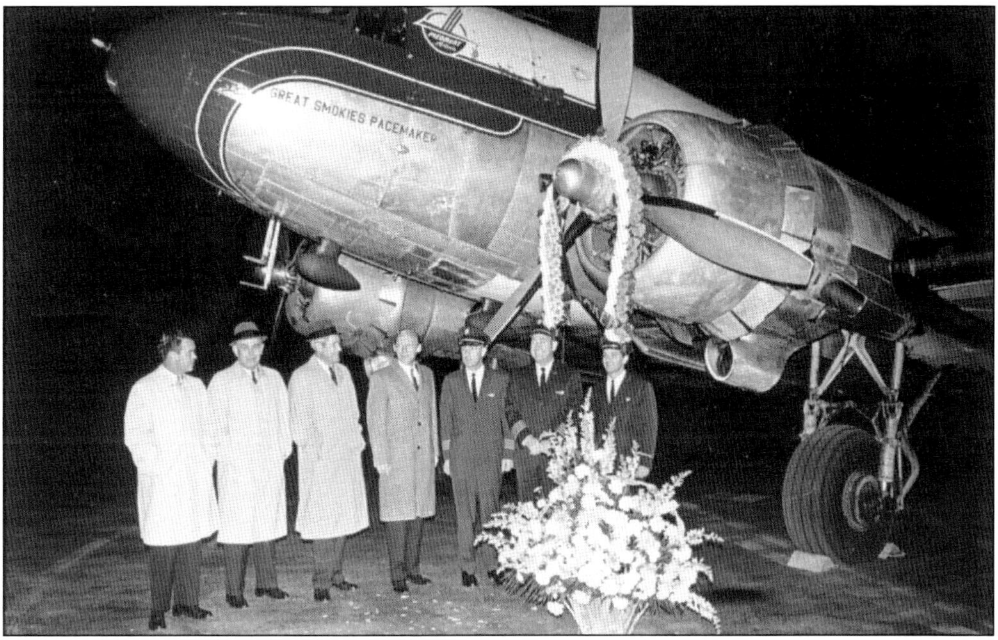

The horseshoe of flowers on the Piedmont DC3 propeller marked the 15th anniversary for Piedmont Airlines. On February 20, 1948, a Piedmont DC3 flew from Wilmington to Cincinnati. To commemorate the anniversary in 1963, and the retirement of the last DC3, the same pilot and copilot were at the controls, following the same route. Tom Davis (center), Piedmont president, was flanked by company officials and crew members.

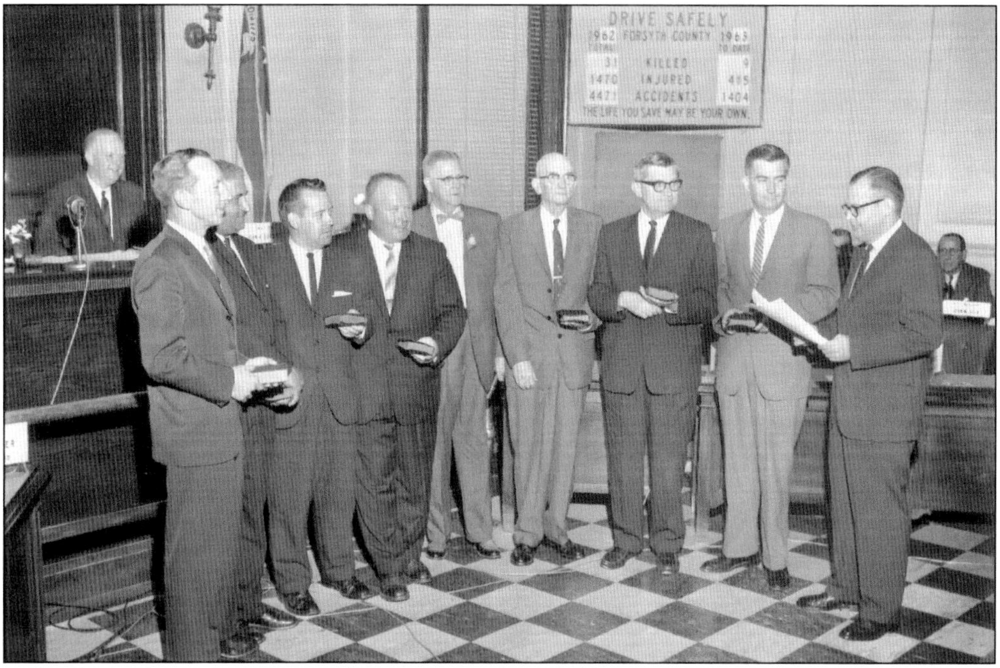

A familiar sight in the Municipal Courtroom of city hall was a changeover in city government officials. The 1963 election resulted in a new mayor, M. C. Benton (far left), and new board of aldermen members. A. E. Blackburn, assistant clerk of Forsyth Superior Court (right), swore in the new officials. Mayor John Surratt, outgoing mayor, and several retiring board members, were recognized for their service to the city.

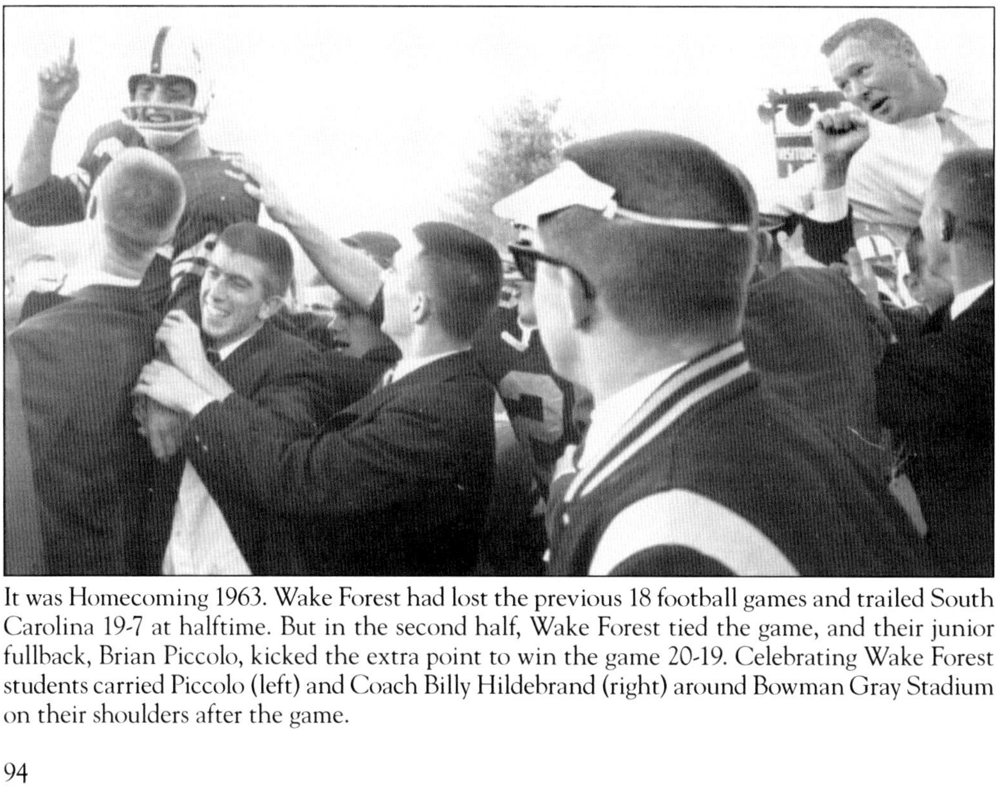

It was Homecoming 1963. Wake Forest had lost the previous 18 football games and trailed South Carolina 19-7 at halftime. But in the second half, Wake Forest tied the game, and their junior fullback, Brian Piccolo, kicked the extra point to win the game 20-19. Celebrating Wake Forest students carried Piccolo (left) and Coach Billy Hildebrand (right) around Bowman Gray Stadium on their shoulders after the game.

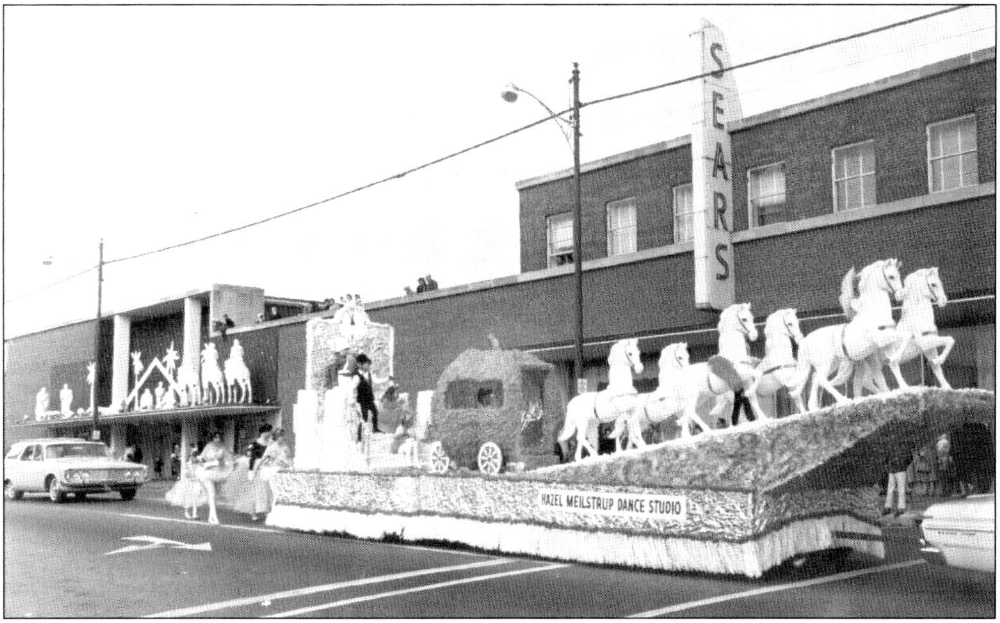

The last day of November 1963 was cold and windy and kept many spectators at home to watch the Holiday Festival Parade on television or ran them into the downtown stores to watch from store windows. The parade passed in front of Sears, bedecked with the large, white Nativity figures that graced the store exterior for many years. The Methodist Children's Home adopted the Nativity figures and displays them on their lawn at Christmas.

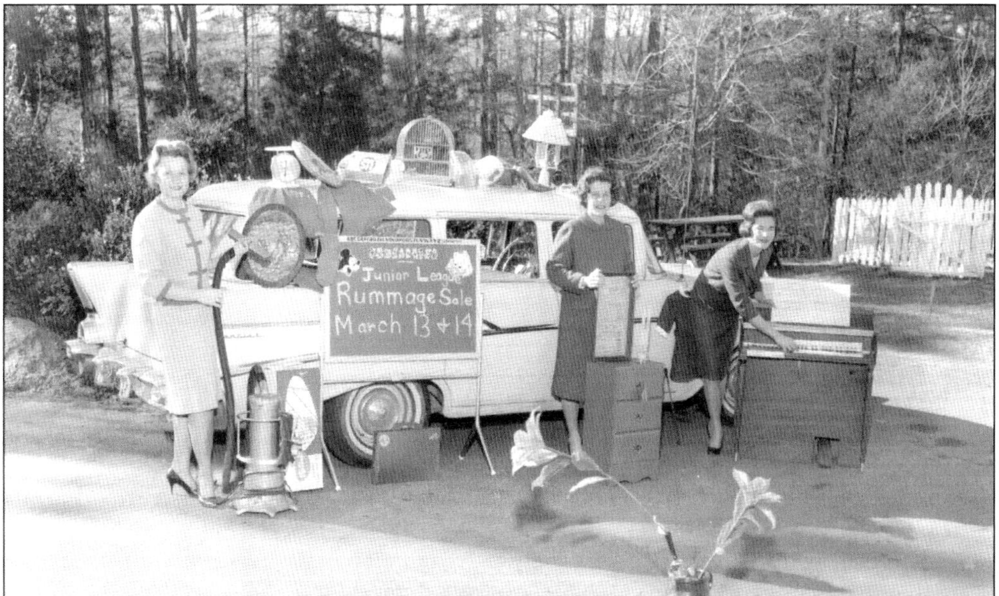

Junior League members began their rummage sale collections early for the upcoming March 1964 event at Taylor's Warehouse on Patterson Avenue. Rummage sale chairman Mrs. John Eller Jr. (left), with Mrs. Bailey Glenn Jr. (middle), and Mrs. Hugh Gramley, pose with some of the items for sale, including the car. The Junior League began in Winston-Salem in 1923, organized by Mrs. J. Edward Johnston, known to many as Katherine Smith Reynolds.

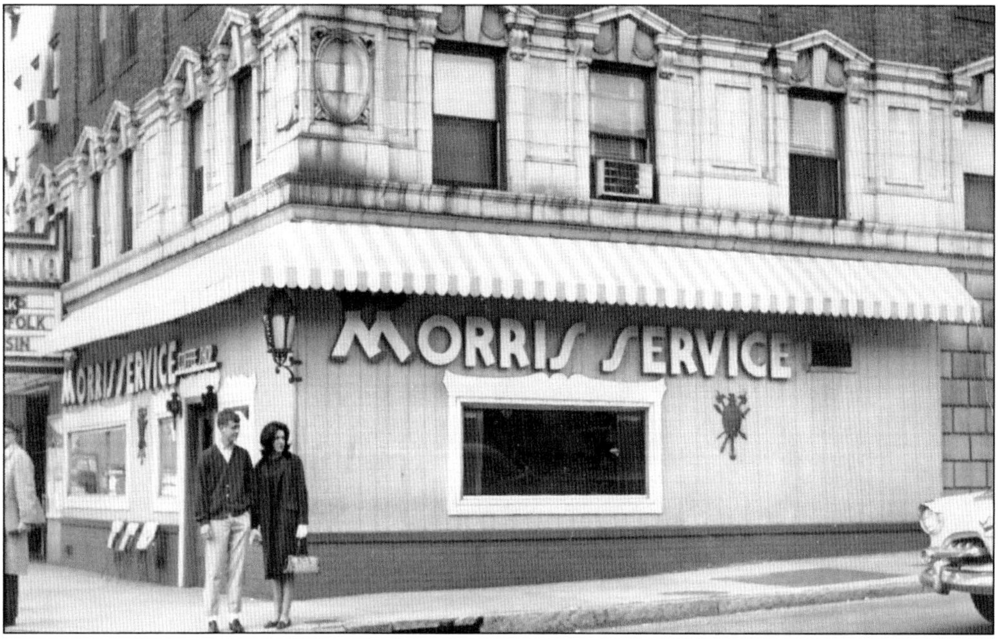

Morris Service opened in 1930 beside the Carolina Theatre on the corner of Fourth and Marshall Streets. The restaurant was named for its first operator, a Mr. Morris, who sold it to Howard Lee within a year. Warner Collier purchased the business in 1944 and operated it until 1964, when this photograph was taken. George Cortesis and Paul Rogatsios of the Little Pep Grill bought Morris Service from Collier.

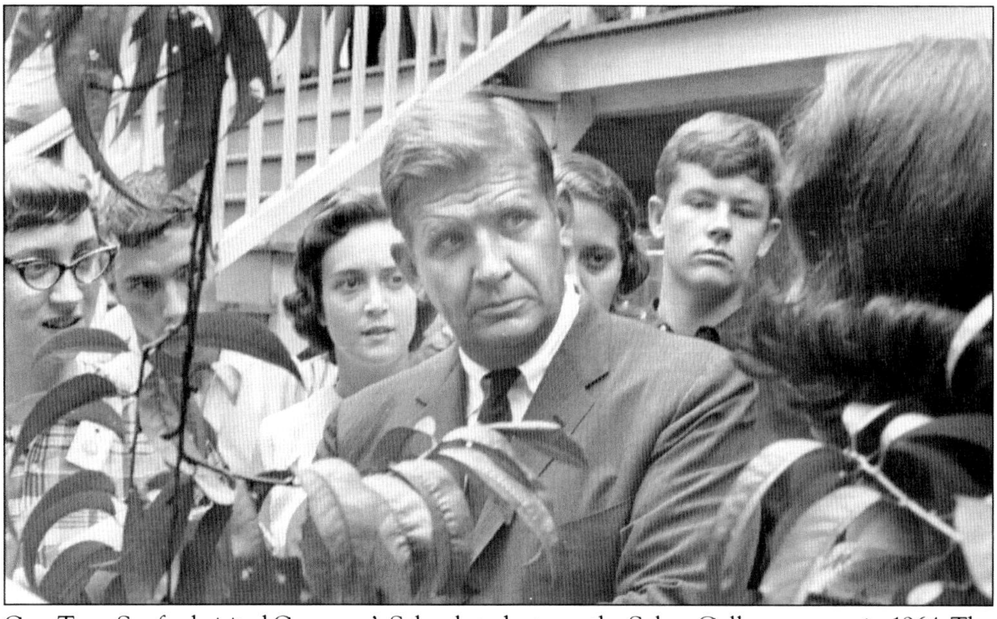

Gov. Terry Sanford visited Governor's School students on the Salem College campus in 1964. The school was in its second year of operation, established through the efforts of Governor Sanford and funded by a three-year Carnegie Corporation grant and matching local funds. The gifted and talented students attending the school were challenged to be concerned for people less fortunate and to share their learning experiences with their local schools.

Wake Forest coach Horace "Bones" McKinney rarely struck such a calm pose during a basketball game, especially when the game was against rival North Carolina. Coach McKinney stood with his son, Kenneth, watching his Deacons trounce the Tar Heels, 107-85, at Memorial Coliseum in January 1965. After the game, Bones gave credit for the win to his starters, Richard Herring, Ronny Watts, Bob Leonard, John Anderson, and Jim Boshart.

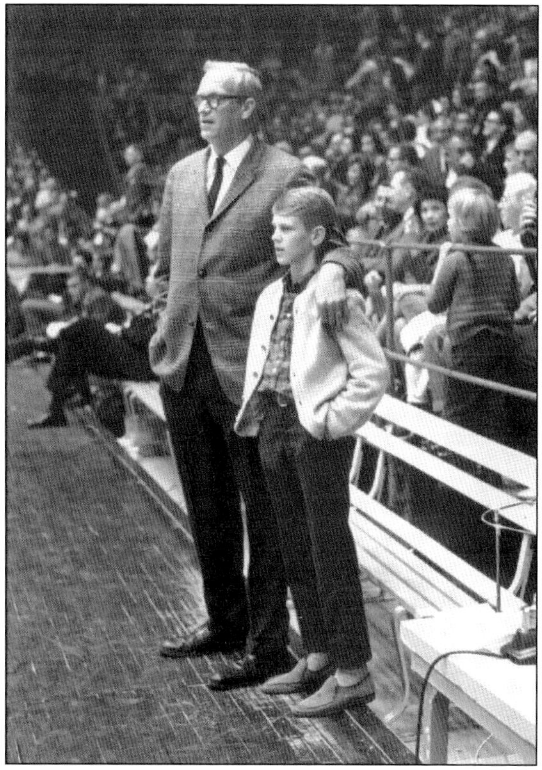

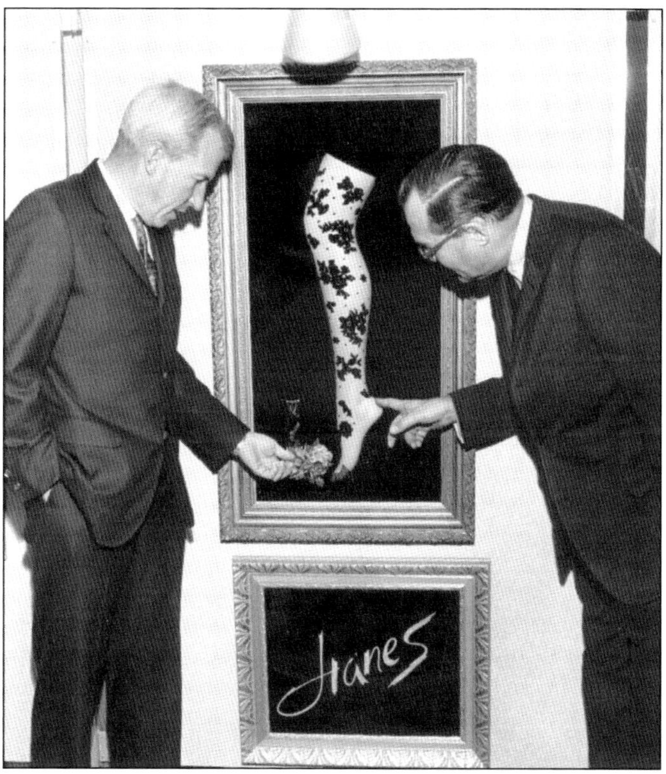

The establishment of Hanes Corporation on March 1, 1965, marked the merger of P. H. Hanes Knitting and Hanes Hosiery Mills. The new corporation was headed by second cousins, Gordon Hanes (left) as chairman of the board and P. Huber Hanes Jr. (right) as president. With 9,000 employees, Hanes Corporation became the second largest employer in Winston-Salem, after R. J. Reynolds Tobacco Company.

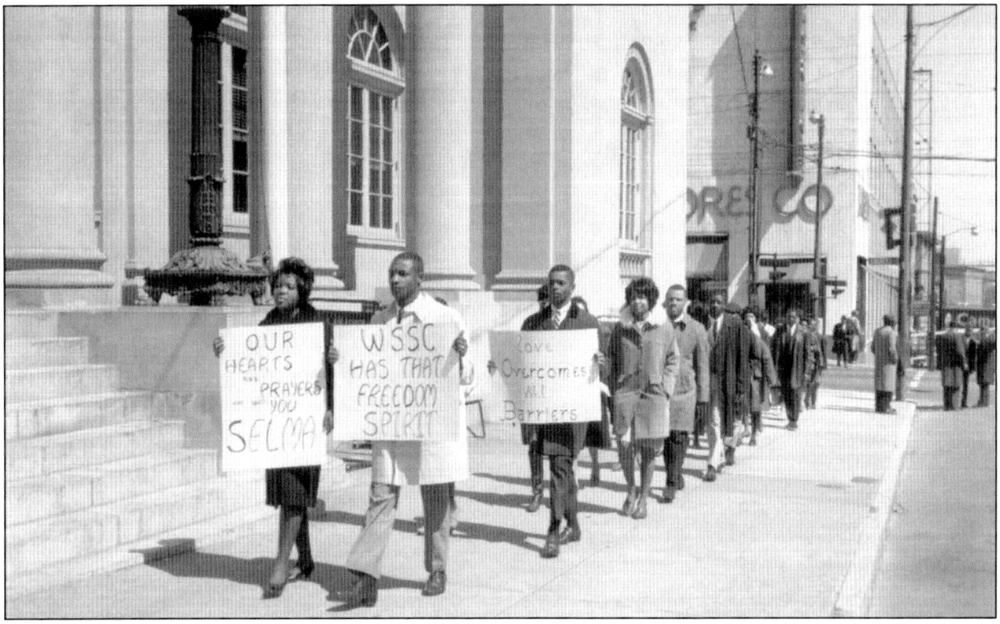

Over 500 Winston-Salem State College students marched silently from the campus to the downtown post office on March 21, 1965, holding placards that spoke their purpose. The march lasted two hours and was held to show sympathy and support for a civil rights march being held in Selma, Alabama. The students gathered at the post office for a brief service, which included prayers by local ministers for the Selma participants.

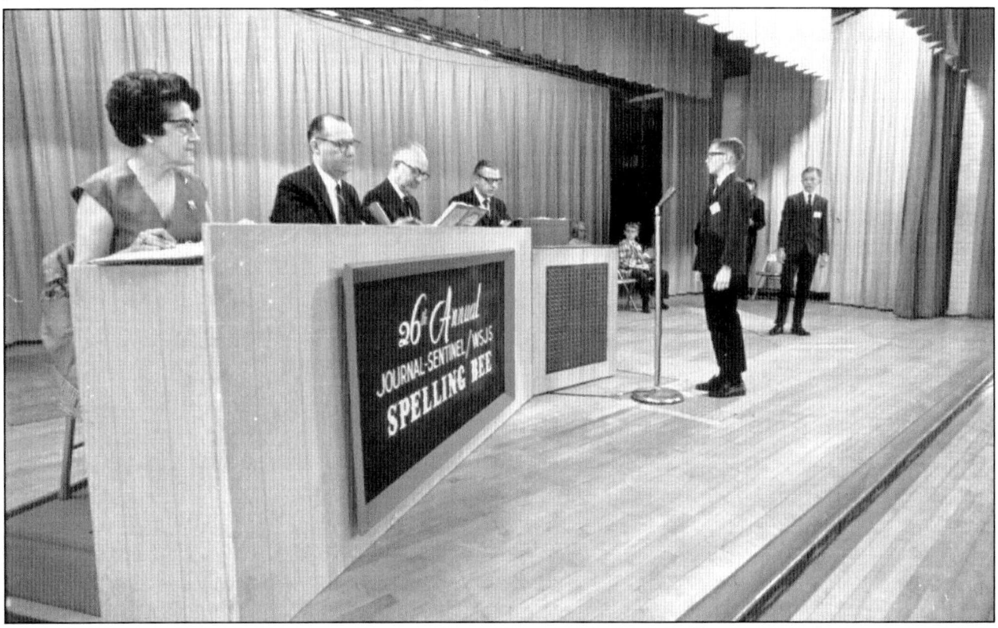

When Marshall Jones of Statesville won the Journal and Sentinel/WSJS Spelling Bee in 1966, he was preparing himself for the record he attained in 1967 when he became the first person to win the bee three times. Marshall was hoping to return the national title to North Carolina. Instead he finished fourth. As the last male to be eliminated, he became the best boy speller in the nation. This photograph shows some of the 1966 contestants.

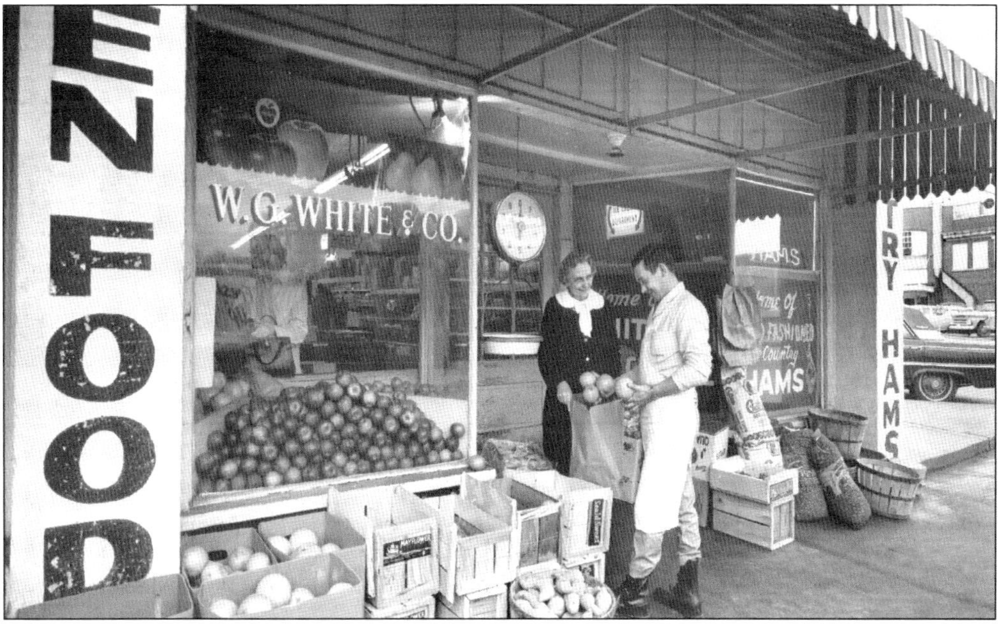

W. G. White and Company was always located on Cherry Street and specialized in country ham, fresh fruits and vegetables, and friendly clerks. Founded by William G. White, the grocery store is shown in a 1966 photograph, when it was located on the same side of Cherry Street as the City Market. After a 1969 fire, the business moved across the street and turned their warehouse location into a retail store.

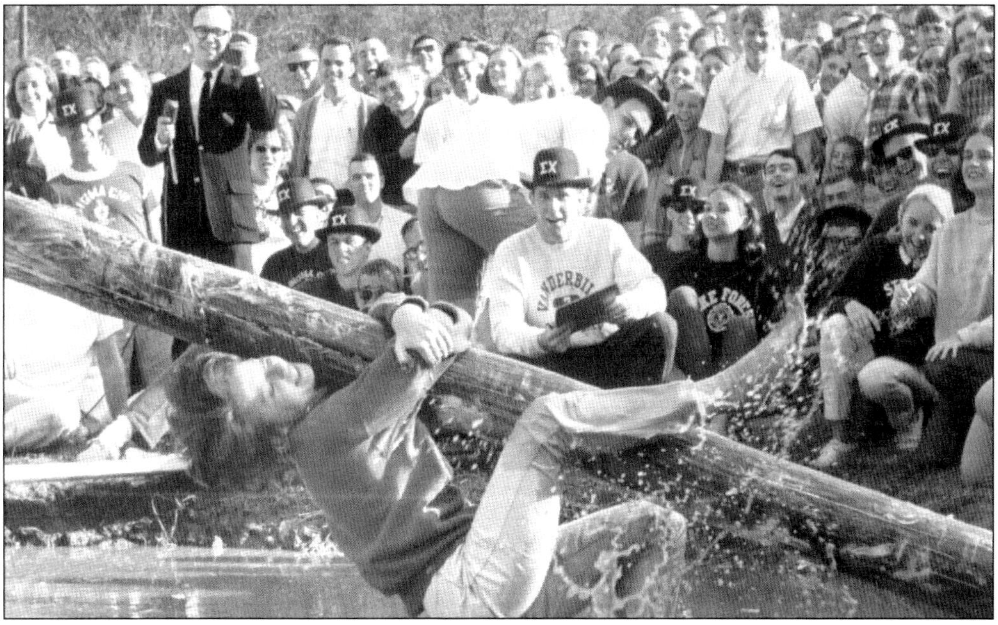

The annual Sigma Chi Derby Day took place on the Wake Forest lawn in April 1965. The spring event attracted a large crowd to see coeds doused with whipping and shaving cream, rotten tomatoes, eggs, and other gooey substances. Coeds ran relay races, tried to cross a board situated over a mud hole, and climbed a greased log. The last contest was to collect the most derbies blindfolded—and with their teeth!

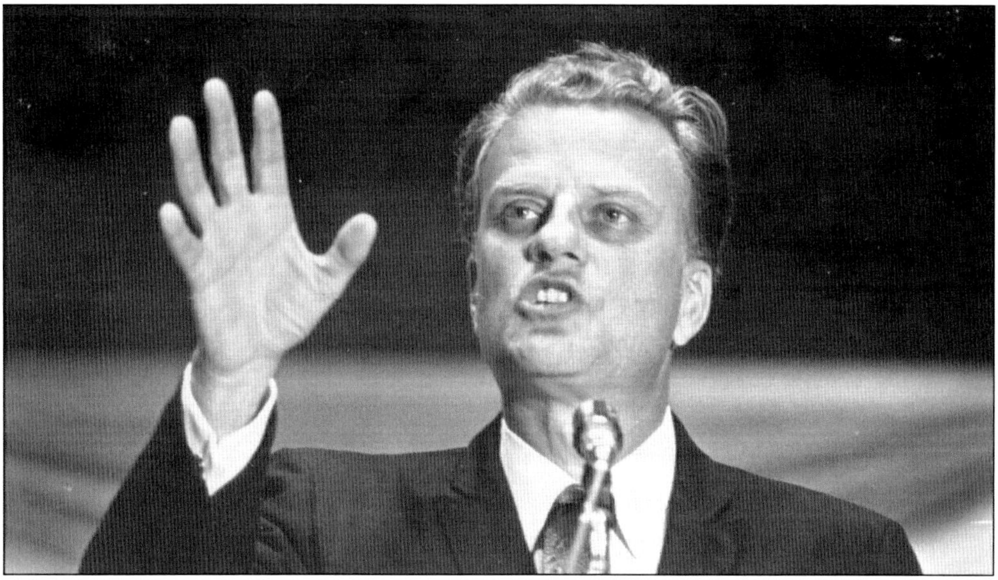

Winston-Salem celebrated its 200th anniversary in 1966 by holding two Festivals of Thanksgiving, one in January and one in November. The January event was held 200 years to the day that the Salem settlement began. The November event featured evangelist Billy Graham as the evening's speaker. Graham spoke about problems facing the country and how residents must recapture the faith of Moravian forefathers to prepare for the future.

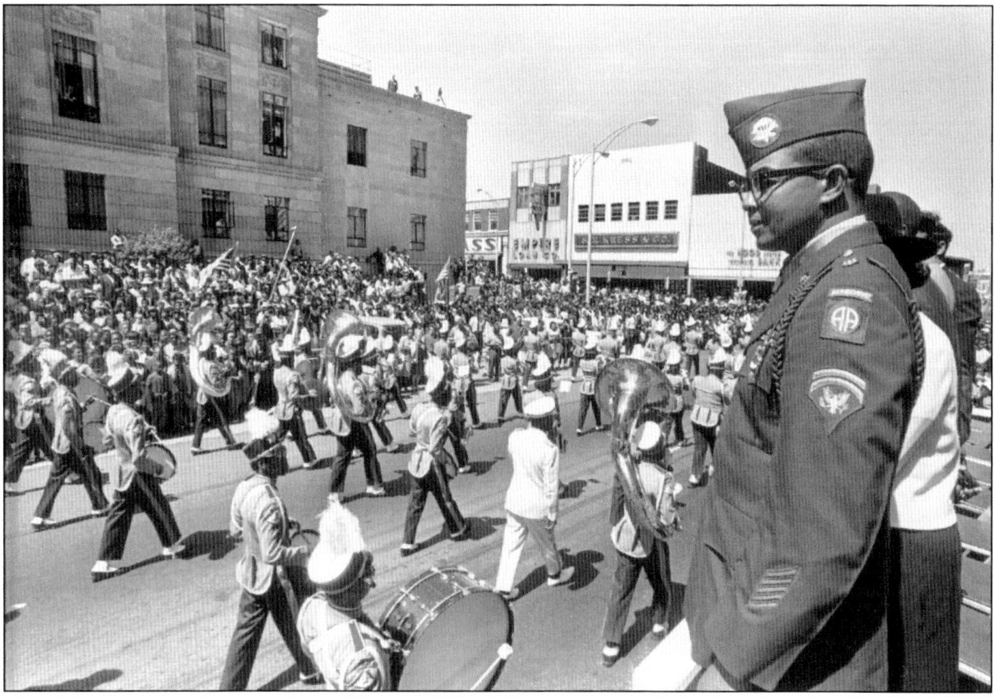

Lawrence Joel stood at attention during the parade in his honor on April 8, 1967. Joel grew up in East Winston and joined the army in 1946. His unit was attacked by a Viet Cong regiment in November 1965, and despite his own wounds, he gave medical aid to his comrades. For his bravery in combat and his wounds, he was awarded the Medal of Honor and the Purple Heart.

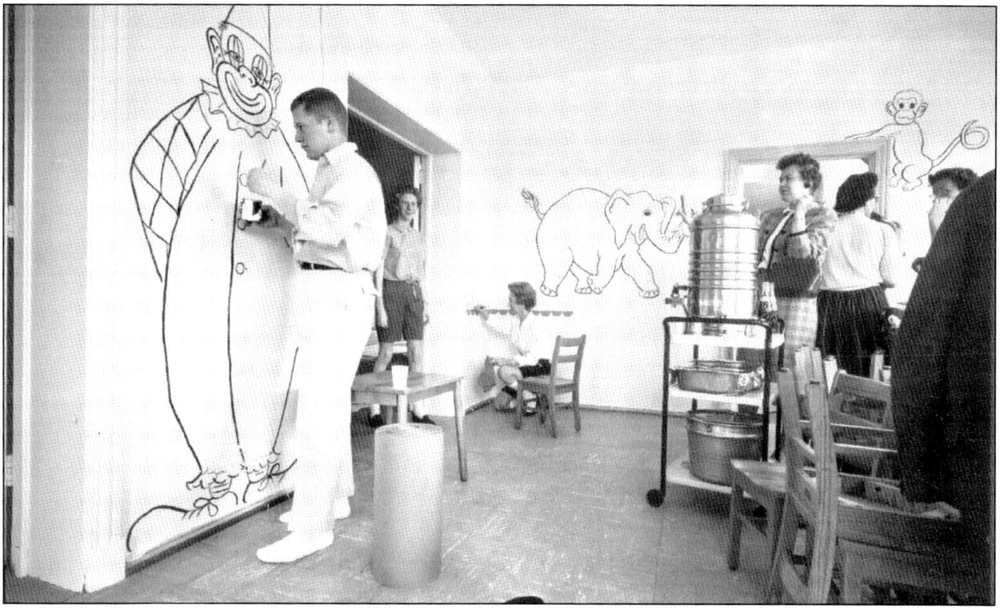

Amos Cottage had been organized about two and a half years in 1961 when funding for the 30-bed center for mentally retarded children was insufficient to keep the center operating properly. The facility was in need of repair and more modern equipment. Supporters of Amos Cottage appealed to the community, and residents responded with cash donations and repair assistance, plus the volunteer artists who brightened the rooms for the children.

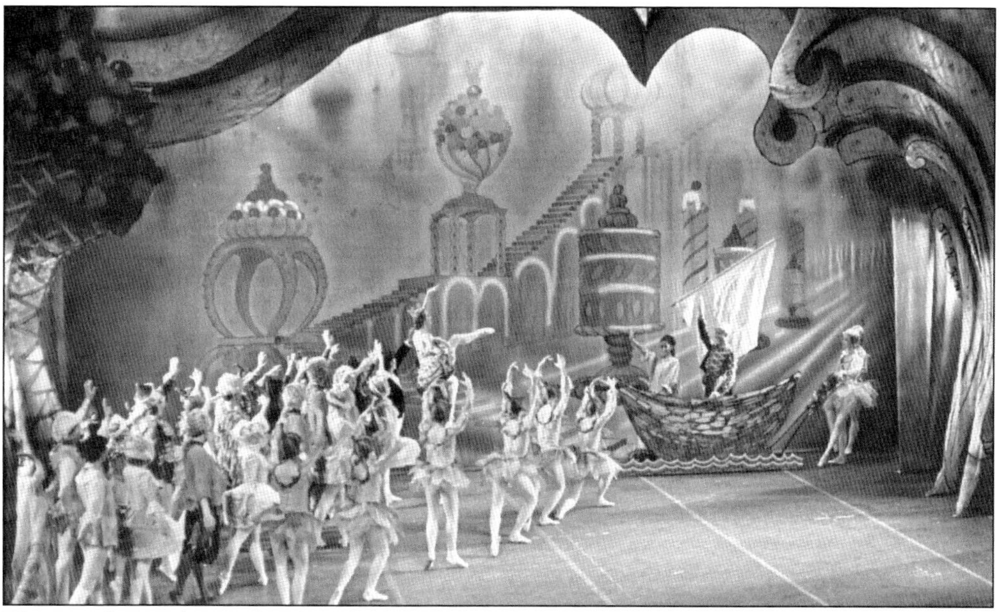

The North Carolina School of the Arts presentation of Tchaikovsky's ballet *The Nutcracker* was in its infancy during this 1967 performance at Reynolds Auditorium. Under the direction of Robert Lindgren, head of the dance department, the matinee and night performances received favorable reviews for the dancing, costumes, and beautiful sets. The one unfavorable area focused on the recorded music, later improved by the musical accompaniment of the Winston-Salem Symphony.

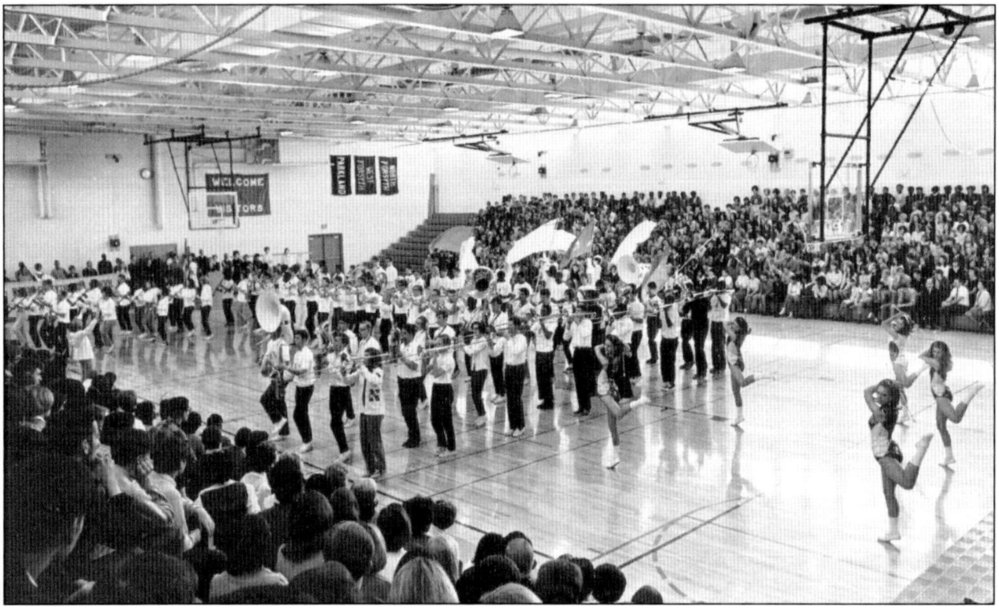

North Forsyth High School opened on Shattalon Road in 1963. The above photograph was taken about 1967 and shows the interior of the gym, probably during a pep rally, led by the Viking band. North Forsyth holds the distinction of being the first Forsyth County high school to hold its graduation ceremony in the Memorial Coliseum. The graduation took place in 1965, with 519 seniors walking across the stage.

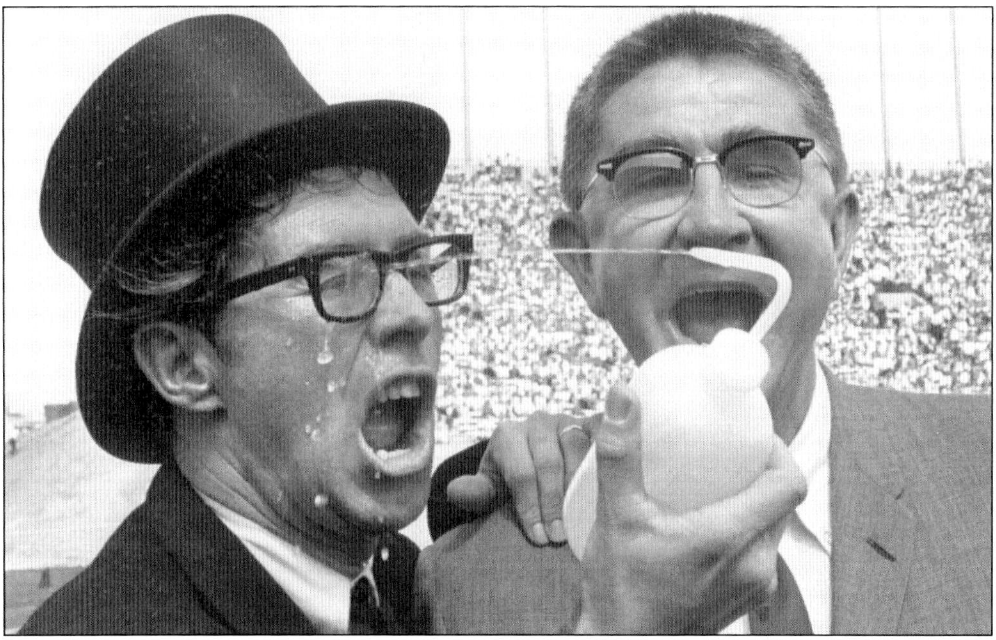

The shovel used by Pres. Harry Truman for the Wake Forest groundbreaking in 1951 was used to break ground for their new stadium in June 1966. The new Groves Stadium was dedicated in September 1968 at the opening game of the season, between Wake and N. C. State. Deacon Bill Shepherd (left) entertained a capacity crowd that heard speeches and listened to the Wake Forest band.

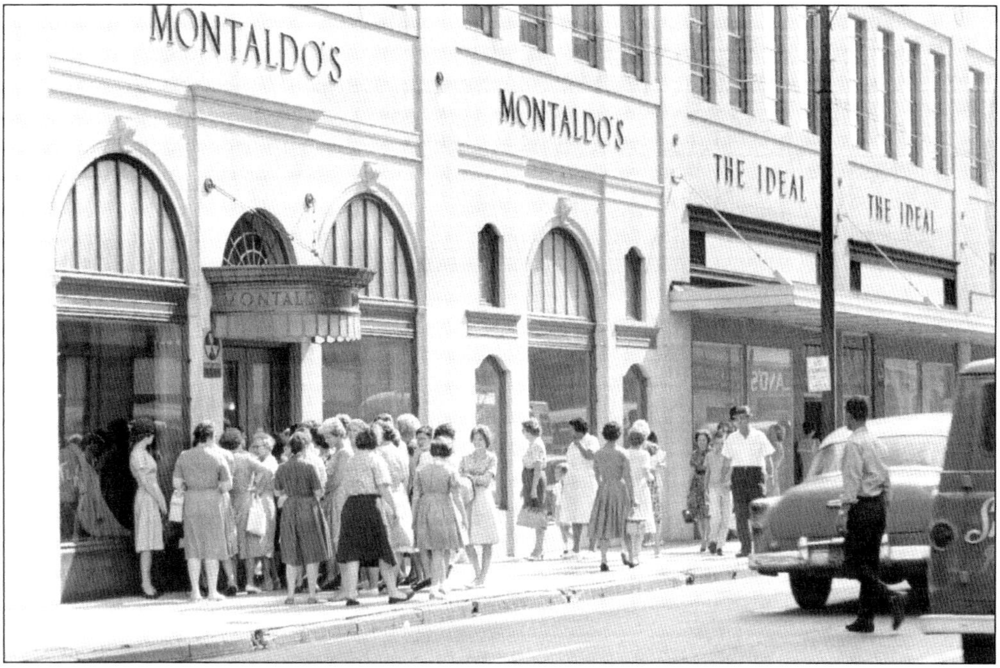

Lines formed early outside the Montaldo's store on West Fourth Street during Winston-Salem Bargain Days. Montaldo's was well known for their fine women's fashions and their specialized service. The local store was established in 1923, founded by Miss Lillian Montaldo of New York. By 1960, there were 10 stores across the United States, all with women managers. Montaldo's frequently held fashion shows in the elegant main salon with its French decor.

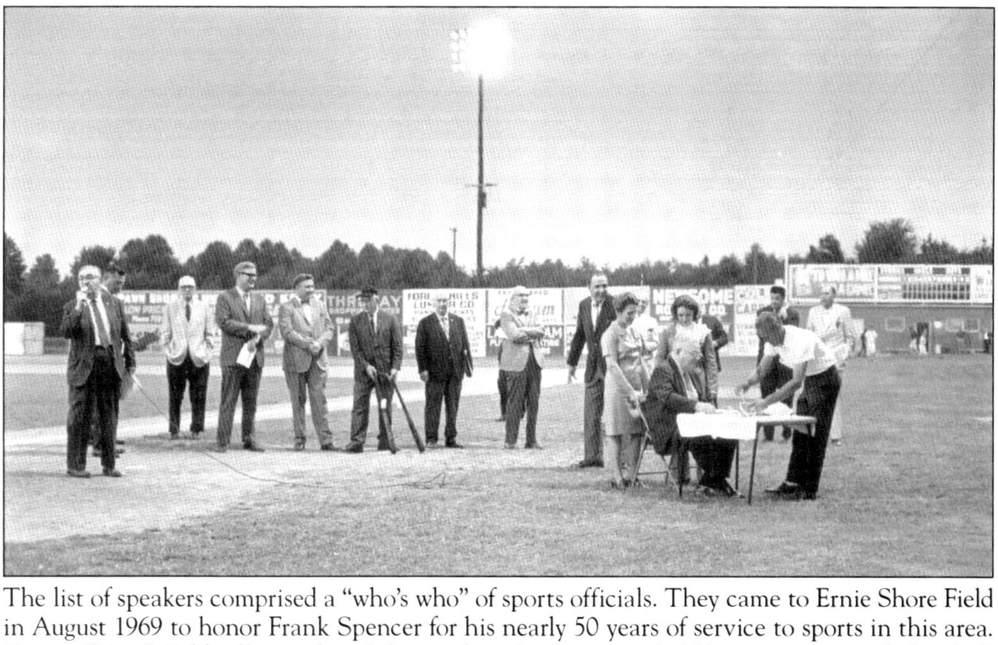

The list of speakers comprised a "who's who" of sports officials. They came to Ernie Shore Field in August 1969 to honor Frank Spencer for his nearly 50 years of service to sports in this area. Gowan "Nutt" Caldwell introduced the speakers for the event, held between games of a baseball doubleheader. Among the many gifts presented to Frank (seated at the table) from friends and colleagues was a new Crown Toyota.

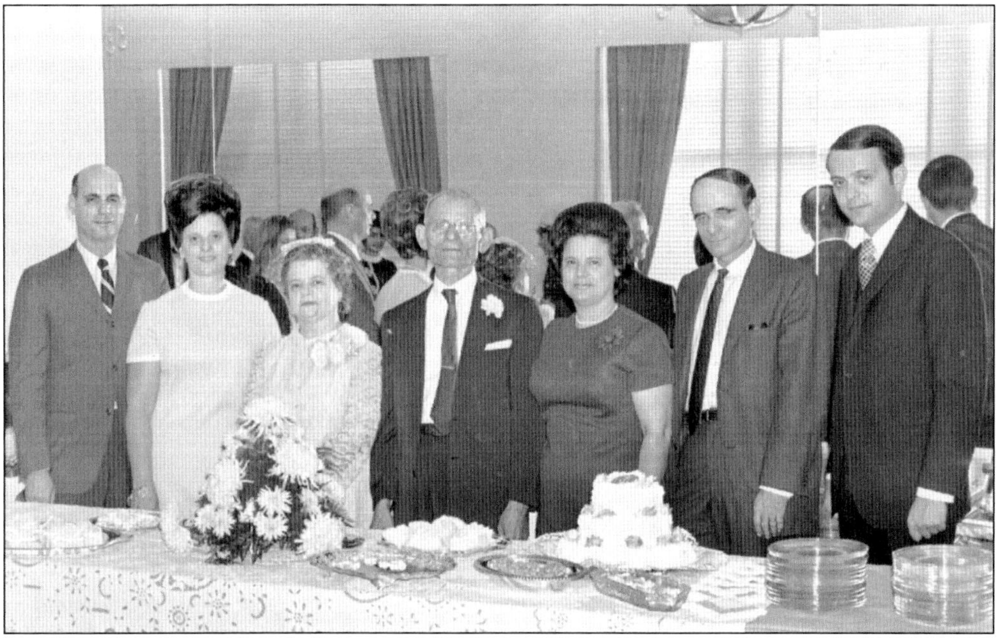

Chrisoula and Arthur Hondros celebrated their 50th wedding anniversary in the Robert E. Lee Hotel's Salem Room in November 1969. Their anniversary article mentioned that their 1919 wedding was the first Greek Orthodox Church wedding ceremony in Winston-Salem. Posing from left to right with their parents are George, Virginia (Lampros), Mary (Pappas), Harry, and Pete. Harry, a friend of Frank Jones, worked as a volunteer for several years with Frank's photograph collection.

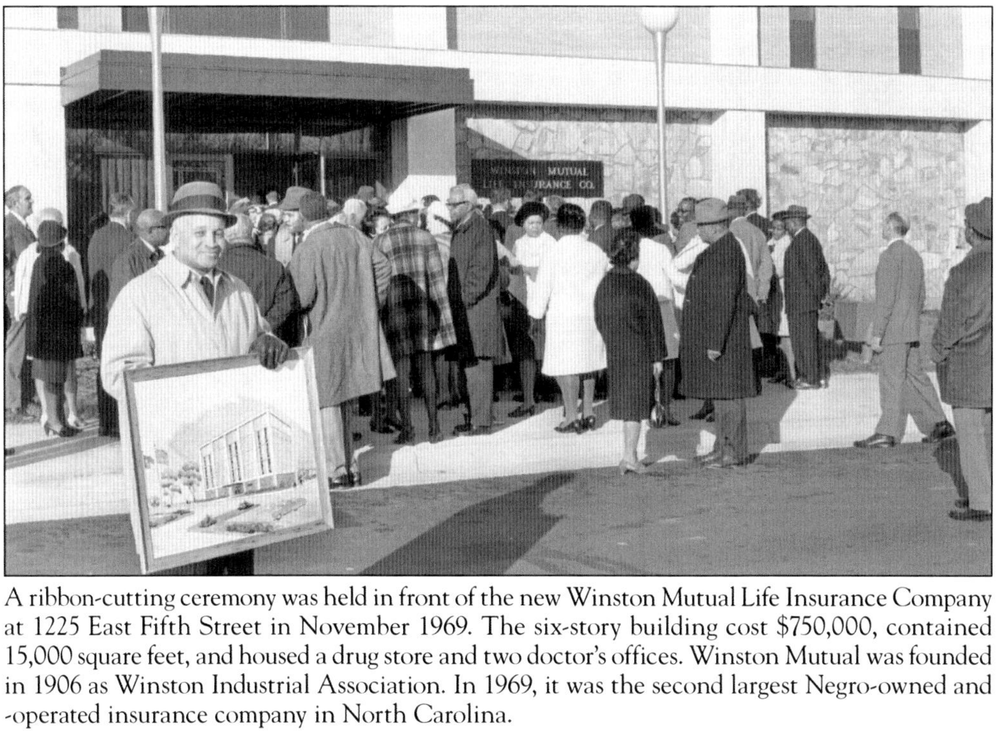

A ribbon-cutting ceremony was held in front of the new Winston Mutual Life Insurance Company at 1225 East Fifth Street in November 1969. The six-story building cost $750,000, contained 15,000 square feet, and housed a drug store and two doctor's offices. Winston Mutual was founded in 1906 as Winston Industrial Association. In 1969, it was the second largest Negro-owned and -operated insurance company in North Carolina.

Six

THE 1970S

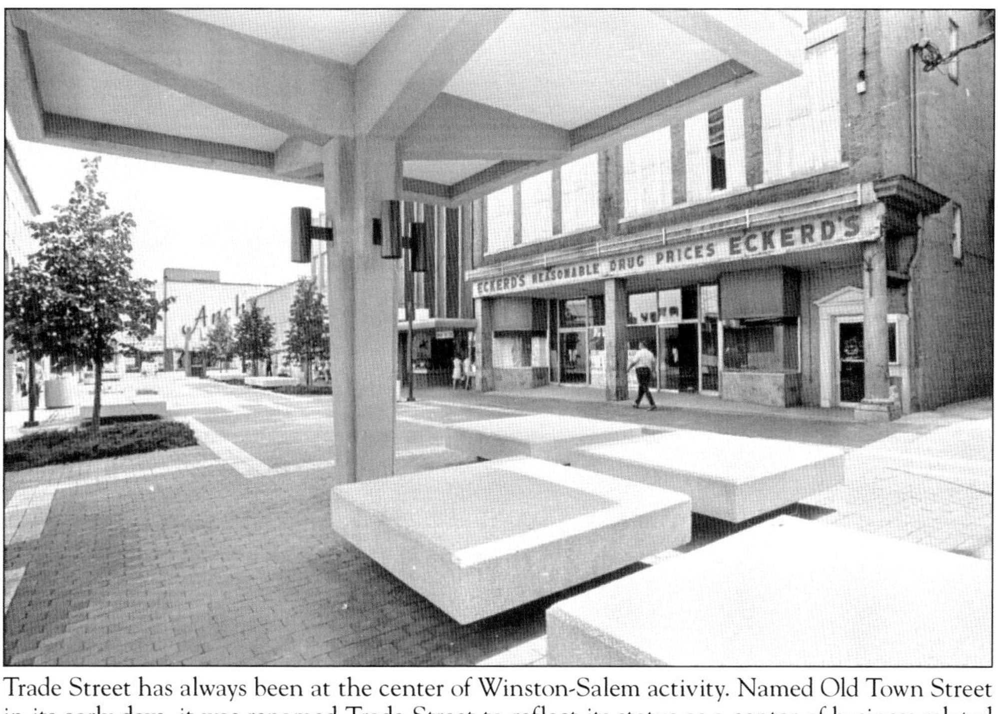

Trade Street has always been at the center of Winston-Salem activity. Named Old Town Street in its early days, it was renamed Trade Street to reflect its status as a center of business related to the tobacco trade. It has been covered with dirt, cobblestone, asphalt, and even brick, when the 400 block was closed to car traffic to create a pedestrian mall in 1970 (shown above). Trade Street reopened to car traffic in 1980.

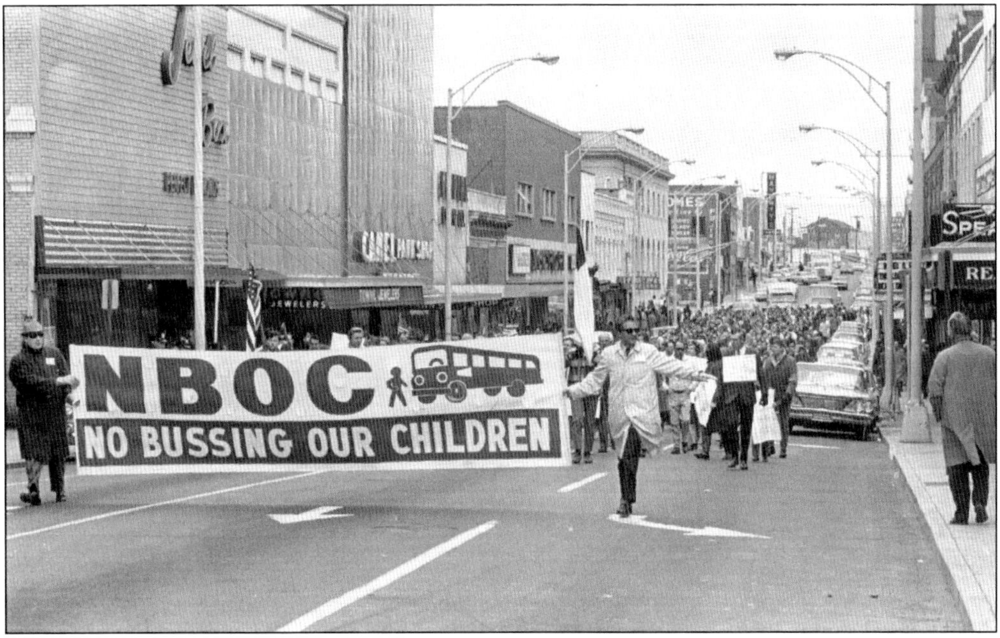

A peaceful, but determined, group of about 4,000 marchers walked through downtown Winston-Salem in February 1970 to oppose cross-busing of students. The demonstration was sponsored by the "No Busing Our Children" group, which was dedicated to the goals of neighborhood schools and freedom of choice in school assignments. Policemen in three-wheeled vehicles led the marchers through the downtown streets for the 20-minute walk in near-freezing weather.

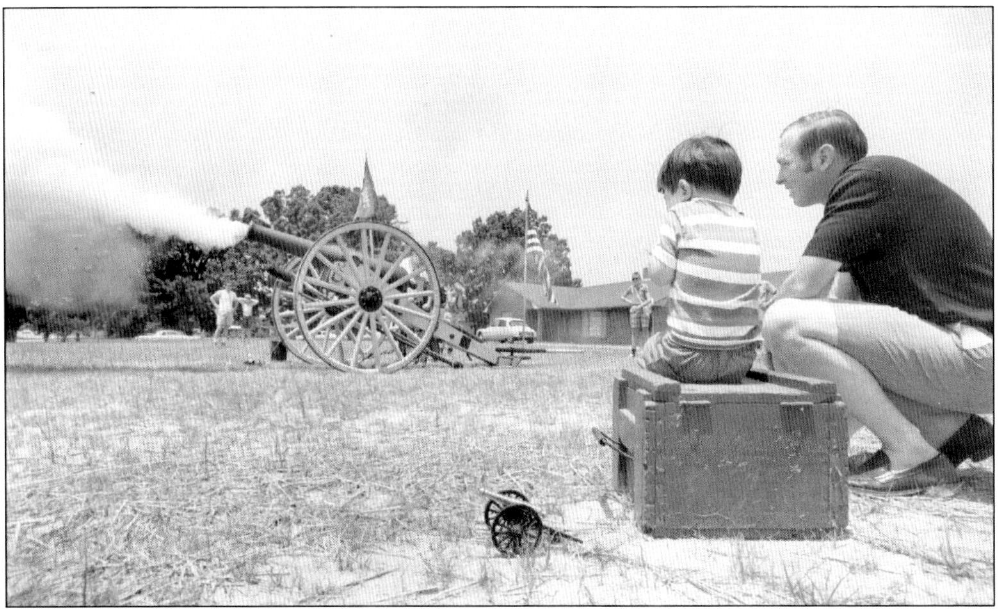

Bands and fireworks are great for celebrating our country's independence day. But Troy Church made July 4, 1970, a memorable day for his Robinhood Road neighbors when he fired the 100-year-old Civil War howitzer in his front yard. Church prepared the cannon and let neighborhood children do the firing. After making the rounds at reenactments, Church sold the cannon, and today it resides in a relic shop in West Tennessee.

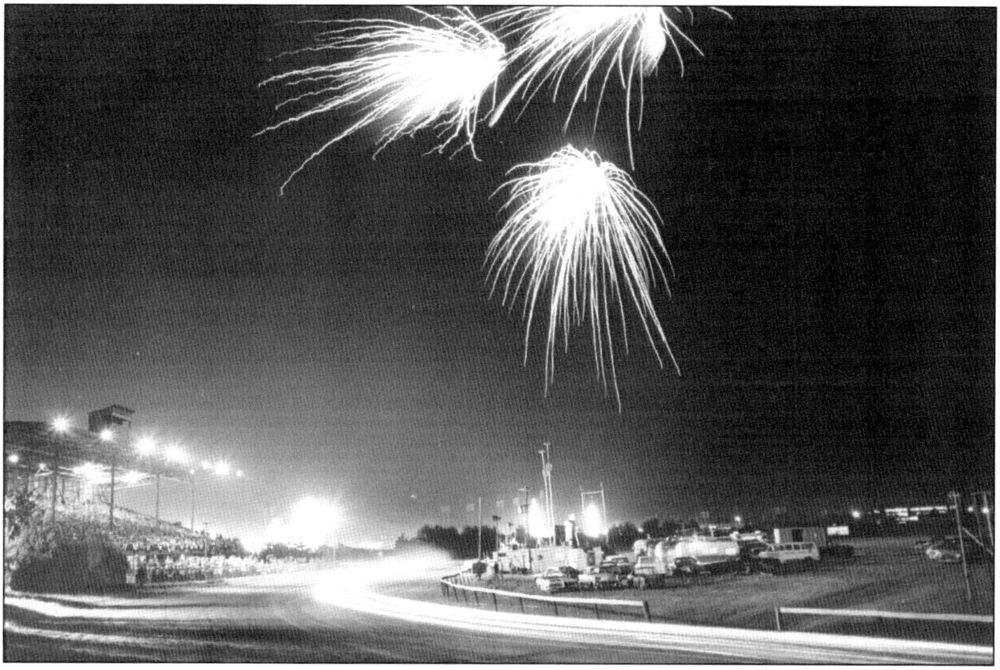

The Dixie Classic Fair ran for five days and nights in October 1970. This composite photograph shows the car lights from the grandstand show and the fireworks that ended the evening's activities. The midway rides featured the Scrambler, Twister, Paratrooper, Tilt-a-Whirl, and Tip-Top. Some of the contests that attracted many entrants as they vied for prizes were tractor driving, rooster crowing, pipe smoking, and chicken barbecuing.

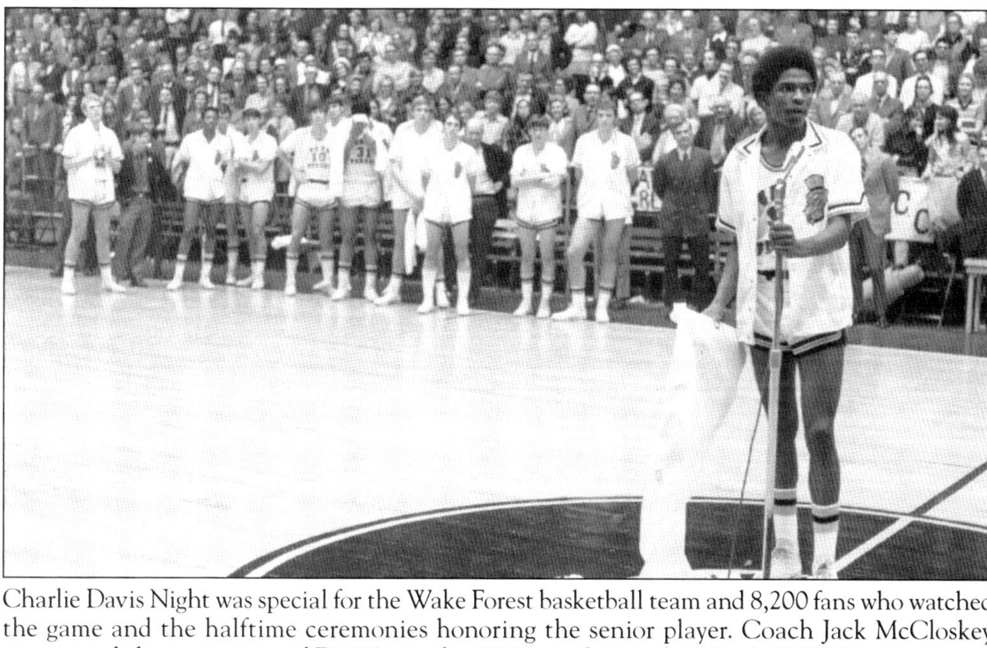

Charlie Davis Night was special for the Wake Forest basketball team and 8,200 fans who watched the game and the halftime ceremonies honoring the senior player. Coach Jack McCloskey announced the retirement of Davis's number-12 jersey during the March 2, 1971, game against Maryland. Wake Forest won the game, 72-66, thanks to Charlie's seven free throws in his last tense minutes as a Deacon player.

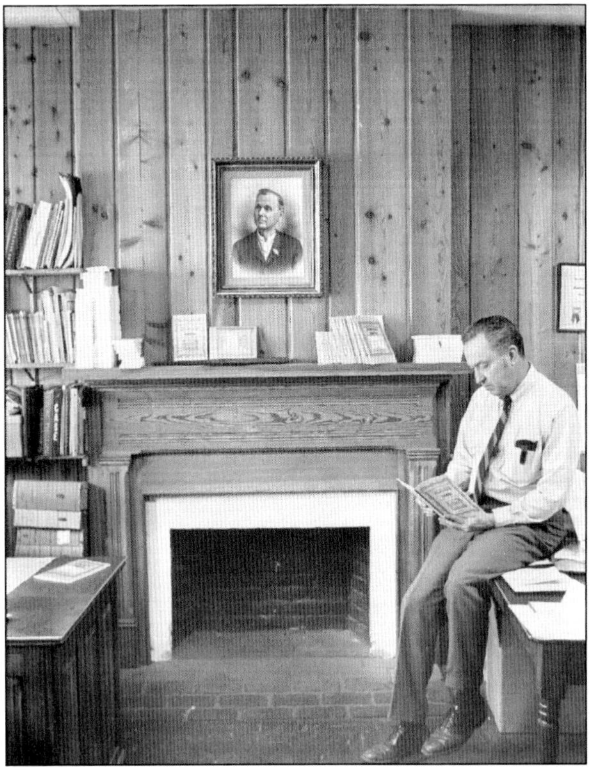

J. B. Goslen Jr. examined the 1971 issue of *Blum's Almanac*, the last issue to be published in the company's North Main Street office. The building housing Goslen Printing Company, built in 1896 by Fogle Brothers, was scheduled for demolition in the city's urban redevelopment project. *Blum's Almanac*, published by three generations of Goslen men since 1926, continued their operation in new offices at Healy and Plaza Drives.

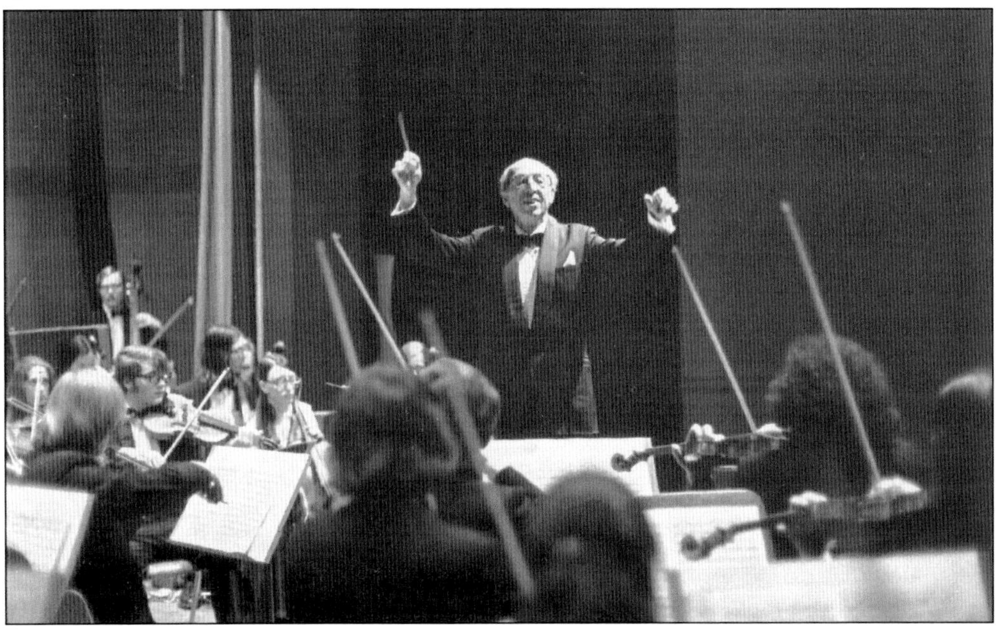

Former North Carolina School of the Arts orchestra students may still recall an evening in March 1971 when they played a selection of music by Aaron Copeland, conducted by the famous composer. The 70-year-old Copeland led the orchestra in three selections, "An Outdoor Overture," his Suite from "Rodeo," and "Lincoln Portrait." The opening piece, "An Outdoor Overture," was composed in 1938 for a high-school orchestra.

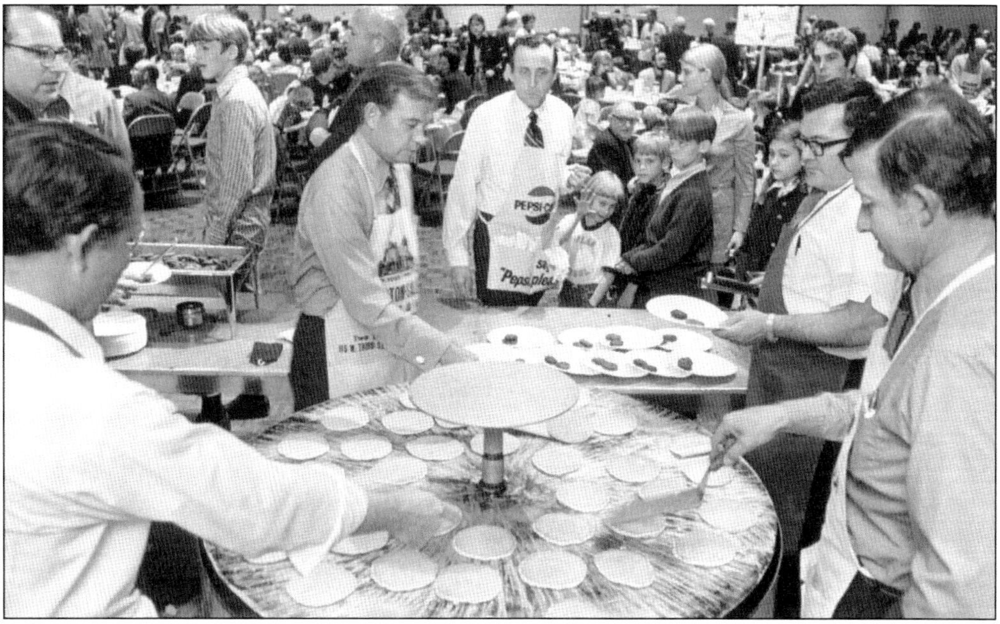

A large, hot griddle and many experienced cooks are a necessity when you plan to cook 15,000 pancakes and 900 pounds of sausage. The Twin-City Kiwanis Club serves up pancakes and sausages every year to raise money for their community service projects. In 1971, the all-day event was held at the convention center in April. A family of two adults and two children could eat their fill for just $3.50.

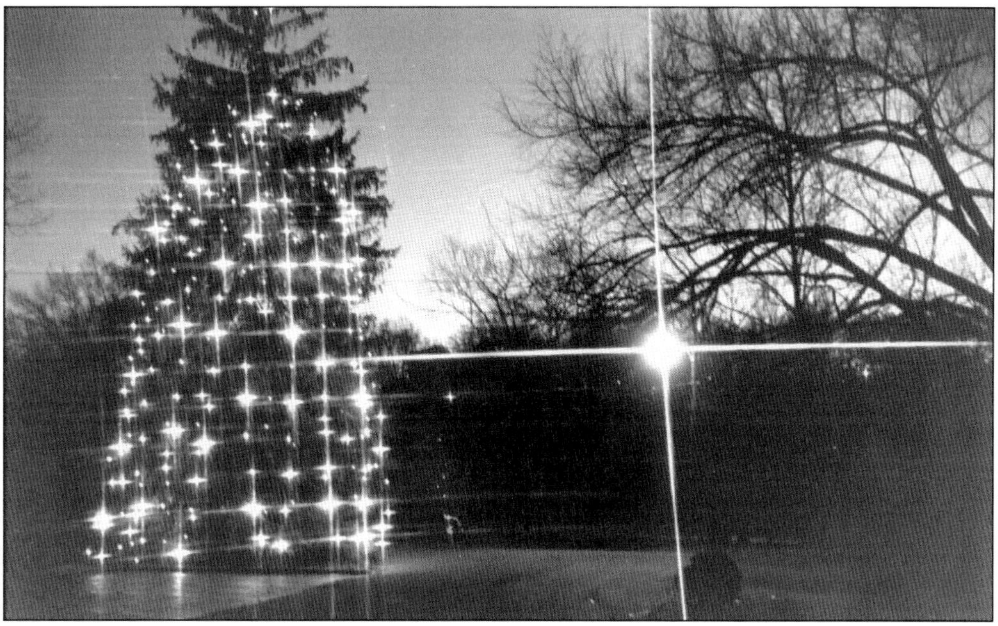

Christmas decorations in town changed frequently over the years. Sometimes plastic reindeer and Santa Claus figures adorned downtown lamp posts. Sometimes Moravian Stars, lanterns, or candy canes announced the yuletide season. Each Christmas since about 1930, a large tree at the Methodist Children's Home has been decorated with colorful bulbs, brightening the evening landscape on Reynolda Road for a few weeks each year, captured in this 1972 photograph.

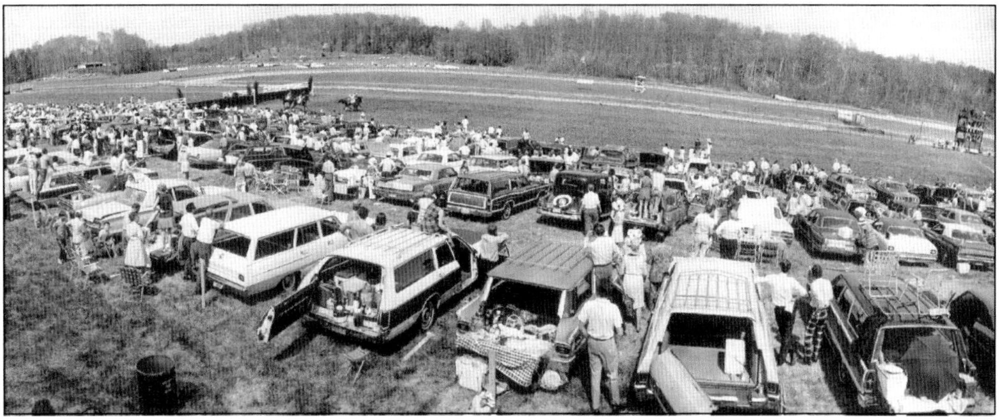

The initial Tanglewood Steeplechase was held on April 27, 1963, at the site that William Neal Reynolds built for racing horses on his farm near Clemmons. The track was in excellent condition in spite of a Yadkin River spring flood just five weeks before starting day, which washed away preliminary track work and fencing. The event was held again in 1964 and then opened in 1970 after a five-year layoff. The fourth Tanglewood Steeplechase in 1971 marked the 50th anniversary of the date that William Neal Reynolds purchased Tanglewood. The beautiful weather attracted a large crowd in all types of vehicles, but the popular station wagons provided both transportation and picnic space. Jeannie Lybrook (below, center), daughter of Tanglewood president Bill Lybrook (below, left), took part in the cup presentation at the close of the races.

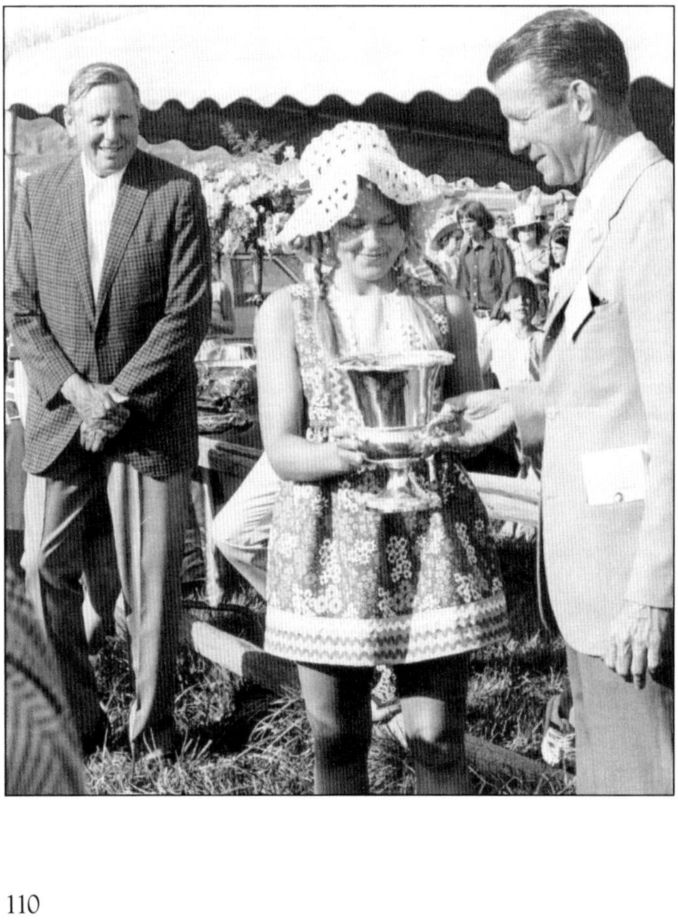

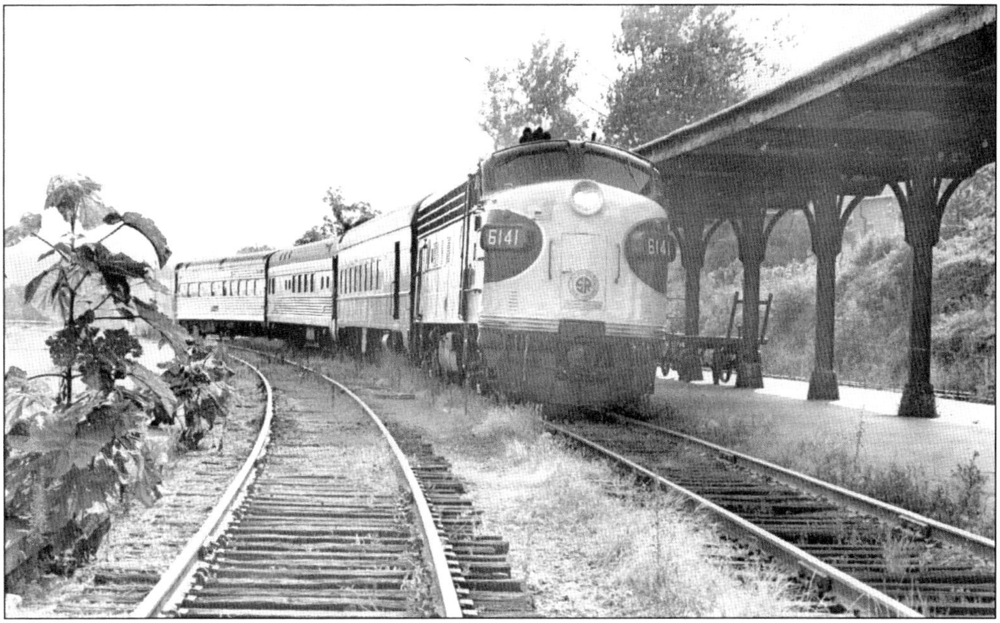

An order issued by the State Utilities Commission on July 9, 1970, eliminated Southern Railway passenger service from Greensboro to Asheville. Train service would be modified to originate from Salisbury, rather than Greensboro, thus ending passenger service to Winston-Salem. On July 21, 1970, the last passenger train from Greensboro to Asheville pulled into Union Station, 97 years after Southern began service to Winston-Salem.

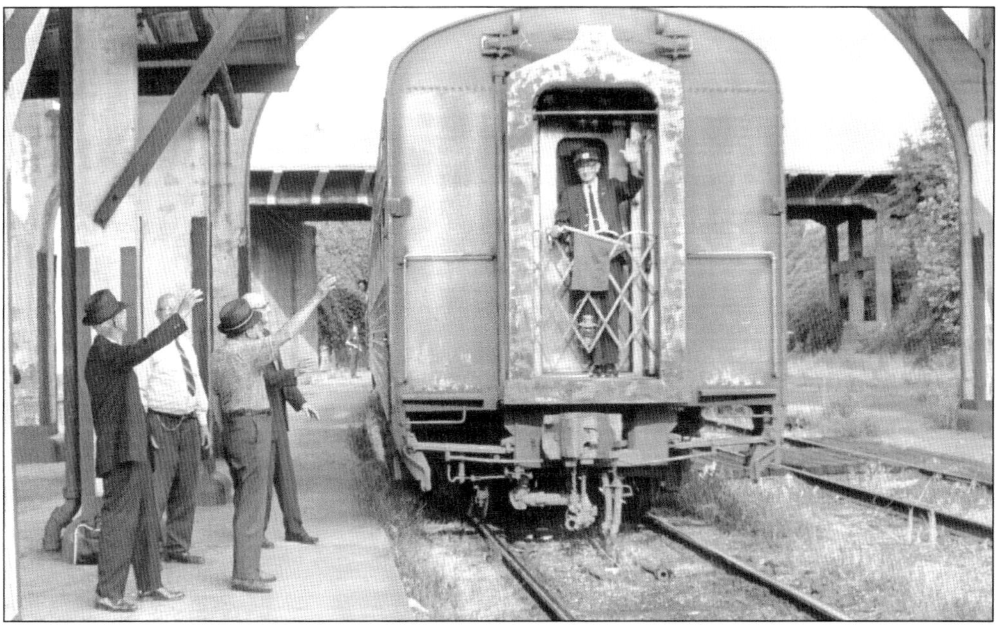

To commemorate the ending of passenger train service to Winston-Salem, more than 100 residents boarded the last train to Asheville. Others came just to see the train enter and leave Union Station on Claremont Avenue. Some of the riders brought picnic lunches, while others just brought their memories, which they shared with riders of all ages. A few veteran trainmen came for a final ride, ending the era with a wave goodbye.

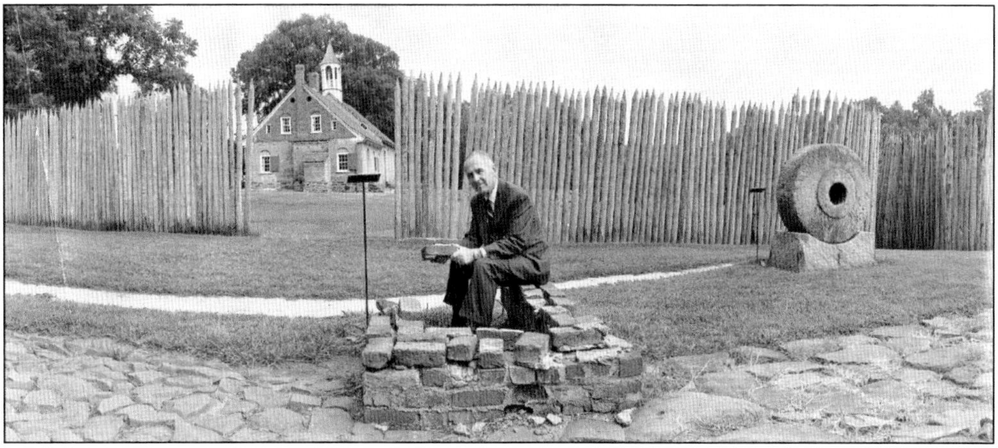

Edwin Link Stockton retired in 1971 as chief financial officer of the Southern Province of the Moravian Church. He succeeded his father, the Reverend Ernest Stockton, in the job in 1935. Among his many accomplishments related to the multi-faceted nature of his job was assembling the land on which the Moravian Home was built and assembling the 50 acres for the Historic Bethabara Park site, which surrounds Mr. Stockton.

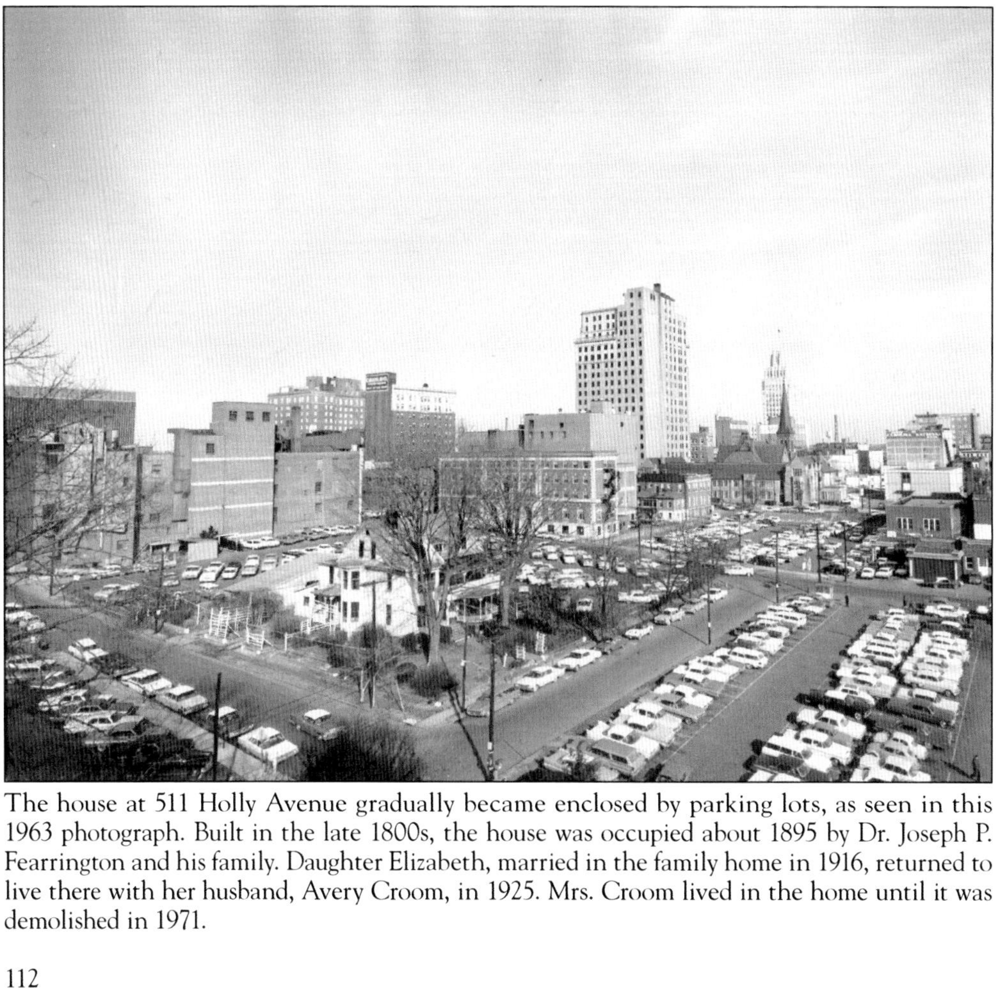

The house at 511 Holly Avenue gradually became enclosed by parking lots, as seen in this 1963 photograph. Built in the late 1800s, the house was occupied about 1895 by Dr. Joseph P. Fearrington and his family. Daughter Elizabeth, married in the family home in 1916, returned to live there with her husband, Avery Croom, in 1925. Mrs. Croom lived in the home until it was demolished in 1971.

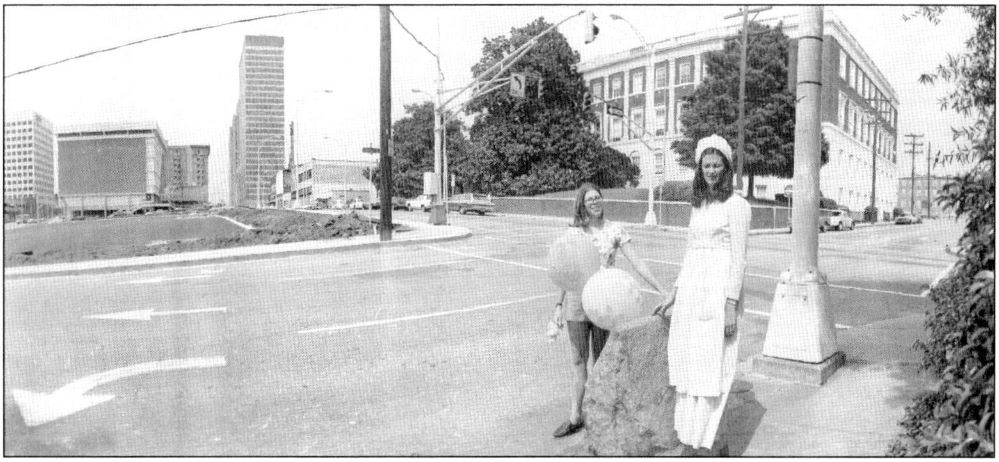

Passersby might easily overlook the historical marker near the corner of First and Main Streets. It designates the dividing line between Winston and Salem before the towns were officially consolidated on May 12, 1913. The marker is a granite block set in the sidewalk, with a bronze plaque announcing the merger. Wendy Reid (left) and Charlotte Pepper (right, in Moravian clothing) stand beside the marker in this 1974 photograph.

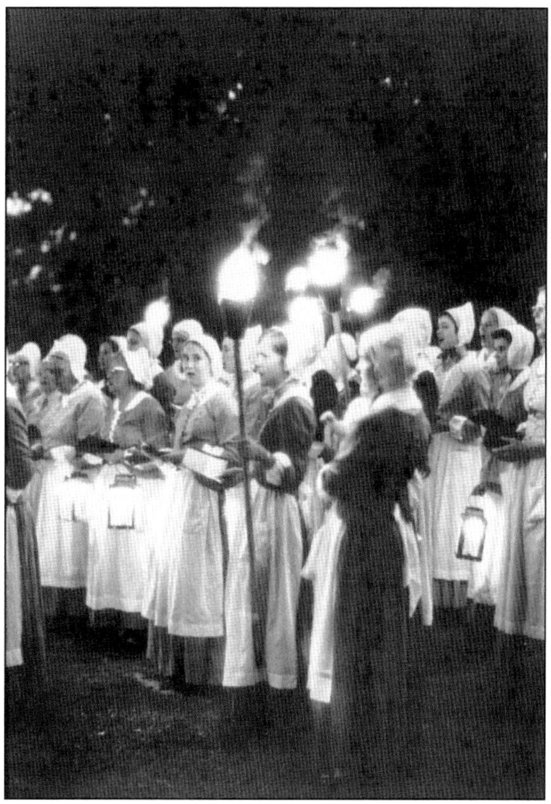

At the stroke of 9:00 p.m. on July 4, 1973, the streets of Salem became filled as men, women, and children reenacted the first official observance of Independence Day in 1783. Torch and candlelight guided the Moravians and other observers to Salem Square, where they gave thanks for peace through song and worship. The night watchman's blowing of a conch shell ended the torchlight parade and the day in Old Salem.

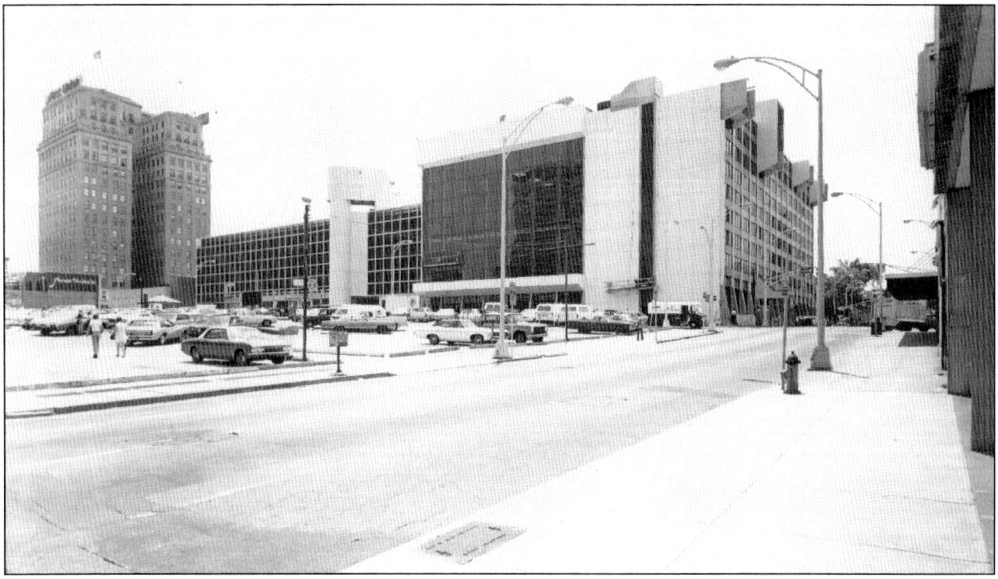

Hotel Robert E. Lee and the bus station were demolished in March 1972 to make way for a new hotel and parking deck. The Hyatt Regency Hotel (center) on West Fifth Street was nearing completion in 1974 when this photograph was taken. The September 1974 opening gala featured music by the Winston-Salem Symphony. Across the street, Les Elgart's Sophisticated Swing filled the Benton Convention Center with big band sounds.

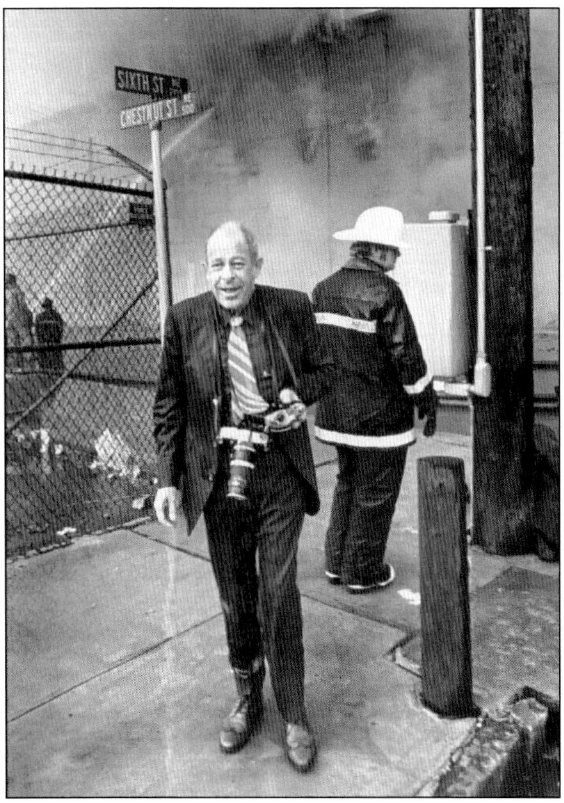

Fire struck the Hinkle Wholesale Company warehouse at Sixth and Chestnut Streets on April 25, 1974. The warehouse served four Hinkle stores and contained office products, such as desks, chairs, files, and office supplies. The fire summoned several fire units, plus newspaper reporters and photographers. Frank Jones photographed the building and the firefighters, getting close enough to the action to be doused by a fire hose. This is one of the last photographs taken of Frank before he died in February 1975.

Seven

THEN AND NOW

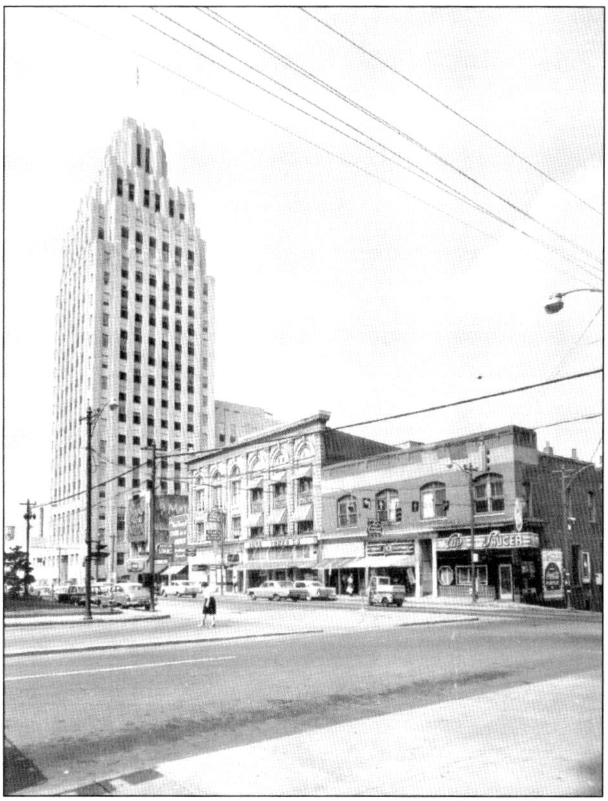

Winston-Salem's skyline changed drastically shortly after this photograph was taken in the late 1950s. Wachovia Corporation announced plans in December 1962 to construct a multi-story office building on the 300 block of North Main Street, across from the courthouse. The entire block of buildings was leveled. Today's view of this area shows the base of the Winston Tower, with the left view obstructed by trees and the 1960 courthouse addition.

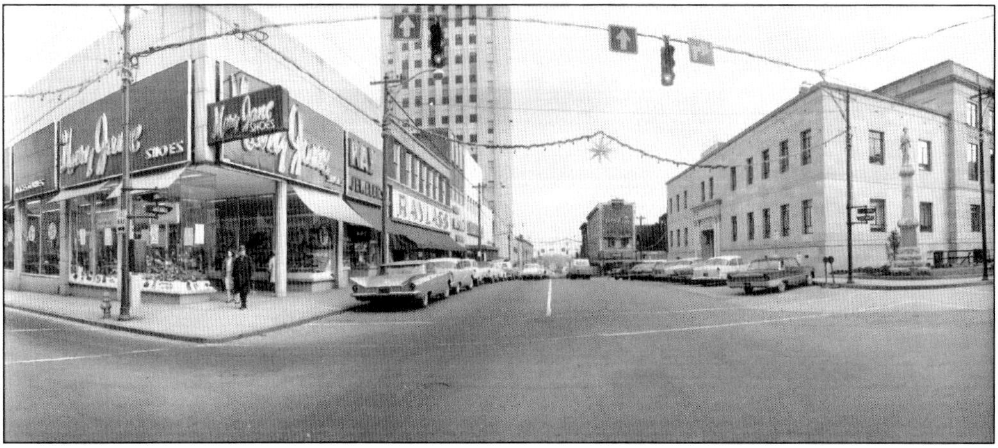

A. S. Beck Shoe Company opened its new store in 1947 on the northeast corner of Fourth and Liberty Streets. The business closed in September 1958, and the two-story building was soon occupied by the John Irvin Shoe Company. This January 1962 view looking east on Fourth at Liberty shows (at left) the Mary Jane Shoe Store, Kay Jewelry Company, Raylass Department Store, S&H Kress Store, and the Hood System Industrial Bank on the far corner. The Reynolds Building occupies the northeast corner of Main Street, with the Masten building on the southeast corner. Across the street, the courthouse fills the entire block. The 2006 view of the same area shows the 13-story One West Fourth Building on the left, built in 2002. The Winston Tower rises above the former courthouse on the right.

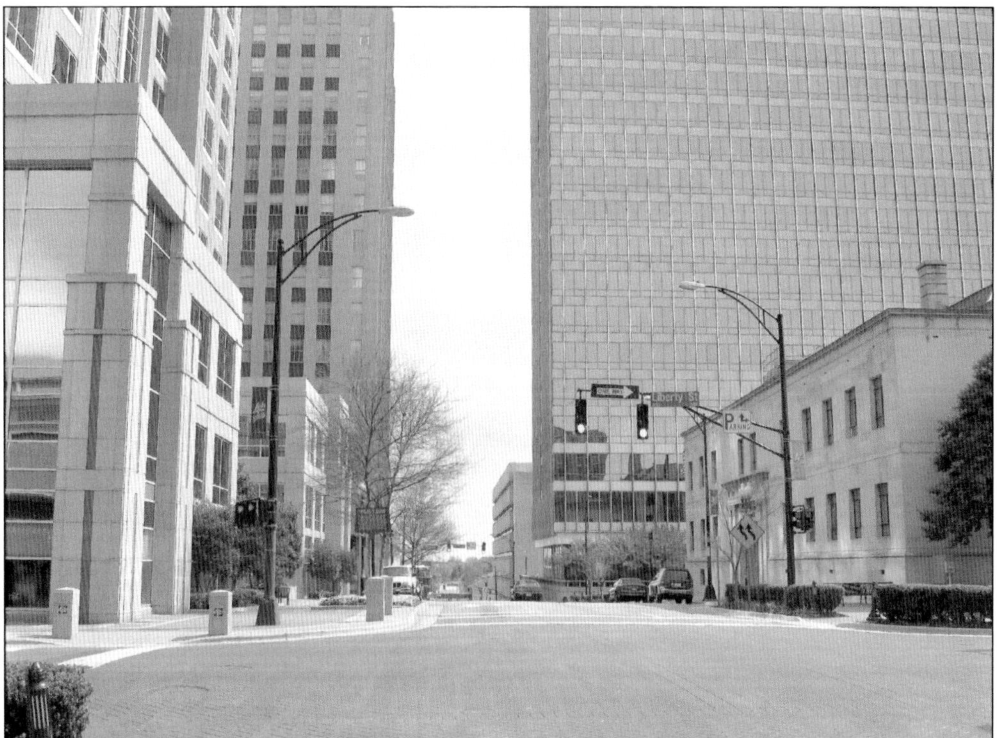

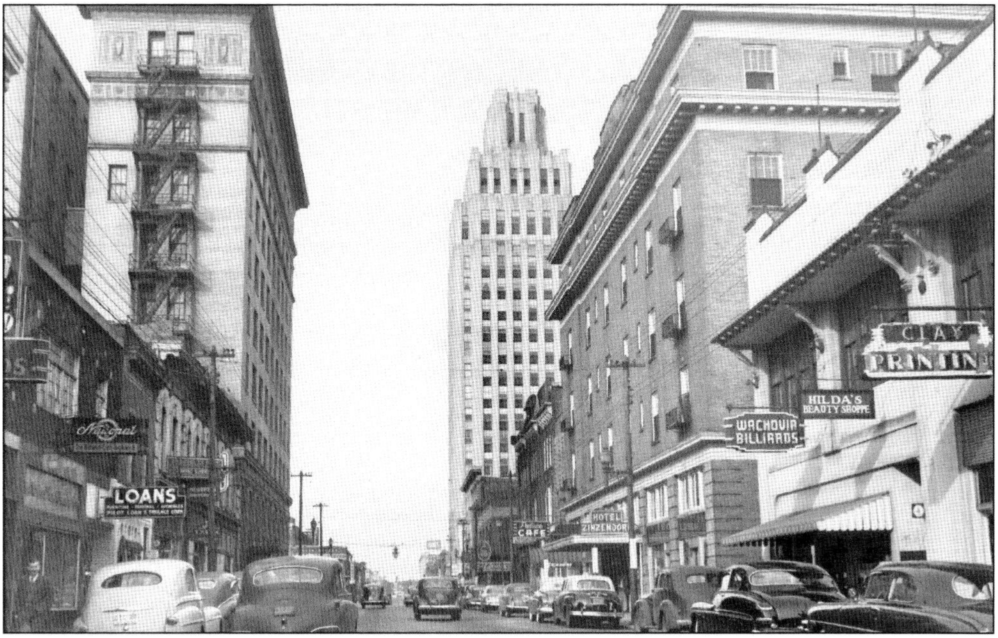

Cars and businesses lined the 200 block of North Main Street in this 1950 view looking north. The Tamplin Building was at right, with occupants Clay Printing, Hilda's Beauty Shoppe, and Wachovia Billiards. Next door was the Zinzendorf Hotel, built in 1906 and enlarged in 1917. The hotel housed Dorminy Studio, where young people learned to dance under the tutelage of Jacqueline Dorminy. The hotel was demolished in 1971, along with other businesses on the block. Located on the opposite side of the street were several small businesses and Standard Building and Loan Association. The eight-story Wachovia Bank and Trust Company (1911) stands on the corner of Main and Third Streets. The 2006 view of this street shows a parking lot beside the Winston Tower (right) and part of the Hall of Justice (left) beside the 1911 Wachovia Bank building.

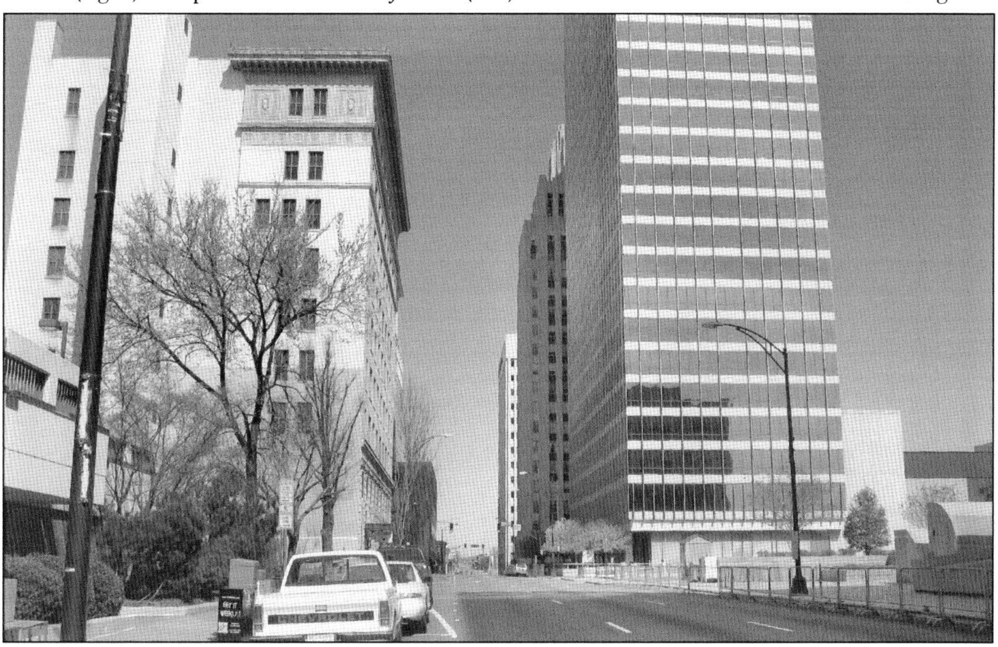

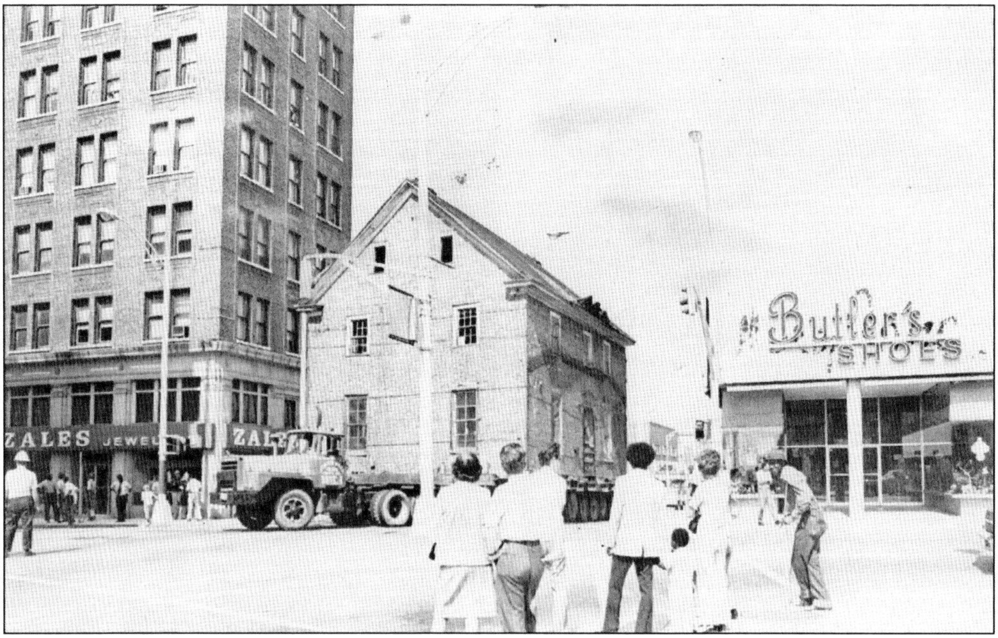

Van N. Zevely, a Salem cabinetmaker, built his house about 1815 in a wilderness area outside of Salem. In 1972, the house at 734 Oak Street was placed on the real estate market with the hope that it would be purchased and restored as a historical house. The purchasers of the house decided that it also needed a new location, so it was moved from Oak Street to the corner of Fourth and Summit Streets in September 1974. The house porches were rotten and stayed behind. Steel beams reinforced the corners of the house and cables were wrapped around the house to prevent cracking. After only a few little hitches, the seven-hour move was completed. In 2006, the historic house is firmly planted as the Zevely House Restaurant.

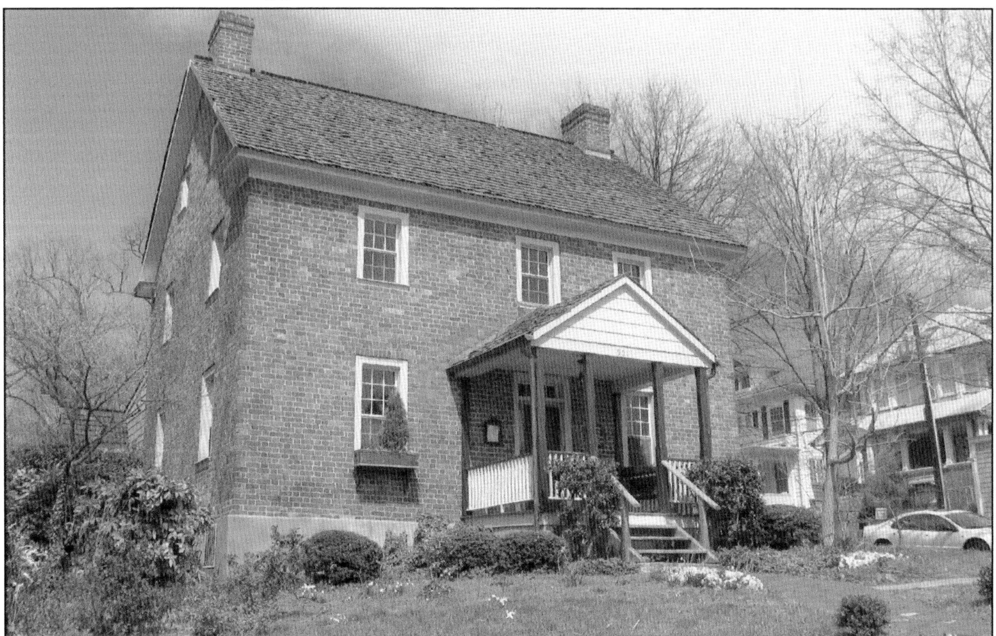

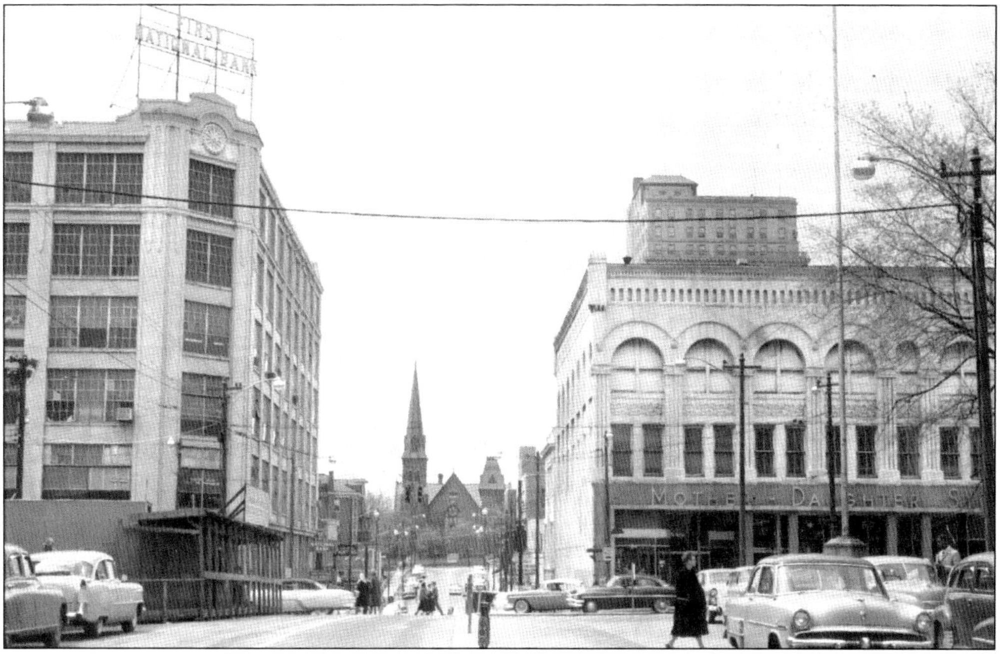

The view down Third Street, crossing Liberty and looking toward Cherry Street in 1956, shows three primary buildings. First National Bank was once situated on the right corner before it moved to the Universal Garage building on the left corner. In 1961, First National Bank merged with North Carolina National Bank, and the building was imploded in 1973. The Mother and Daughter Store on Liberty Street expanded into the old First National Bank building (right). First Presbyterian Church is seen in the distance before the sanctuary was demolished and rebuilt in 1972. The 2006 view shows a parking lot at right where Mother and Daughter stood. First Presbyterian Church has a new look and a new steeple. The Forsyth County Sheriff's Department is housed in the building at left, with a cross-over to Fourth Street.

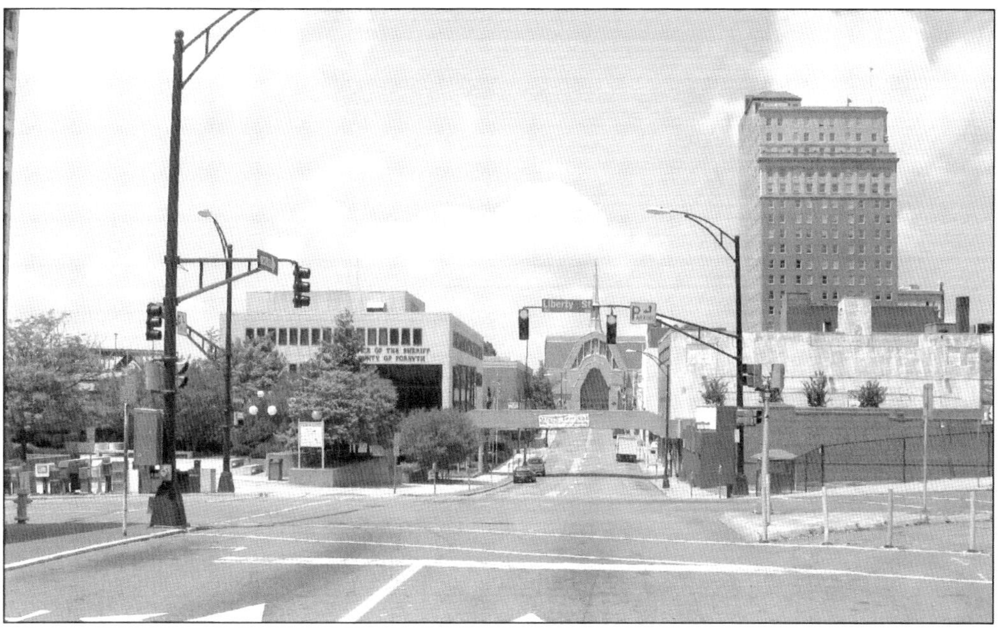

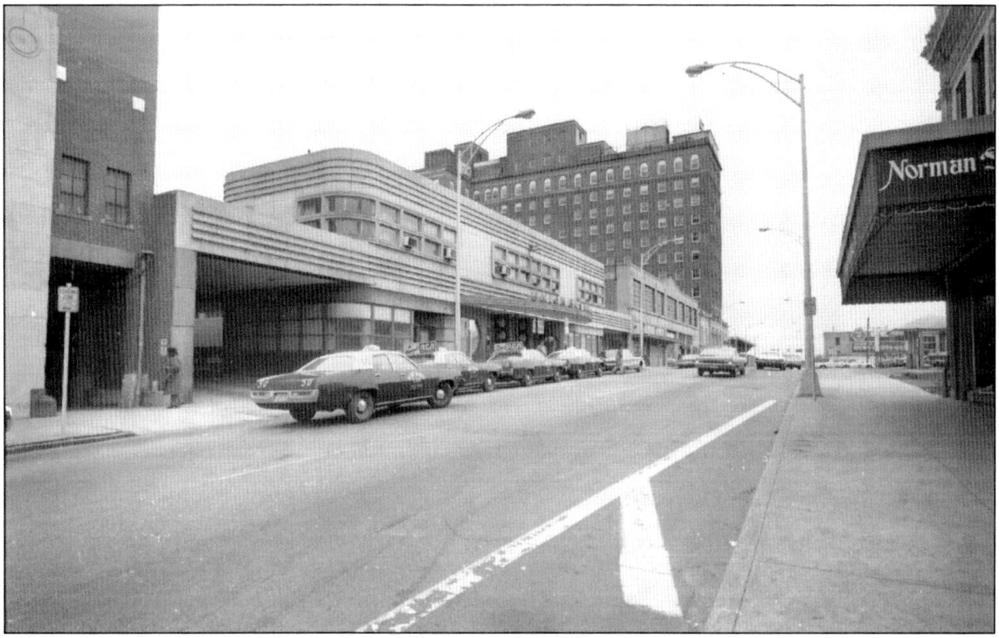

Greyhound buses traveled into the downtown area, pulling into the bus station on Cherry Street near the Hotel Robert E. Lee and the K&W Cafeteria. The buses would unload and load passengers, then exit onto Marshall Street and head out of town. The bus station (left) is shown in 1972, just one month before the hotel and station were demolished. Across the street was the Norman Stockton store, with a parking lot to the side. The 2006 view shows a parking garage at left, built to accompany the Hyatt Regency Hotel, which was constructed on the former Hotel Robert E. Lee site. Embassy Suites is located there today, linked by a crosswalk to the Marriott Hotel, located across the street. The two previous hotels were renovated and refurbished and opened under new ownership in 2005.

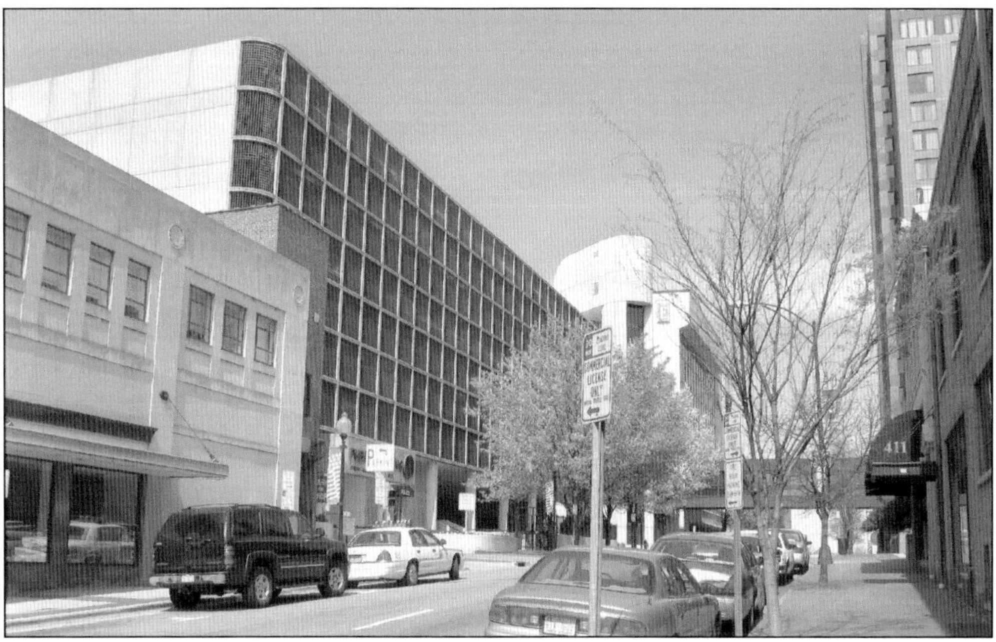

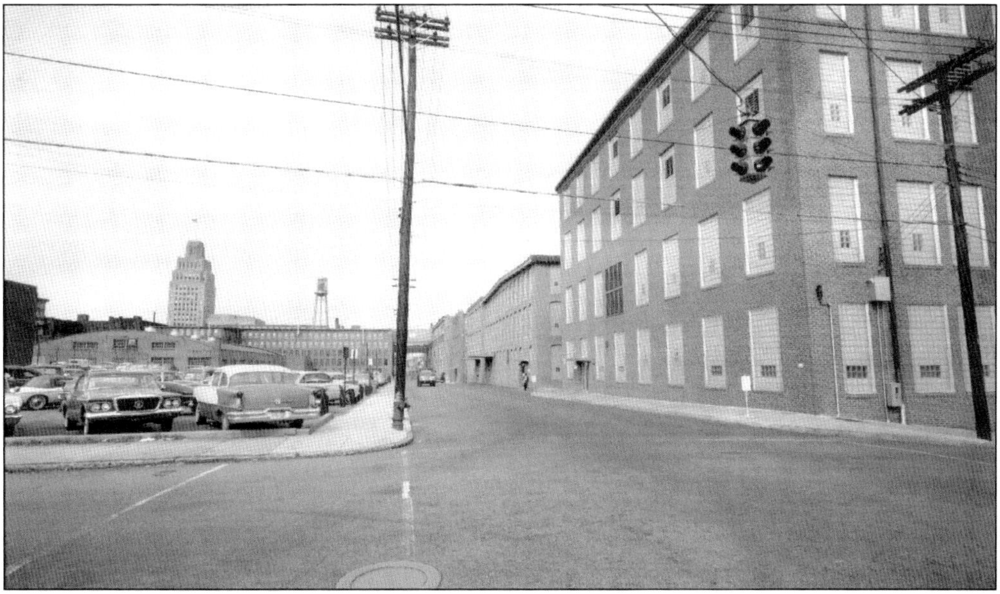

R. J. Reynolds Tobacco Company factories lined the right side of Chestnut Street, from First to Third Street, in 1963. Parking lots for tobacco workers were on the left. When tobacco operations moved to other locations, the factories were sold and found new use as offices and condominiums. On August 27, 1998, fire claimed the 256-factory complex, including Victoria Hall, and damaged the Albert Hall building on the corner at right. In 2006, Victoria Hall is rebuilt and, along with Albert Hall, is again used for offices and condominiums. R. J. Reynolds Factory Number 12 was located in the 200 block of Chestnut Street. Although not damaged in the fire, it was completely refurbished and today is the Forsyth County Government Center. A parking deck replaced the one-level parking lot at left.

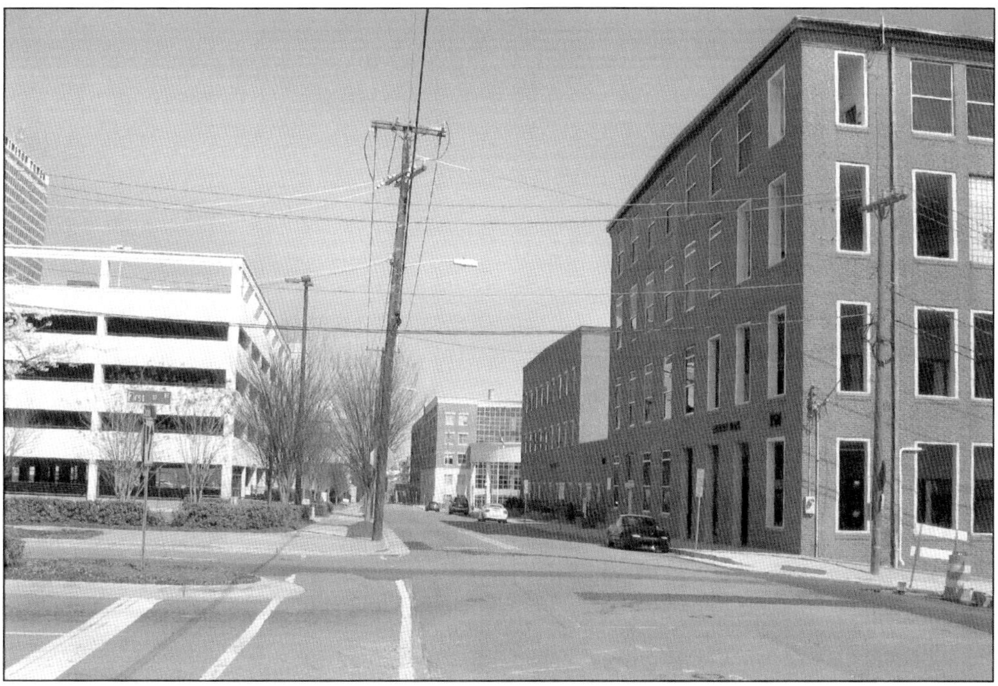

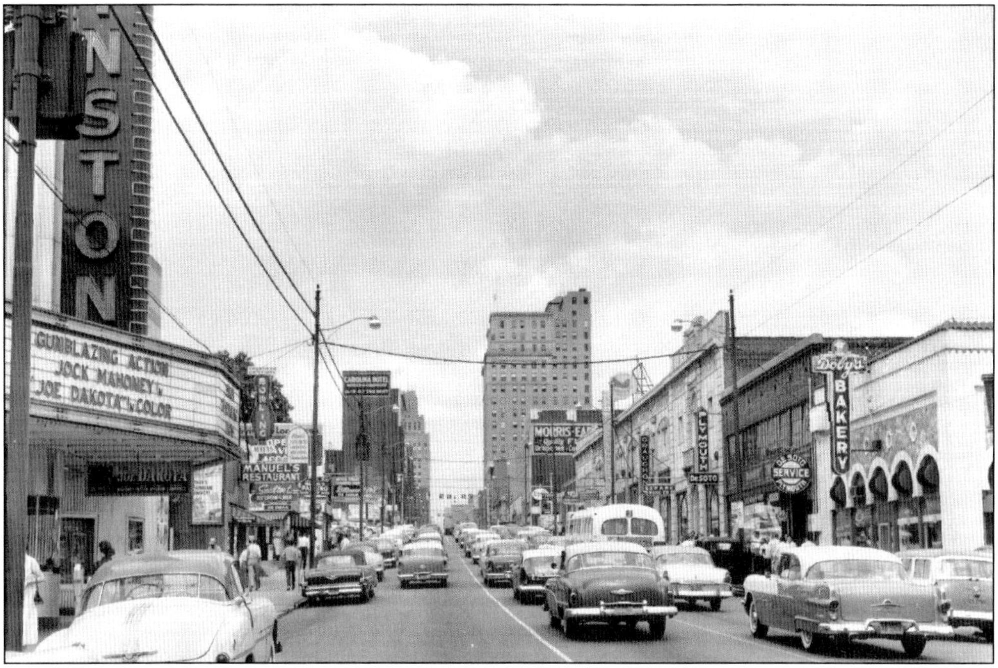

Fourth Street was a busy one-way thoroughfare in 1958, shown by passing traffic in the 600 block of businesses. Doby's Bakery, with the arched windows and founded in 1937, was on the right. Odell Matthews Motors was the next business and then the Separk Music Company. At left, the Winston Theatre marquee announced the current movie. The Winston Theatre opened in 1949 and was refurbished in 1968. Next door was Manuel's Restaurant and the Twentieth Century (Bowling) Lanes, and beside it was the Dutch Treat Sandwich Shop. Traffic travels two-ways in 2006, and trees line Fourth Street. Separk Music is in its same location. Next door, Foothills Brewing opened in 2004. Across the street, the Winston Theatre location was renovated in 1982 to accommodate City Center West offices. A warehouse next door was also renovated for offices.

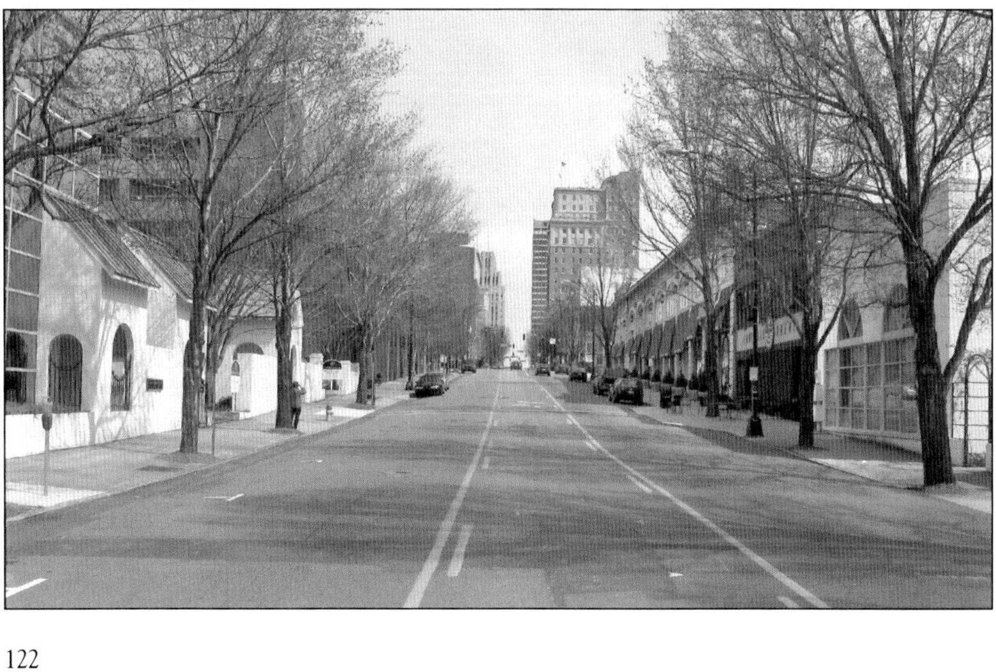

Frank B. Jones Jr. Chronology

1914, March 26	Born in his grandfather's (Wiley Keith's) house on Brookstown Avenue.
1926, April 4	Made profession of faith and joined the membership of Calvary Moravian Church.
1932	Graduated from R. J. Reynolds High School.
1934–1936	Worked for Barber Photo Supply.
1937	Joined *Winston-Salem Journal* as staff photographer.
1941, October	Carrie Jones, Frank's mother, died.
1942, October	Enlisted in the navy.
1944, September	Awarded special citation by the navy.
1945, December	Returned from service in the navy. Bought home on Brookstown Avenue.
1946, August	Trip to Nicaragua (returned October 7, 1946).
1947	Photograph selected by Wilmington Junior Chamber of Commerce and Carolina Press Photographers Association as best photograph of 1947 Miss North Carolina.
1947, August	Frank's services were donated by the *Journal* to make a film for the Community Chest.
1949, August 27	Frank Jones Sr. died.
1951, May	Joined the delegation that was retracing the Trail of Tears as pilgrimage photographer.
1954, June	Trip to Nassau.
1955, August	Built a greenhouse onto his Brookstown Avenue house. In the greenhouse were plants and birds.
1960	Named senior photographer at *Journal.*
1960, May 27	Left for trip to Russia (returned about July 2).
1964, June	Trip to Bucaramanga, Columbia, Winston-Salem's sister city.
1965, October	Moravian Study Tour.
1966, January	Over 200 photographs prepared for an exhibit as part of the 200th anniversary of the founding of Winston-Salem.
1968, January	Another trip to Bucaramanga. Frank hurt his knee in a ski accident shortly before leaving on the trip.
1975	Named *Winston-Salem Journal* chief photographer.
1975, February 20	Died at age 60 while at work in the *Journal* newsroom.
1975, October	Exhibit of Frank's photographs was the first exhibit for the new Winston-Salem Museum.
1983, May 26	Wachovia Historical Society Board voted to put the Frank Jones Photograph Collection on permanent loan at the Forsyth County Public Library.
1990, February	Molly Rawls hired to identify, organize, and catalog the Frank B. Jones Jr. Photograph Collection.

BIBLIOGRAPHY

Crews, C. Daniel, and Richard W. Starbuck. *With Courage for the Future: The Story of the Moravian Church, Southern Province.* Winston-Salem, NC: Moravian Church in America, Southern Province, 2002.

Interviews and telephone conversations with Tim Cahill, Mary Davidson, Joe Dudley, George Hege, Keith Hege, Art Hondros, Jane Pepper Masich, and Gertrude Clay Norris,

Memoir for Franklin Buxton Jones, Jr. Prepared by Rev. David R. Burkette and delivered at Jones's funeral at Calvary Moravian Church, February 22, 1975. Winston-Salem, NC: Moravian Church Archives of the Southern Province.

Winston-Salem Journal and the *Twin City Sentinel.* Winston-Salem, NC: Piedmont Publishing Company, various issues.

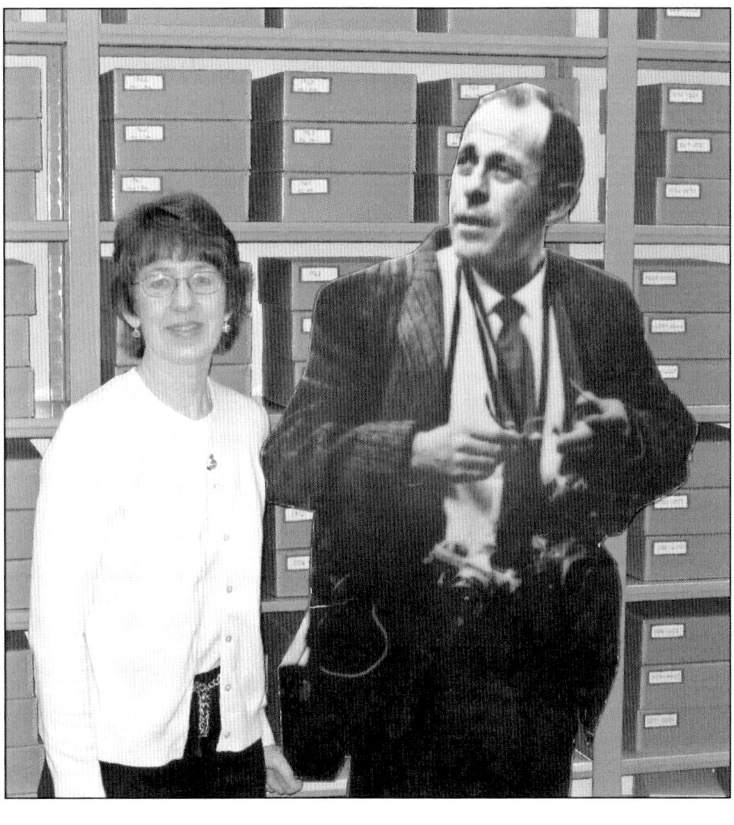

Author Molly Grogan Rawls poses with a life-size cut-out of Frank Jones in front of boxes containing Jones's photograph collection at the Forsyth County Public Library. Rawls is a second-generation Winston-Salem native, graduating from North Forsyth High School and from the University of North Carolina at Chapel Hill with an undergraduate degree in English and a graduate degree in library science. Rawls is also the author of *Winston-Salem in Vintage Postcards*, published in 2004 with Arcadia Publishing.

INDEX